BUILDING and IMPLEMENTING a SECURITY CERTIFICATION and ACCREDITATION PROGRAM

OFFICIAL (ISC)²® GUIDE to the CAP℠ CBK®

OTHER INFORMATION SECURITY BOOKS FROM AUERBACH

AUERBACH PUBLICATIONS
www.auerbach-publications.com
To Order Call: 1-800-272-7737 • Fax: 1-800-374-3401
E-mail: orders@crcpress.com

BUILDING and IMPLEMENTING a SECURITY CERTIFICATION and ACCREDITATION PROGRAM

OFFICIAL (ISC)²® GUIDE to the CAP™ CBK®

Patrick D. Howard

(ISC)²®

SECURITY TRANSCENDS TECHNOLOGY®

Auerbach Publications
Taylor & Francis Group
Boca Raton   New York

Published in 2006 by
Auerbach Publications
Taylor & Francis Group
6000 Broken Sound Parkway NW, Suite 300
Boca Raton, FL 33487-2742

International Standard Book Number-10: 0-8493-2062-3 (Hardcover)
International Standard Book Number-13: 978-0-8493-2062-0 (Hardcover)
Library of Congress Card Number 2005053005

Library of Congress Cataloging-in-Publication Data

Howard, Patrick D.
    Building and implementing a security certification and accreditation program / Patrick D. Howard.
        p. cm.
    ISBN 0-8493-2062-3 (alk. paper)
    1. Electronic data processing personnel--Certification. 2. Computer security--Examinations--Study guides. I. Title.

QA76.3.H693 2005
005.8--dc22   2005053005

Taylor & Francis Group
is the Academic Division of Informa plc.

Visit the Taylor & Francis Web site at
http://www.taylorandfrancis.com

and the Auerbach Publications Web site at
http://www.auerbach-publications.com

Dedication

To Annemarie: my biggest fan; my master motivator; my loving wife

Contents

Section I Building a Successful Enterprise Certification and Accreditation Program

Section II Certification and Accreditation Processes

Section III Certification and Accreditation Case Study

Section IV The Future of Certification and Accreditation

Section V Appendices

Foreword

There are many elements that make system certification and accreditation (C&A) complex. This book focuses on the processes that must be employed by an organization to establish a certification and accreditation program based on current federal government criteria. Although the roots of this book address various federal requirements, the process developed and presented can be used by nongovernment organizations to address compliance and the myriad laws, regulations, and standards currently driving information technology security.

The key to reaching C&A nirvana is understanding what is required and then implementing a methodology that will achieve those requirements. The top-down methodology presented in this book provides the reader with a practical approach for completion of such an undertaking. By demystifying government requirements, this book presents a simplified, practical approach to certification and accreditation.

Pat Howard is one of those few individuals who can create processes that work in the real world. I discovered this by working with him — one of those wonderful times when you find someone who is more skilled than you are. Our collaboration was brief but we were able to take complex issues and distill them to the point that senior management could understand what was being presented. Since then we have stayed in touch, and I watched this book evolve over the past two years.

Pat accepted the challenge to create a book that would answer the burning question: Can certification and accreditation be explained in a manner that will allow agencies and businesses to readily implement the process? The answer to the question is a resounding YES! By being actively involved in this process for over 15 years, Pat has created a practical guide that can be used by security professionals, auditors, and business-people alike.

What Pat brings to the process is his background in the public and private sectors. Because he has been a manager of tasks and people in the public and private sectors, Pat is able to present a clear and concise blueprint for what needs to be accomplished. The book has the unique perspective of implementing requirements while still meeting the business objectives or mission of the organization.

I first met Pat Howard a number of years ago when he and I went to work for the global security practice of a company called Netigy. I was the "big picture" person who needed someone well grounded in project management principles. Because Pat had a strong background in information security, we were able to converse on ideas and concepts from the very first day we met at Boston's Logan Airport.

One of the first projects we collaborated on was the creation of a training infrastructure for the security consultants who would implement the products and services of our company. Pat was able to take the ideas and concepts discussed by eight different security professionals and then build a meaningful framework for implementation. The results of this work were so detailed that we are still able to use the training process with clients today.

Pat has structured this book to address the key issues in certification and accreditation, including roles and responsibilities, the life cycle, and even a discussion of pitfalls to avoid. As with all of Pat's work, he provides the reader with practical information on what works and what does not. I am pretty sure he learned what is right firsthand and what goes wrong by observing people like me.

This smooth-as-syrup, "ah shucks" gentleman from Oklahoma has spun a story that security professionals need to read and heed. Even if government certification and accreditation is not your concern, the new ISO 27002 (formerly ISO 17799) will require all of us to look for a process to make certification and accreditation bearable. Pat has succeeded in doing just that with this practical and readable book.

Thomas R. Peltier

Preface

Certification and accreditation has become a major topic of discussion in the information security arena over the past two to three years, at least in U.S. government circles. Many government organizations are currently engaged in employing certification and accreditation processes in response to the requirements of the Federal Information Security Management Act (FISMA). FISMA, with its emphasis on measuring progress in the implementation of information security within the federal government, has elevated certification and accreditation into the preeminent position of being the government's primary risk management approach in the field of information technology security. Although certification and accreditation is not new, its preeminence is, and its newfound acceptance promises to solidify its position for many years to come. Certification and accreditation has been employed in government for over 20 years, and it is becoming recognized outside government for the promise it holds as a practical approach for identifying and documenting business requirements for security, for ensuring that cost-effective controls are functioning appropriately, and for ensuring that weaknesses in protective controls are managed effectively. This book demonstrates the practicality, comprehensiveness, and effectiveness of certification and accreditation as a risk management methodology for information technology systems in both public and private organizations.

Acknowledgments

I would like to express my gratitude to four people who were instrumental in the creation of this book. First, to Tom Peltier, president of Peltier and Associates, friend, and mentor, for planting the seed that led to this volume and for convincing me that I had something to say on the subject. To Victoria Lord, director of Enterprise Information Technology Security Division at the U.S. Department of Transportation, for allowing me to apply the concepts and processes described in this book and for her trust in my capabilities as a program manager and security professional. To Kelvin Taylor, of Titan Corporation and a fellow traveler in the unending quest for certification and accreditation perfection, for serving as my sounding board on these principles and practices and for being one of the most positive people I have ever met. And, finally to Lisa Schlosser, chief information officer at the Department of Housing and Urban Development, for her encouragement to strive for the impossible, for her confidence in my certification and accreditation expertise, and for the opportunity to apply it under her guidance on numerous occasions over the past 13 years.

Introduction

On the day I turned 16, my sister drove me to the Department of Motor Vehicles Office in Anadarko, Oklahoma, to take my driving test. This first attempt at the test failed as did the second; I was finally able to pass the test on the third try and obtained my much-cherished license to operate a motor vehicle. This license meant that the state certified that I had met minimum driving standards and it served as my authorization to drive a car in the state of Oklahoma and wherever else the license was recognized. The subject of this book is similar to the drivers' licensing process that I experienced firsthand in 1965 in that the certification and accreditation methodology includes testing against an established standard, and authorization to operate is given on the basis of this testing. Although certification and accreditation relates to information systems rather than to anxious teenagers awaiting their fate, these processes have much in common.

Background

In December 2002, Congress passed the Federal Information Security Management Act (FISMA). This new federal law has done more to elevate the importance and visibility of certification and accreditation than any other single event in the history of U.S. government. Certification and accreditation did not begin with FISMA. In fact, it had been established as a formal information technology security methodology with the publication of Federal Information Processing Standard (FIPS) 102 in 1983, and it was elevated in significance with the enactment of the Computer Security Act of 1987 and with the publication of Office of Management and Budget Circular A-130, which implemented the act. However, certification and accreditation had never truly taken off in government outside of the

Department of Defense (DOD) where DOD had implemented its DOD Information Technology Security Certification and Accreditation Process (DITSCAP). Unfortunately, the DITSCAP process, though ideal for the highly sensitive systems operated in support of the national defense mission, was never broadly adopted for use elsewhere in government. This was only partially remedied by the National Information Assurance Certification and Accreditation Process (NIACAP), which was published in 2000. It was only with FISMA (which was followed closely by publication of NIST Special Publication 800-37 on the topic) that certification and accreditation was given the boost that has effectively raised its visibility across government and into the consciousness of federal executives and managers.

Defining Certification and Accreditation

Before proceeding further, it will be necessary to define our terms. Certification and accreditation is the methodology used to ensure that security controls are established for an information system, that these controls are functioning appropriately, and that management has authorized the operation of the system in its current security posture. Although these two terms are in most cases used together to define a comprehensive process, certification and accreditation are distinct processes, which must be performed separately by different entities at different times for different but related purposes. Certification is the process by which the effectiveness of security controls is assessed, and accreditation is the management decision (based on that assessment) to permit an information system to operate at its current security posture. It is possible to perform each of these two processes by itself, but it would be either incomplete or risky. Performing certification on a system without continuing on to an accreditation decision misses an opportunity for fixing accountability for remediating weaknesses uncovered in the certification process. On the other hand, an authorizing official who chooses to accredit a system without first having the adequacy of security controls certified is taking a very large risk.

The Systems Security Approach

It should be noted that the objective of certification and accreditation as used in this volume is to ensure the security of an information technology system. It is not meant to ensure the security of an organization, a security program, a person or persons, or a manual process. There are other processes available to measure and ensure the effectiveness of these, but

Figure I.1   Viewing systems as islands of security.

the focus of our attention will be on computer systems, which are viewed as distinct units in the construction of a successful information technology security program. As depicted in Figure I.1, this approach considers systems as secure islands in a sea of risk. With this model a security perimeter is established for individual critical resources according to system boundaries, rather than constructing a single, extended security perimeter to protect all critical resources the organization chooses to protect. The approach works because systems are distinct and their limits can be defined in practical terms and security is comparatively easy to implement at the system level. On the other hand, the enterprise security is more difficult to define and implementation of security controls enterprisewide is far less practical. This approach envisions the implementation of an organizationwide security architecture through the identification and implementation of its aspects at the system level.

Perhaps the key aspect of the certification and accreditation methodology described in this volume is its concentration on systems as building blocks for an organization's information security program. This is based on the notion that it is more practical to define security requirements for an individual system than for an entire enterprise.

The Problem with Certification and Accreditation

To many, certification and accreditation are dirty words because they equate them with expensive and time-consuming paperwork foisted on them by unknowing and uncaring bureaucrats. The process is viewed as an unnecessary requirement that provides no return on investment, challenges managers with a need to dip into already limited resources, preventing them from meeting other more pressing priorities with which they must contend. When being confronted with requirements to implement certification and accreditation for the first time, the natural reaction is to wonder why it is needed because the system has survived without it beforehand. Most consider it "a government thing" that is not really relevant to the private sector. Those more familiar with certification and accreditation carp that it is too heavy on assessment and not heavy enough on remediation, or that concentrating security on systems is too granular to be effective. Others who have no familiarity with certification and accreditation think that it relates to individuals and miss the point entirely.

Benefits of Certification and Accreditation

In this guide I hope to effectively address these concerns about certification and accreditation and make a case that certification and accreditation can provide significant benefits to an organization. Some of the most obvious include:

- Helping to maintain the visibility of the information technology security program by drawing attention to it at multiple organizational levels.
- Effectively being used in the exercise of due diligence, allowing management to prove that it is doing the right thing in protecting its assets, and providing a process for meeting requirements and managing risk.
- Providing a means for integrating security across all of its computer systems, allowing consistency in the implementation of security controls.
- Permitting fulfillment of requirements of the information technology security program by helping focus on a unified objective. All the elements of the program — security planning, vulnerability assessment, risk assessment, controls testing, etc. — aim toward achievement of a common goal: the protection of the organization's information technology systems.
- Ensuring that minimum security controls requirements are being met.

- Ensuring that appropriate, risk-based security controls have been identified and are implemented and functioning as designed.
- Promoting management involvement through the designation of program-related roles and responsibilities, by fixing accountability for the secure operation of the system, and by measuring the effectiveness of managers in mitigating risks to the system.
- Saving effort and resources by consolidating individual processes into an integrated program.

External Program Drivers

There are certainly internal drivers for establishing a certification and accreditation program, but there are also external requirements pointing to the need for one as well. In recent years public laws, such as Sarbanes–Oxley, the Health Insurance Portability and Accountability Act, the Gramm–Leach–Bliley Act, Clinger–Cohen, as well as FISMA, have pointed toward the need for more effective implementation of security in government organizations and have increased the need for organizations to concentrate on regulatory compliance as a primary business driver. The fervent work of the National Institute of Standards and Technology staff in the United States as well as the development of ISO 17799 and its spread throughout the developed world have accompanied this renewed emphasis on security and accountability. In the private sector, successful prosecution of executives in large American corporations like Enron, WorldCom, and Global Crossing have pointed to the need for management accountability and due diligence. Additionally, since September 11, 2001, the war on terrorism and the establishment of the Department of Homeland Security have heightened awareness of security in general and management's role in the protection of its resources, especially its critical infrastructure and personnel.

Why Read This Book?

The primary reason that one should take the time to read this book is that it describes a usable approach for top-down implementation of information technology security in an organization. This book aims to define a practical approach to certification and accreditation that can be successfully implemented in most organizations, both public and private. The book will help readers make sense of official guidance that has been published on certification and accreditation and on its related processes. What I seek to define in this volume is not only a practical approach but also one that simplifies the certification and accreditation process while still following federal guidance. Because of the number of guidelines in this area that have been published over the years and in particular the last five years, those wishing to gain an introduction into the world of certification and accreditation are struck by the relative bounty of information, some of which appears to be in conflict. This book will help readers understand how various, seemingly disparate processes, some old and some new, are combined into a coherent, unified risk management methodology. The book provides a consistent view of those processes through the perspective of an enterprise information technology security manager, or chief information security officer (CISO), with a view toward following U.S. government guidance on the subject. In so doing, it provides nongovernment CISOs guidelines on why and how certification and accreditation can be implemented in their organizations even though they are not subject to federal information technology security statutes and directives. Finally, the book is based on real-world experience in certification and accreditation and it describes the most current thinking on the topic based on my personal involvement in certification and accreditation activities over the past 15 years, and in particular over the past two years.

Target Audience

This book is intended to benefit those who are classified as security practitioners or those charged with implementation or evaluation of security controls at either the system or security program level. This is translated to mean information system security officers (ISSOs), security managers, certifiers, and developers both in the public and private arenas. Those who are charged with developing an information security program for an organization will benefit from this volume most because it provides an overview of all of the various components of certification and accreditation. After reading this book, those tasked with certifying an information system should be able to document the status of security controls of a system. Those charged with securing a system at the system security officer or system administrator level can benefit by gaining an appreciation for how security for a system can be ensured through standard, repeatable processes. Those who own a system can benefit from reading this book and gain an appreciation for approaches to ensure that their system has been properly secured. The processes described in this book apply to security professionals both inside and outside of government organizations. Program managers and system developers can also gain insights from this material that will help them in effectively developing secure systems.

On the other hand, this volume is not intended to serve as an introduction to the information technology security field, and individuals who are new to information security may have difficulty understanding this material until they have grasped the concepts, practices, principles, and definitions used in the business.

Author Qualifications

I am qualified to write on this topic because of my active and continuous involvement with certification and accreditation since 1989. My first experience with this subject was as an officer in the U.S. Army, when I was charged with responsibility for the security of the local area network and three major applications my office used. In 1992, I became a full-time security consultant and began certifying systems and assisting government agencies in establishing certification and accreditation programs. Since that time I have performed certification and accreditation–related tasks for 20 federal and state departments, agencies, and institutions. My description of security process described in this book is further based on my experiences in the private sector where I have performed policy development, risk assessment, business impact analysis, vulnerability assessment, and certification testing for more than ten major corporations. In these engagements I developed a direct working knowledge of Federal Information Processing Standard 102, Office of Management and Budget Circular A-130, Appendix III, ISO 17799, and most NIST Special Publications. I was recently engaged as a full-time certification and accreditation practitioner for a department-level U.S. government agency and performed the role of certification and accreditation program manager on a full-time basis for that department for over two years. I currently serve as chief information security officer for the Department of Housing and Urban Development and have served in that position since May 2005.

Among my years as an information technology security professional, I have had many opportunities to design and develop information technology security programs and document program guidance and policies. This has included establishment of guidelines and processes for certifying and accrediting information systems. My varied experiences as a manager in government as well as in the private sector have allowed me to broaden my perspective beyond that of a mere information technology security analyst. Understanding the management point of view allows me to place information technology security program planning and certification and accreditation into a broad context and to respect the difficulties that managers have in prioritizing resources.

Organization of the Book

This book consists of four main sections. It begins with a description of what it takes to build a certification and accreditation program at the organization level. Then the discussion progresses toward describing various certification and accreditation processes and activities and how they interrelate. The next section provides a case study of the successful implementation of certification and accreditation in a major U.S. government department. Finally, the book provides a collection of helpful samples in the appendices.

The Author

Patrick D. Howard, CISSP, CISM, was assigned as the first chief information security officer at the U.S. Department of Housing and Urban Development on May 2, 2005. He has over 20 years' experience in information security and has been involved in the security profession since 1972. A former military police officer, Pat successfully served in military positions in law enforcement, operations, physical security, information security, and security management, retiring from the U.S. Army in 1992. Since then he has served as an information security consultant with several government contracting firms in the Washington, D.C., area, including the Comsis Corp., PRC Inc., and Troy Systems. He has also provided support to the Nuclear Regulatory Commission, U.S. Coast Guard, Bureau of the Census, Bureau of the Public Debt, House of Representatives, and Departments of Agriculture, Veterans Affairs, Labor, and Defense among others. Pat was formerly employed as a senior manager for Ernst & Young, LLC, where he developed security consulting methodologies for E&Y's national information technology security practice and created policies and standards for a variety of commercial clients. He has also performed consulting services for Netigy and Quinetiq Trusted Information Management, where he was charged with developing security consultant certification programs, developing and delivering CISSP® preparatory training, creating corporate security consulting methodologies, and delivering consulting services to commercial and government organizations. Pat has also served as an instructor for the Computer Security Institute, has written articles on the security policy development, and is co-author of a CISSP preparatory handbook. Most recently Pat was employed by the Titan Corporation and was assigned full time to the Department of Transportation, Office of the Chief Information Officer, where he served as the department certification and accreditation program manager. Pat has a B.A. degree from the University of Oklahoma and an M.A. degree from Boston University. He lives with his wife, Annemarie, in Bel Air, Maryland.

BUILDING A SUCCESSFUL ENTERPRISE CERTIFICATION AND ACCREDITATION PROGRAM

I once made the acquaintance of an information system security officer in a federal department who had what he defined as airtight security for his application system. During my assessment I found that he had implemented government certification and accreditation guidance for his application as well as could possibly be imagined and had fully documented all the controls protecting the system. Three years later when I returned to assess the system for reaccreditation I was somewhat surprised that the system could not be recertified. When I was told that the ISSO had been transferred, the problem became quite clear to me. The process that the ISSO had used to protect his system was limited only to his single, well-protected application and had not been institutionalized elsewhere in the organization.

To be effective, a certification and accreditation program must be greater than the efforts of isolated, well-intentioned individuals like this ISSO and must be implemented on an enterprisewide level. A program implemented at this highest organizational level first and foremost permits consistency across the entire organization. Further, the implementation of a successful enterprise certification and accreditation program can greatly promote the implementation of a likewise effective information security program for an organization.

An enterprise certification and accreditation program can be considered successful if it provides an effective means of identifying and meeting requirements, permits efficient oversight of its activities, and provides assurance that necessary controls are implemented at the system level. For the purposes of this discussion an enterprise program is one that supports the entire organization and that is either independent of any other program or has a significant degree of independence to implement guidance of a higher level program. This equates to a corporate- or department-level government organization. An enterprise program is distinct from its business unit–level components, which relate to elements of the overall enterprise program. Certification and accreditation for a line of business will normally focus on an interrelated grouping of information technology systems that support a tightly focused business function.

The information contained in this section applies to efforts to build an enterprise security certification and accreditation program from the ground up, as well as efforts to expand an existing program with additional capabilities or with a revised orientation. This section will discuss the ingredients necessary to construct a successful enterprise certification and accreditation program, provide a detailed discussion of certification and accreditation roles and responsibilities, explain how certification and accreditation is incorporated into the system life cycle, and describe causes of the failure of many certification and accreditation programs over the years.

Chapter 1

Key Elements of an Enterprise Certification and Accreditation Program

A certification and accreditation program is comprised of people, processes, and technologies of a wide variety. Each of these various elements is important, but there is a small subset of program components that can truly be classified as essential to the success of the program. These are the deal breakers. If they are not in place or do not function effectively or completely, implementation of the program will be hampered, and the success of the entire program may be jeopardized. In the following paragraphs I identify and explain several program elements that are critical to the success of any certification and accreditation program. Because of their importance to the success of the program, the following components should be designed into the program from its inception.

The Certification and Accreditation Business Case

The establishment of an enterprise certification and accreditation program has to be based on a strong business case that documents its key benefits to the organization. This business case highlights for management the reasons why the program is necessary for the organization, and it establishes early on that there is a business need for the program. These benefits of an enterprise certification and accreditation program include:

- *Due Diligence*: The certification and accreditation program provides a means for exercising due diligence. It assures management that security has been appropriately addressed through the implementation of a comprehensive, documented process that produces evidence of this assurance.
- *Accountability*: The program provides mechanisms for making executives, managers, and employees at multiple levels of the organization accountable for the security of the systems that they either use or are responsible for.
- *Implementation*: Certification and accreditation facilitates the management of risks. It provides a mechanism for ensuring that security issues are addressed by means of its requirements for remediation plans and oversight of corrective action. The program provides a road map for fixing as well as identifying weaknesses and formalizes security control identification, implementation, and evaluation.
- *Visibility*: The certification and accreditation program provides visibility to information technology security across the organization by addressing issues at several levels.
- *Cost-Effectiveness*: Finally, the certification and accreditation program provides a cost-effective approach for securing systems through the establishment of repeatable processes that regularize security tasks, and lend themselves to management oversight.

When developing the business case for the program, it is important for the chief information security officer (CISO) or security program manager to enlist the support of allies. By building partnerships with other organization managers, the CISO can build a more convincing case for the program. Although the CISO must play the role of program champion, he or she needs to seek support of other influential individuals as co-champions. This can be done by meeting with and working closely with managers of other organization programs and operations to convince them of how the certification and accreditation program can help them meet their business needs. Building these relationships is discussed further in Chapter 2.

Certification and Accreditation Goal Setting

In designing a certification and accreditation program for the enterprise, goals and objectives for the program must be established and effectively communicated across the enterprise. When considering program goals it is important to understand that the program must be:

- *Realistic*: The program must solve a realistic business problem. Small organizations or those without significant investments in information technology resources realistically do not need a formalized certification and accreditation program like those described in this volume. In such cases, less elaborate programs that include risk assessment and acceptance will probably meet the needs of such organizations.
- *Comprehensive*: The certification and accreditation program needs to leave no stone (or system) unturned. One of the program's greatest benefits is standardization of processes, requirements, and outcomes. Failure to require all organizational elements to comply with program requirements risks the loss of this standardization.
- *Integrated*: The program must integrate requirements from multiple sources under a centralized authority. Requirements that impact security must all be brought into the certification and accreditation house so that they can be addressed as part of an integrated program.
- *Achievable*: The program must be achievable with resources that are or will be reasonably available. There is no need to design an elaborate program that is impressive to behold but that can never be implemented due to its complexity or cost. The program must be able to harness the skills of those readily available in the organization.
- *Effective*: An ineffective certification and accreditation program may very well be worse than no program at all because of the basic planning and implementation required to initially establish the program. If the certification and accreditation initiative does not achieve its goals, then the effort that has been expended on it has been wasted with no obvious benefit, further deteriorating any element of goodwill that may have existed previously.
- *Supported*: The certification and accreditation program must have genuine support to work effectively. If no one supports it, or if it is only supported by a limited number of individuals in a minimal number of organizational elements, it will fail. Executives must provide their active support especially in its early stages by providing resources to the initiative; business managers must exercise continuing support; technicians must understand the benefit of the program and support it through their day-to-day control of system controls; and users must see evidence of enhanced security provided by the program to perform the security functions inherent to their jobs.
- *Enduring*: A certification and accreditation program must be designed for the long term. It is not a temporary solution for a

short-term problem. The program must be designed to permit continuous improvement in the security posture of the organization. And, because of the threats inherent in the nature of the modern workplace, an optimum security posture can probably never be achieved; even if it is, this posture cannot be maintained without a certification and accreditation program.

The most effective approach to setting program goals and objectives is for the organization information technology security director or CISO to be the individual charged with this responsibility, because he or she is the rightful owner of the program. Goal setting must be closely tied to the development of the business case for the program and must be underwritten by senior organization management. Knowledge of the organization, its culture, its personalities, and its security posture is essential in this process. Other areas that the CISO should consider as part of the program goal-setting process are the effect that other programs and initiatives may have on certification and accreditation (e.g., strategic enterprise information technology planning, mergers and acquisitions, etc.), and the resources available. There is no need to plan a two-week vacation in Maui when you can't afford the trip to the airport.

Establishing Program Tasks and Milestones

For the program to be effective the CISO or dedicated program manager must establish tasks that need to be performed and a schedule for their completion. These tasks must be established from the perspective of identifying how approved program goals and objectives will be achieved. Both short-term (immediate certification of systems) and long-term goals (achieving an established performance objective as an organization) need to be addressed. Tasks and milestones need to be consolidated into a coherent high-level program management plan that is disseminated to program participants and other organization managers under the authority of executive management. This program-level plan cannot simply be developed and then reviewed annually. It must be a driver itself that is used frequently in monthly and quarterly updates, and it should provide the basis for development of objectives for individual performance plans of key program players.

Overseeing Program Execution

The execution of the certification and accreditation program must be constantly measured to ensure that it is being implemented effectively and to ensure that established program requirements are being met. The program oversight function must be responsive to the needs of the organization and this is best served through a dedicated tracking process established by the CISO or certification and accreditation program manager. Metrics that can be used to measure the successful implementation of the program are outlined later in this chapter. The CISO should seek frequent feedback from program participants on their view of the program and ways in which it can be improved, and the CISO must be responsive to their concerns either by making suggested changes or by explaining why their recommendations cannot be employed. Program requirements must be subject to a well-defined enforcement mechanism and schedule. The enforcement effort should not be half-hearted, capricious, or irregular. System owners and business managers should know how compliance inspections will be performed and when they will be conducted.

Oversight of the program also needs to include provision of assistance and advice to program participants. This assistance should extend to the area of problem escalation on either an immediate or periodic level. The CISO or certification and accreditation program manager should either create or be part of an escalation plan where issues related to the program can be identified, reported, and resolved on an immediate basis. Additionally, the CISO should schedule regular meetings to explain program initiatives and their impact. Such meetings should be conducted for systems owners, ISSOs, and also authorizing officials when necessary.

Should one exist (and one should), a security oversight committee can assist in performance of the certification and accreditation program oversight function. This group will probably meet on a periodic basis with representation of broad organizational elements well suited for oversight of program compliance and for establishing program goals. To be effective the security oversight committee must have access to performance metrics to perform its program evaluation function and must have the authority to establish or recommend changes to program objectives and strategies. The CISO should closely coordinate with this group as it reviews objectives and goals and assesses progress toward those goals, and as best possible use its findings as justification for resources for the program.

Maintaining Program Visibility

Without consistent management support, the certification and accreditation program will lose effectiveness and will eventually die. To maintain the attention it needs, the CISO will have to work hard to maintain management support by providing frequent updates on program status, needs, and benefits. As part of his or her participation in regular organization staff meetings, the CISO should make reporting on certification and accreditation one of the hot buttons. The CISO should brief executive management on project plans for significant program initiatives (e.g., recertification of a large number of systems due to a facility upgrade) and should consider couching problem resolution in terms of certification and accreditation program implementation. For instance, implementation of a biometric solution can be presented not just as another control that provides security to information systems, but also as a means of mitigating residual risks in the operation of the system that were previously identified during certification testing.

The CISO should take every opportunity to maintain the interest of upper management because it has control over the lifeblood of the program: resources. The CISO must offer upper management frequent written updates, involve them in program issues during routine staff meetings, and get on their schedule to brief them when their direct input is required on program issues. In addition to offering formal briefings to keep C-level executives in the loop, brief, well-written electronic mail messages can also be an effective means of communicating program status to upper management, and these messages keep the program visible. Focusing such messages on the program's support to other ongoing initiatives helps elevate the program's usefulness in their eyes. This is most effective when concrete metrics can be pointed out, such as delays in schedules or the number of security weaknesses that can be resolved through the selection of a particular course of action. In addition to topical electronic mail, certification and accreditation program status should be integrated into other reports as much as possible. For instance, weekly reports from the CISO should most assuredly include a paragraph on program status, and information technology security input regarding the status of an organizational initiative like implementation of a new accounting system should use certification and accreditation terms and program objectives as fully as possible.

CISOs should remember that in their drive to gain the ear of chief executives, they should avoid using any increased visibility or influence to draw unnecessary attention to the failures of individual program participants. Although this may very well be required on occasion, this tactic should be rarely employed and only after making every effort to personally resolve the difficulty first. Seeking the cooperation of system owners and business unit managers involved in the program must be maintained at a high priority, and using upper management to hammer them into cooperation, may be effective in the short term but is detrimental to the program in the long run.

Table 1.1   Man-Hour Planning Estimates

Certification Level	Duration of Testing	Number of Personnel	Man-Hours
Low	1 day	1	8
Moderate	2–3 days	2	32–48
High	5–10 days	4	160–320

Resources

Funding for certification and accreditation initiatives is the lifeblood of the program. The decision to establish an enterprise program must be followed with a commitment to invest in the people, processes, and technology required to implement and maintain the program. This begins with a realistic definition of program requirements, not a wish list. A realistic budget for the program can be developed by first estimating the man-hours needed to perform project tasks because labor and personnel costs will make up the lion's share of program expenditures. Costs to certify individual systems vary greatly, but reasonably realistic man-hour estimates based on system type and level of effort are provided in Table 1.1. Other costs include program management costs (addressed in Chapter 6), costs for developing program guidance, training costs, and costs for the purchase of development-automated tools. Once the program is established and operating, the program manager must continue to develop, submit, and justify program budget requirements. When the program manager anticipates resistance in initial funding for the program, the program manager should consider a salami-attack-like approach, where program objectives are quantified individually, allowing them to be funded incrementally depending on funding available. Using the repeatable processes and quantifiable metrics described in this volume, program operating costs can be readily estimated, making the job of defending the program budget much easier.

Developing Guidance

Once program goals, objectives, tasks, and milestones have been developed, and resource requirements have been identified, then it is time to begin documenting what the program is and how it will be implemented. This is achieved through the development and publication of certification and accreditation guidance. By guidance I mean documented policies,

Table 1.2   Certification and Accreditation Guidance Development Life Cycle

Phase	Task	Activity
Development	Creation	Plan for, research, and write the policy
	Review	Complete an independent policy review prior to approval
	Approval	Obtain management approval of the policy
Implementation	Communication	Disseminate the policy
	Compliance	Implement the policy
	Exceptions	Manage cases where full implementation is not possible
Maintenance	Awareness	Ensure continued awareness of the policy
	Monitoring	Report and track compliance with the policy
	Enforcement	Handle violations of the policy
	Maintenance	Keep the policy current
Disposal	Retirement	Retire the policy when it is no longer required

standards, guidelines, and procedures. This set of documentation establishes mandatory program requirements (policy, standards, and procedures) and offers useful but optional advice (guidelines). As a reminder, guidance documentation should always stress that the purpose of the certification and accreditation program is to meet an organizational business requirement and is based on a combination of legal, contractual, operational, and other business drivers; it is not simply a security program for its own sake.

Certification and accreditation guidance documentation is developed at the CISO level using the existing organization guidance structure (i.e., policy library) to give program documentation added authority and credibility. As part of this guidance development process, the CISO needs to assess any existing security guidance documentation to determine if it can be used to establish the program by updating it or if it needs to be replaced entirely. The CISO should also look to follow a guidance policy life-cycle approach, shown in Table 1.2. Program guidance begins with developing a policy statement. This is a brief, no more than one page, document signed at the highest level of the organization that establishes the program. A sample enterprise-level certification and accreditation policy is provided in Table 1.3. Program-related terms and definitions must be described in a certification and accreditation glossary, preferably at this highest level where it will be most visible.

Table 1.3   Sample Enterprise Certification and Accreditation Policy

On the basis of a certification package that contains an up-to-date security plan, risk assessment, security test and evaluation (ST&E), and plan of action and milestones (POA&M), each XYZ Agency general support system and major application will be evaluated for authorization to process. The XYZ Agency senior management official, who is responsible for the business process supported by the system and who exercises budgetary control over the system, must authorize the system prior to its being allowed to go into production for newly developed systems or those undergoing major updates, or must authorize systems in production to continue to operate. This authorization must be made in writing based on implementation of its security plan before beginning or significantly changing processing in the system. Use of the system shall be reauthorized at least every three years.

Based on the policy establishing the program, enterprise-level certification and accreditation standards are developed to establish particular program requirements. These standards facilitate implementation of the high-level policy by elaborating on program requirements in more detail. Standards should be set for the entire spectrum of the program to establish minimum security baseline requirements that must be met. Minimum security baseline standards are addressed in detail in Chapter 10.

The next type of program guidance to be developed is enterprise-level certification and accreditation guidelines. These are written as work aids, templates, samples, checklists, and instructions that are designed to assist in the development of program documentation and in meeting program requirements. This type of documentation is highly valuable because it facilitates consistency in program documentation. Although the use of guidelines is optional, they should be so well written and so easy to use that their use will be practically universal. They should represent the simplest, most effective, and best ways to perform a task. Ensure that when templates and samples are provided that users understand that these need to be tailored to their own specific needs. Otherwise, the use of out-of-the-box certification and accreditation products without thought can lead to the organization being held liable for noncompliance with rules that are actually nonapplicable.

The final component of an integrated set of certification and accreditation policies is security procedures. Development of security procedures is accomplished on several levels. At the enterprise level, responsible organizations develop procedures that apply to all systems throughout the organization. At the business-unit level, managers prepare procedures that apply to only those systems in their area of responsibility, but with which all systems must adhere. Finally, at the system level, the system owner is responsible for creating procedures that implement program policies, standards, and procedures of higher level organizations. These system-specific procedures apply only to a particular information technology system and present the most detailed requirements of all policy documents. The development of security procedures is addressed in more detail in Chapter 12.

The certification and accreditation guidance must describe a methodology for performing program tasks. This means that it must present a flow of how certifications and accreditations will be performed and how program processes, tasks, and activities interrelate. An example of certification and accreditation process flow is presented in Figure 1.1. Program guidance documentation must describe each process, what each is designed to achieve, the output from each, responsibilities for the process, and timelines for completion.

Certification and accreditation policy and guidance should be precise, clear, and as brief as possible to enhance understanding and to limit confusion. It should be located in the same repository and should be tightly controlled by the CISO. For every new policy document created, an old one should be removed to avoid its continued use. Stability of documentation is a useful goal, particularly in light of the fact that certification and accreditation documents are being used at very low levels of the organization. System administrators rely on clear and stable documentation in developing security plans, minimum security baseline self-assessments, and other documentation, and they expect that once they learn how to comply with the rules, the rules will not be changing frequently. Other desirable characteristics of certification and accreditation policy documentation include ease of access (preferably it will be accessible from the corporate intranet); seamless integration into the organization's policy structure; consistency with other policy documentation, particularly other certification and accreditation policies and standards; readability by an average reader; that it is up to date; and applicability to the needs of the organization.

Limiting the amount of certification and accreditation policy documentation in circulation will facilitate ease of maintenance as well as making it more readily accessible and useful. The golden rule of policy documentation — "less is more" — should be adhered to because an overly abundant set of rules and regulations stifles application of discretion in the security of systems as well as innovation in identifying solutions to control implementation.

Program Integration

CISOs will have to integrate the certification and accreditation program with other organization programs and activities, both those that they

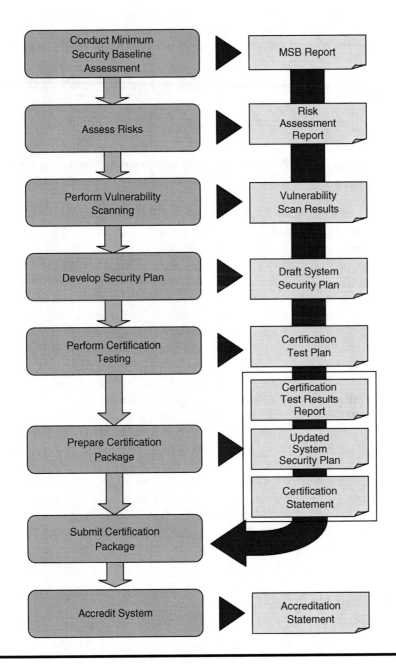

Figure 1.1   Certification and accreditation process flow.

control as well as those they do not. High on the list of priorities will be initiating discussions with individuals responsible for incident response, disaster recovery, system development, auditing, resource management, personnel security, human resources, physical security, general counsel, the security oversight committee, education and training, the configuration control board, and contracting. The relationships of these contacts to the certification and accreditation program will be detailed further in Chapter 2.

Establishing Certification and Accreditation Points of Contact

Although the CISO has direct responsibility for the success of the organization's certification and accreditation program, he or she has to rely on many others to be successful. One of the first objectives for achieving success in building a program is the development of a certification and accreditation workgroup. Such an informal organization would consist of key players across the organization who can contribute to the effectiveness of the program. The CISO should strive for the involvement of system owners, points of contact from key lines of business, adjunct members from external sister organizations, and points of contact from interconnected systems.

Individuals who function most effectively as members of a certification and accreditation workgroup are those who have knowledge of the organization's operations, management structure, leadership hierarchy, business strategies, and initiatives and plans, as well as its systems and information technology architecture. Security qualities that point to success as a workgroup member are a basic understanding of security principles and practices, sound knowledge of certification and accreditation policies and processes, and a general knowledge of risk management principles, as well as knowledge of specific risks to organization information technology assets. Therefore, the team should have a good mix of members with business, information technology, and security backgrounds.

Measuring Progress

An effective certification and accreditation program requires defined metrics to allow the CISO to know how well it is functioning. The CISO should establish a process for measuring the effectiveness of the program so that he or she can rapidly determine shortfalls and redirect efforts to trouble spots. The certification and accreditation processes described in this volume are designed to produce information that the CISO can use to monitor the progress of the program at several levels throughout all the stages. Common measures of success that can be used in monitoring program effectiveness include:

- *Time*: Measuring the completion of program requirements according to a predetermined schedule to determine if they are being completed in a timely and efficient basis.
- *Task*: Measuring discrete program elements such as preparation of security plans, risk assessments, certification tests, etc. Tasks of this nature have established start and end dates and follow a measurable development process, allowing the security manager to determine if they are being performed on time and according to standards.
- *Cost*: Measuring the amount of financial resources expended in performance of program requirements. This is primarily related to man-hours utilized in performing program tasks but also includes expense elements such as contracting, training, travel, and supplies. Costs are measured against an established program budget and deviations are readily discernable.
- *Number of Systems*: Measuring the scope of the program is achieved by measuring the number of general support systems and major applications within its scope. The system inventory process will produce this metric and is addressed in detail in Chapter 6.
- *Sensitivity and Criticality*: Measuring a system's relative need for protection and its relative importance to the organization permits the manager to determine if the system's security protection requires additional emphasis, more resources, increased priority, or elevated scrutiny. Chapter 7 defines the process for assessing system sensitivity and criticality.
- *Risk*: Measuring the number and severity of weaknesses in information systems that are certified and accredited. The identification of risks and determination of their severity follow a well-defined process that produces consistency in findings. The risk assessment process is described in Chapter 11.
- *Level of Effort*: A measure used to establish the amount of time and expertise required to perform certification testing. The level of effort is defined in predetermined standards and is applied according to the sensitivity and criticality of the system. This ensures that the rigor of certification testing is commensurate with the needs of the system. Certification levels of effort are discussed in Chapter 13.
- *Improvements*: Measuring the status, rate of completion, and adequacy of corrective actions taken in response to correct deficiencies

in security controls. The plan of action and milestones or remediation plan is normally used by the security manager to measure the success or failure of remediation efforts, and the process is further discussed in Chapter 14.

■ *Number of Systems Accredited*: This measurement gives a direct indication of the bottom line. The goal of the certification and accreditation program is to accredit 100 percent of the organization's systems. Counting the number of signed, approved system accreditation packages readily allows the security manager to establish the level of progress toward this goal. Documentation and approval aspects of the accreditation process are defined in Chapters 15 and 16.

Use of these metrics allows CISOs to measure progress toward accomplishment of program requirements and gives important feedback that can be used to inform management of the security posture of the organization's information systems. These metrics permit a comparison of different organizational elements to establish where increased emphasis and priority are needed. They allow identification of trends that require resolution at the enterprise level, such as implementation of a strong authentication solution. And, because easily quantified, common metrics are used, they allow CISOs to benchmark the status of their organization's program with that of other organizations. FISMA has been effective in its establishment of useful metrics that allow Congress to compare the level of security in major government departments and agencies.

Tracking Program Activities

At any given time CISOs will have a wide variety of certification and accreditation projects and activities taking place, and they have overall responsibility for the adequacy of their results and the timeliness and cost-effectiveness of their completion. A tracking process allows CISOs to use the metrics described above to monitor the progress and status of these activities to identify problems before they become bigger problems. Key elements of project tracking include:

■ *Problem Forecasting*: Program managers as much as possible should aim to forecast difficulties for management, allowing them to be the bearer of bad news but also the providers of an accompanying solution. Knowing the dependencies related to a project progress allows CISOs to project potential difficulties before they occur, and focusing on the critical path allows them to concentrate on the tasks that matter most to the successful completion of the project and ensures that they are not distracted by minutiae.

■ *Tracking External Projects*: CISOs must also be aware of and track the progress of ongoing projects for which they do not have responsibility but that have an impact on the certification and accreditation program. This could include development of new systems, consolidation of existing systems, or interconnection with external systems. Processes that address events such as these are discussed in more detail in Chapters 3, 9, and 16.

■ *Reporting*: The information that the CISO gathers to maintain visibility of program activities should be translated into reports to apprise management, supporting elements (e.g., certifying agents), and supported elements (e.g., system owners) of project status. Regular status reporting to management helps to maintain management support and aids in team building when dependably communicated to other program participants.

■ *Resource Tracking*: Close tracking of resources expended in the performance of program activities allows the CISO to monitor and respond to deviations in the budget estimate. This helps him or her identify requirements for additional resources to ensure that critical projects can be completed even when over budget.

Management of certification and accreditation projects is further described in Chapter 5.

Tracking Compliance

If the program manager only needed to meet certification requirements by identifying weaknesses and risks, his or her job would be more simple but incomplete. After a system has been certified, the CISO needs a process to monitor the system's continued compliance with requirements, measure progress in implementing corrective actions to address weaknesses, and track risks that authorizing officials have accepted. The process needs to include the following capabilities.

■ *Vulnerability Scanning and Checking*: The compliance tracking process needs to include the use of automated vulnerability scanning tools to periodically verify the ability of a system's technical controls to protect against known exploits. These should be performed as often as weekly for the most sensitive systems, but no less frequently than quarterly for any system. In addition to automated scanning, physical spot checks of security practices should be performed to ensure compliance. This includes reviews of documentation (such as audit trails, facility access logs, system change request forms), as well as observations of how system personnel comply with documented procedures.

■ *Recertification Tracking*: The process must provide for tracking the need for periodic recertification of systems to ensure that full and interim accreditations are not allowed to expire. Associated with this is the CISO's need to monitor systems for which accreditation has been denied to ensure that the systems do in fact terminate processing or do not begin processing.

■ *Monitoring Accepted Risks*: The CISO should maintain an inventory of all risks that accrediting authorities have accepted and do not plan to mitigate due to cost or other operational considerations. The purpose of this is to ensure that these risks do not present exposures to other systems in the enterprise and to allow them to be reassessed when changes in the environment occur.

■ *Tracking Changes in the Environment*: The tracking process must provide for monitoring changes to systems environments to identify additional requirements for protection. This process must be closely tied to the incident response capability to allow knowledge of incidents that may impact the enterprise.

■ *Tracking Audit Findings*: The CISO must be able to maintain visibility of security-related findings from internal and external audits and must ensure their integration into remediation plans developed through system certification.

■ *Reviewing Security Documentation*: The process should track the currency of security documentation (i.e., security plans), by reviewing it to ensure it has been reviewed and updated by system owners annually to account for changes to the system and its security posture.

■ *Validating Corrective Action*: Once system owners report through the plan of action and milestones process that corrective action has been completed, the process must provide the capability to spot check reported corrective actions to provide assurance that they fully mitigate the weakness and that they will prevent the weakness from reoccurring.

Providing Advice and Assistance

From the perspective of the senior manager, one of the primary services rendered by the certification and accreditation program manager is offering advice and assistance. Advice and assistance is important to others in the organization, so this is essential both vertically and horizontally. The CISO needs to establish a process that maximizes consistency while minimizing ad hoc readings and opinions that may not withstand scrutiny when applied enterprisewide or over time. Other considerations for the certification and accreditation program manager when providing advice and assistance include:

- *Knowledge of the Program*: The program manager is expected to be the absolute subject matter expert and resident guru who offers the most reliable information on the certification and accreditation program and how it works. Advice provided regarding processes, policies, and products must be based on a thorough knowledge of all aspects of the program based on personal experience.
- *Understanding*: When offering advice or providing assistance, the program manager must avoid the urge to rule from "on high." Though he or she may be charged with establishing program requirements and enforcing compliance, the manager must understand the perspective of the individual seeking advice and should offer solutions rather than simply responding that there will be no alternative but compliance. It is always better to offer advice and assistance with an aim toward relationship building based on an understanding that compliance starts from the bottom up, not from the top down.
- *Limiting Assistance*: The program manager must understand that many requests for assistance are based on a desire by the requestor to avoid responsibility. Be on the lookout for this tactic and avoid the trap of doing the work for system owners, ISSOs, and authorizing officials.
- *Accepting Suggestions*: Program managers should also understand that just because an idea does not originate with them that it is not a good one. Program managers must be open to suggestions, recommendations, and new ideas received from program participants and give them credence because they may very well be based on hard-earned experience.
- *Making Promises*: Certification and accreditation program managers must be careful in making promises in response to requests for advice and assistance. Promises may be difficult to keep once they are made, particularly when they have not been well thought out. Program managers must not promise an authorizing official that they will recommend that a system be certified until certification testing has actually been performed and results have been reviewed. Breaking promises is a quick way to lose credibility with those for whom it is most important. Program manager should

work to manage expectations with honest answers rather than with easy promises.

■ *Seeking Advice*: Program managers, though they may be the resident experts, will not always have all the answers. When this happens they should seek external advice and assistance by approaching an expert outside the organization. This might range from a phone conversation with a counterpart in a sister organization to discuss how a similar problem there may have been solved or presentation of a proposal to a higher level organization (for government agencies perhaps this will be approaching NIST for more detailed guidance).

■ *Recording Agreements*: Agreements made as a result of offering advice and assistance, which commit the program manager to provide assistance in the future, need to be recorded to ensure that they are met when the time comes. If the CISO offers to expedite his or her annual review of security compliance as requested by a system owner, then the work must be scheduled to ensure that it happens. Once again, credibility is an asset that is difficult to reestablish once it is lost.

Responding to Changes

Another essential ingredient to the success of certification and accreditation is ensuring compliance with external requirements. To do this, program managers must establish a process for ensuring they are aware of changes that affect the program and that permit them to develop an understanding of the changes' impacts. Examples of changes that could change the ground rules for the program might include the passage of new laws and dissemination of new regulations; requirements associated with new business agreements and contracts; new business models and initiatives; mergers and acquisitions; and new operating locations. If not careful, external changes can lead to requirements for major changes in the certification and accreditation program, even a potential program reinvention if these changes are not fully researched and understood. Having a process that allows them to be proactive in addressing potential impacts, program managers must know when and how to contest proposed changing conditions when warranted. Frequently, threatened changes are based on changes of personnel in the hierarchy and are made without knowledge of their impacts. CISOs must revisit the program business case and use it to present a convincing case for maintaining the status quo.

Program Awareness, Training, and Education

Developing and managing certification and accreditation–related awareness, training, and education is also an essential element to sustain the program over the long term. A certification and accreditation program can be implemented in the short term with the use of external resources (i.e., contractors and consultants). However, to maintain the program its requirements have to be internalized so as to be performed by assigned personnel. Program awareness ensures that every individual in the organization is familiarized with program objectives, processes, and benefits so that they understand the value of the program to their own work. Next, training provides more specialized training to program participants in certification and accreditation requirements specific to their program roles. System owners, ISSOs, system administrators, managers, and executives form the target audience for this training. Finally, education should be provided to those involved in the program who, because of the nature of their program roles, require professional-level expertise in certification and accreditation concepts, principles, and best practices. The CISO, others performing program manager functions, certifying agents, and certain ISSOs who are responsible for highly sensitive systems should receive professional certification and accreditation education.

In developing and delivering awareness, training, and education opportunities, the program manager should work with the organization's training function to ensure it is fully integrated to allow the use of existing mechanisms for documenting attendance, posting to personnel records, requesting funding, etc. As they always say, there is no need to reinvent the wheel. Once certification and accreditation requirements have been integrated into the organization's training program, there will be less difficulty in scheduling time to train employees and to obtain resources required to present the training. Table 1.4 provides planning estimates for establishing certification and accreditation awareness, training, and education requirements.

Use of Expert Systems

Another essential element of the enterprise certification and accreditation program is the evaluation, development, and utilization of automated tools to assist in the implementation of the program. Expert systems can be useful in developing program documentation and ensuring consistency. The program manager must decide which processes are ripe for automation and whether useful tools can be acquired or developed within the limits of available resources. Processes that lend themselves most readily

Table 1.4   Example of a Certification and Accreditation Training Plan

Priority	Target Audience	Description of Training	Duration
1	System owners/ project managers	Overview of certification and accreditation and the role of the system owner/project manager	2 hours
2	Approving authorities	Overview of certification and accreditation and the role of the approving authority	1 hour
3	System security officers (ISSOs)	Implementing certification and accreditation at the system level and the role of the ISSO	4 hours
4	IT Security Oversight Board	Overview of certification and accreditation	1 hour
5	Business unit security POCs	Oversight of certification and accreditation activities	4 hours
6	System administrators	Compliance with minimum security baseline controls	4 hours
7	System developers	Integration of certification and accreditation into the system development life cycle	4 hours
8	General users	Awareness of certification and accreditation	1 hour

to automation are those related to identification of controls, assessment of risks to those controls, documentation of vulnerabilities in the controls, and correction of weaknesses in these specific controls; in other words the security plan, risk assessment, certification testing, and remediation planning processes. There is an array of products available that automate certification and accreditation processes, including the minimum security baseline assessment, security plan development, risk assessment, aspects of certification testing (i.e., vulnerability scanning and baseline configuration checking), and remediation planning. However, care must be taken to ensure that the output of these various tools can be integrated to allow compliance with program requirements in a coherent way.

The tools that most effectively support certification and accreditation are those that centralize data collection, permit assessment of security posture against established standards, ease calculation of risks, consolidate development of security documentation (e.g., generation of security plans and certification test results reports), generate action plans, permit tracking of individual project work, and facilitate periodic reporting on program status (e.g., quarterly and annual FISMA reporting). The cost to purchase or develop tools is a key consideration, and costs to provide continuing training to users must be factored in because there is normally a significant need to train new program participants. When establishing a program and assessing the viability of using automated tools, it is important to determine first who the prospective users are going to be. Will they be employed for external certifying agents or system owners and ISSOs? The answer to that question impacts requirements for ease of use and consistency. When selecting a tool, the CISO needs to make sure that program requirements are used to drive the selection and that tool capabilities are not used to drive the program.

Waivers and Exceptions to Policy

Although not as essential as the other elements listed previously, a process for considering waivers and exceptions to program requirements is normally a part of a successful certification and accreditation program. As a component part of program enforcement, the CISO must know how to identify when waivers of program policies and standards are warranted in the interest of the overall mission of the organization. Considerations relating to schedules and costs have to be weighed to see if they can be accommodated without unduly jeopardizing the security of the system and the enterprise. There may be short-term circumstances that give rise to waivers of program requirements. For instance, it may make sense to honor a request to delay development of a system contingency plan for the system until the organization has decided on an organizationwide recovery strategy. Another example would be to grant a waiver to requirements until the organization has completed its plans for relocation to a new data center. Both of these examples relate to circumstances beyond the control of the affected system owner, are relatively short term in nature, and have established dates by when the security deviation will no longer apply.

On the other hand, there may be cases when an exception is appropriate for a security deviation because of other long-term conditions. This could relate perhaps to minimal cost benefit in meeting program requirements (i.e., implementation of strong authentication on a company parking space registration system). A formal process for reviewing and approving waivers for short-term deviations and exceptions to policy for long-term deviations can be established and managed, but it may prove to be time-consuming and eventually unwieldy due to the fact that tracking of waivers and exceptions is a labor-intensive process and by definition requires management by exception. The CISO will be better served in addressing these deviations using an existing certification process: one that is used to identify risks to systems assets that are acceptable and that leads to executive management acceptance of those risks.

Although the system owner and the authorizing official are the primary players in the risk acceptance process, the CISO can still exercise authority in this process through oversight of risks that have been accepted across the organization's information systems. The CISO should establish a basis for evaluating accepted risks to ensure that decisions are consistent and coherent in a broad context and are realistic and achievable at the system level. A decision-making framework for the CISO should be based on knowledge of the organization, its business processes, and business drivers. The CISO must also apply his or her evaluation based on expertise of the organization's security architecture. Finally, it must be based on a firm commitment from management to provide backing to the decisions the CISO makes regarding risks that should not be accepted. This will allow the CISO to stick to his or her guns when pressure mounts.

Summary

This chapter highlights essential processes and tools necessary to establish an effective enterprise certification and accreditation program. Of course, it is possible for a program to crash and burn even if all of the essential elements that have described are present. However, chances of success are greatly improved when a program has effectively addressed these elements. Although a successful program needs processes and technologies, it also requires people for their implementation. And it is people that will be addressed in the following chapter.

Chapter 2

Certification and Accreditation Roles and Responsibilities

One's view of the certification and accreditation program will be driven by perspective and needs. The program from the perspective of the approving authority may appear to be a means of ensuring that the operation of the system poses no significant risk to the organization. To the system owner, the program may be viewed as a management process that provides assurance that his system is safe from intruders, viruses, and other adverse events. To the security officer, the program may be considered as an approach for facilitating the implementation of essential security controls. And to the system administrator, the certification and accreditation program will appear to be a vehicle for defining security requirements and measuring the security posture of the system. The utility of the certification and accreditation program can then be said to be in the eye of the beholder. However, for the program to be effective, the roles and responsibilities for these individuals and others need to be set down in writing to prevent overlap while ensuring that all are addressed comprehensively.

Primary Roles and Responsibilities

There are five primary roles associated with the certification and accreditation program: the chief information security officer (CISO), the system owner, the information system security officer (ISSO), the certifying agent, and the approving authority. These are considered the primary roles because they are the players who have the greatest impact on the success or failure of the program.

- *Chief Information Security Officer.* The CISO is the organization's senior information system security manager who exercises overall responsibility for the organization's information technology security–related programs such as risk management, policy development and compliance monitoring, security awareness, incident investigation and reporting, and often contingency planning. The CISO is normally charged with responsibility for the enterprisewide certification and accreditation program as well. The CISO's certification and accreditation responsibilities include establishing the program and ensuring enforcement of program-related policies.
- *System Owner.* The system owner is the official who bears the primary responsibility for the security of an information system. The system owner establishes the sensitivity level of the system on the basis of the data it processes and thus establishes the basis for the kinds of controls needed to protect the system. The system owner exercises this responsibility over the full life cycle of the system from its initial development to its final disposition. The system owner ensures that controls are implemented, requests resources to ensure implementation is accomplished, and oversees the continued effectiveness of controls day to day. The system owner initiates certification and accreditation activities and also monitors preparation of certification and accreditation packages from their initiation to final system accreditation. The relationship between the owners of major application and general support system owners must be close and well defined. Because major applications are normally connected to or hosted on a general support system, the owner of the major application must to a large degree rely on the owner of that supporting system to provide a substantial amount of the security for his or her application.
- *Information System Security Officer.* The ISSO serves as an agent of the system owner who appoints him or her. Under the system owner's authority, the ISSO is responsible for securing the system. The ISSO closely monitors the day-to-day security of the system as well as routinely monitors the effectiveness of controls. He or she operates security mechanisms, performs security activities and tasks, follows up on incidents, and advises the system owner on security-related matters. The ISSO plays the most significant role

in the certification of the system by serving as the point of contact for the certifying agent.

- *Certifying Agent*: The certifying agent is the independent authority charged with measuring the effectiveness and completeness of security controls protecting a specific information system. The certifying agent is normally an individual assigned to another part of the organization or is a contractor tasked with performing this function on a short-term basis.
- *Approving Authority*: The approving authority, authorizing official, or designated approving authority (DAA) is the senior management official who is responsible for deciding if a system should be allowed to operate. Inherent in this role is the responsibility for accepting any residual risks to the system.

It is important that different individuals are chosen to perform these primary roles in order to ensure separation of duties. Emphasis on this important security principle means that independence is maintained and that a structure that promotes checks and balances is established. The relationships between these positions must be clearly spelled out in organizational policy so that there is no duplication of effort while ensuring that responsibilities and accountability for all critical tasks are assigned.

Other Roles and Responsibilities

Secondary certification and accreditation roles include the chief information officer (CIO), the information technology security program steering committee, the auditing staff, data owners and custodians, system administrators, business unit managers, project managers, facility managers, and executive managers. Individuals serving in these positions are indirectly involved in the program and support those in primary positions by performing the duties specified in the following paragraphs.

- *Chief Information Officer*: The CIO has overall responsibility for the execution of an organization's information technology security program and delegates authority to the CISO for the management of the enterprise certification and accreditation program. The CIO supports the program through oversight, maintaining visibility of the program across the organization and with senior management, and through the provision of resources for its execution.
- *Information Technology Security Program Steering Committee*: The committee provides high-level oversight of the organization's information security program and provides direction on program goals,

resources, and initiatives. In this context, the committee provides indirect supervision and oversight of the enterprise certification and accreditation program.

■ *Auditor:* This function provides for an independent assessment of the viability of the overall program by looking at the effectiveness of individual program components. Auditors ensure that the certification and accreditation program provides an adequate level of security assurance by reviewing program practices and procedures to ensure that controls are documented, that risks are identified and prioritized, that controls are tested, that weaknesses are identified and corrective actions are specified and are tracked, and that systems have been authorized to process by a senior management official.

■ *Information Owner/Custodian:* The owner of the information processed by an information system and the custodian who serves as the owner's agent are responsible for ensuring that the system owner is aware of requirements for protecting his or her information on the basis of its sensitivity. Most often the information owner and the system owner are one and the same, but the information owner is distinguished as the official who is best positioned to know the impact of the information's unauthorized disclosure, its corruption and loss of integrity, and its unavailability. The information owner should establish these impact levels, which are then used to establish security controls requirements.

■ *System Administrator:* The system administrator is charged with the day-to-day administration and operation of the system and is responsible for the implementation of many of the technical and operational controls employed to protect the system. Primary security-related functions performed by the system administrator include activating, deactivating, and monitoring user accounts; performing backups; implementing hardware and software changes; and monitoring system performance. The system administrator works for the system owner; works closely with, but separately from, the ISSO; and demonstrates controls to the certifying agent during certification testing.

■ *Business Unit Manager:* Although business unit managers often function as system owners, their certification and accreditation responsibilities generally include dissemination of security information to subordinate personnel, reporting and response to security incidents, determining priorities and resources for implementing corrective actions to mitigate identified risks in relation to their areas of responsibility, and enforcement of security controls and associated personnel actions. Generally, the business unit manager's role relates to the implementation and maintenance of security controls.

- *Project Manager:* For the purpose of this discussion, the project manager is the official who is tasked with performing system owner–related functions for a system in development. The project manager fulfills all the certification and accreditation responsibilities of the system owner described above relative to a system in the development phases of its life cycle.
- *Facility Manager:* The individual performing this role is responsible for the implementation and maintenance of physical and environmental controls protecting information technology systems located in facilities he or she manages.
- *Executive Management:* Executive managers play a crucial role in overseeing the certification and accreditation program, establishing policy, apportioning resources, and enforcing requirements. Most important, senior executive management can increase visibility of the program and ensure its success through support and emphasis.

Documenting Roles and Responsibilities

As we will see later in Chapter 8, roles and responsibilities must be documented in the security plan for each system. The specific tasks that must be performed by these certification and accreditation players are also identified in system-level and program-level procedures. In such documents it is normally better to make reference to the position rather than to the individual holding the position to avoid the need for revisions of the procedures when individuals change jobs or otherwise depart. As we will see in Chapter 4, responsibilities for certification and accreditation organizations also need to document and continually update these roles and responsibilities in program policy documentation to ensure they are mutually supporting. Other roles and responsibilities are typically fluid and short term in nature. As such, they need only be documented in general terms as conditions warrant.

The CISO should document as many certification and accreditation positions as possible. This may be achieved through the use of assignment orders or letters of appointment for each individual involved with the program. This cannot be achieved without management support, and a policy or directive signed by senior management will normally be required for this. At the very least, those functioning in the five primary program roles should be formally designated in writing. Others involved on the periphery of the program should also be identified, perhaps in a less formal way by being listed on the CISO's intranet site. The certification and accreditation program manager will find it beneficial to maintain up-to-date lists and matrices of personnel performing program functions, and this is best supported through creation of a contacts database. An example is shown in Table 2.1.

Job Descriptions

Generally, it's a good idea to stipulate certification and accreditation responsibilities in the position descriptions of those involved in the program. The value of including security requirements in an individual's job description is that it sets expectations for performance of security functions and provides a basis for holding the individual accountable for the performance of those duties. However, unless an individual performs certification and accreditation functions at least 50 percent of the time, there is little need to specifically cite these responsibilities in their job descriptions. However, security responsibilities should be prominently included for those holding any of the five primary certification and accreditation roles described above. Examples of job description wording for each of these key positions are provided in Table 2.2.

Position Sensitivity Designations

The positions of individuals holding key certification and accreditation positions should be designated as highly sensitive due to the need for them to have access to all vulnerability information for information technology systems, knowledge of security controls functionality, knowledge of the system's security posture, and their involvement in the mitigation of system security weaknesses. This access and involvement requires reliable and trustworthy personnel, and consequently their background information should be screened more thoroughly and more frequently than for other employees. Because of the costs associated with screening of this nature and the high level of trust involved, organizations should consider performance stipends for personnel holding such positions to encourage stability and to avoid frequent turnover.

Personnel Transition

When individuals holding these positions do depart, the primary concern is ensuring that a capable individual is available to assume the responsibilities. When possible, a replacement should be identified before the

Table 2.1 Example Contacts Database

Name	Position	Organization	Phone	E-Mail
Hector Blanco	Nutria System Owner	Research Division	x8650	hblan@acme.com
Roberta Jones	Security Manager	Finance Division	x8740	rjones@acme.com
Thomas Wild	Payroll ISSO	Administration	x8634	twild@acme.com
Frank Hostler	Security Manager	Administration	x8552	fhost@acme.com
Murray Booker	LAN ISSO	IT Operations	x8907	mbook@acme.com
Felix Gottlieb	Security Manager	Southern Region	345-678-9012	fgott@acme.com

Table 2.2   Sample Job Description Wording

Position	Job Description Entry
CISO	Establish the organization certification and accreditation program and develop program policy; assist in the implementation of the program; oversee program activities and provide management regular reports of program effectiveness.
System Owner	Implement organization certification and accreditation policy through identification and implementation of risk-based security controls for assigned systems; manage the security of IT systems by monitoring system activities and controls effectiveness.
ISSO	Assist the system owner in complying with the organization certification and accreditation program by identifying and implementing risk-based controls, monitoring controls status, and managing corrective actions.
Certifying Agent	Perform independent testing of IT system security controls and make recommendations regarding the potential accreditation or reaccreditation of the system.
Approving Authority	On the basis of certification testing of security controls, approve assigned IT systems for operation with regard to residual risks to the operation of the system, and specify risks for which acceptance has been granted.

incumbent departs to provide overlap and smooth the transition. The incumbent should give the incoming individual an overview of the organization's certification and accreditation policies, procedures, and activities to include pending remedial actions, the certification/recertification schedule, compliance review schedule, and any other pending issues and activities. In the case of very sensitive systems, the ISSOs and system owners should review all certification and accreditation–related documentation (i.e., the system security plan and risk assessment) to ensure that they are familiar with the contents of documents that describe risks to their system and the controls implemented to protect it. Although a transition of this nature does not require that the documents be updated, a formal indication that the incoming individual has reviewed the documents is a clear need. A signature on a document review sheet as described in Chapter 8 will serve this purpose. The CISO should closely monitor personal transitions affecting assigned approving authorities and be prepared to brief replacements to ensure they understand their new roles as accrediting officials.

Time Requirements

At the system level, certification and accreditation–related duties do not normally require full-time concentration. These duties are generally performed as collateral duties by an individual assigned to complementary functions (i.e., system administration, system management, database administration, etc.). In such cases the individual has to make his or her system certification tasks priorities at key stages of the certification and accreditation process. At times, depending on the size of the organization, certification and accreditation will be full time. However, there may be months when no significant certification and accreditation activity occurs at all. As an alternative, organizations may find it advantageous to make computer security activities for a group of several systems the full-time responsibility of a single, dedicated employee. This permits the individual to concentrate on performing security-related tasks (including certification and accreditation) specifically, and it provides the organization consistency of performance and greater assurance that security functions are being properly administered. The decision to employ a full-time security manager in this fashion must be based on resource considerations. However, the sensitivity and criticality of the systems for which the individual may be responsible should also be factored into determination of resource priority setting. A job analysis should be conducted to determine if a full-time security position is necessary, and it should consider elements such as separation of duties, need for independence, level of compliance required and consequent scrutiny necessary, and the security posture of the systems; those with extensive remediation plans will most benefit by the assignment of a full-time security officer at least on a temporary basis.

Expertise Required

Specialized knowledge, skills, and abilities are required to perform certification and accreditation tasks. Project management expertise is essential for the security manager or any other individual who provides dedicated certification and accreditation program leadership. Individuals at this level of program management must know system development principles and practices to promote integration of certification and accreditation efforts into the organization's system development life-cycle methodology and into individual system development projects. All personnel involved in primary certification and accreditation positions must be familiar with platform-specific technical controls and operations, and they must understand particular hardware and software products used in the organization's processing environment. Further, each certification and accreditation specialist needs familiarity with the organization, its structure, its leadership, its mission and goals, its culture and language, and with key business or mission initiatives that it is pursuing. General expertise in the areas of administrative staffing and coordination, information technology security terminology, practices, methodologies and procedures, interpersonal communications, and technical writing skills are also key attributes for individuals assigned to these positions. Additionally, personnel must meet organizational background screening requirements and must be able to receive and maintain appropriate security clearances and access credentials required to perform their functions. In all positions involved in the certification and accreditation program, individuals must have educational credentials commensurate with the level of responsibility required. Perhaps most important of all is the individual's level of credibility.

Credibility of certification and accreditation personnel can be further established through reliance on professional certification. Although there are many to choose from, the professional certifications that are most useful to certification and accreditation practitioners are those related to security management such as the Information Systems Audit and Control Association's (ISACA) Certified Information Security Manager (CISM) credential and (ISC)²'s® Certified Information Systems Security Professional (CISSP)® certification. However, when engaged in certification testing, certification in specific technologies is often beneficial.

Using Contractors

In most cases certification and accreditation functions will be performed by organization employees. This is almost always the case with the CISO, system owner, and the authorizing authority positions, and is only somewhat less so for the ISSO. Use of employees in these positions provides an element of stability, thereby minimizing training time required, fostering competence in duty performance, and reducing the amount of personnel background screening required. However, because of the need for independence inherent in the position, the role of the certifying agent is often performed by consultants or other individuals under contract. The use of contractors for this function is sound not only because of the independence they offer but also because of the breadth of experience and knowledge of certification and accreditation activities, practices, and methodologies their specialization may permit. Requirements for contractors need to be well defined in statements of work and contract terms to ensure the scope of their work is clearly defined, the methodology to be used is specified, timetables for performance are detailed, and deliverables to be produced are clearly documented. Although contractors are not suited to perform all certification and accreditation functions, they can be effective partners in certification and accreditation efforts and can offer checks and balances in program execution. Building a good partnership with supporting contractors can lead to an effective working relationship that is as stable, reliable, and consistent as one experienced with assigned employees. The use of contractors is the most cost-effective approach for the role of certifying agent and should also be considered for other less significant certification and accreditation roles such as data custodian, system administrator, and project manager.

Routine Duties

A day in the life of an individual assigned to a certification and accreditation role involves a wide variety of activities that must be performed routinely and performed well to provide the level of consistency necessary for an effective program. A typical manager involved in certification and accreditation will be regularly involved in the following types of tasks:

- Scheduling tasks to be performed and coordinating work that is underway.
- Reporting on the status of certification and accreditation activities on a recurring basis to include both report submission and face-to-face updates with the management staff.
- Providing routine certification and accreditation–related advice and assistance to members of the organization.
- Attending periodic and ad hoc meetings with system owners whose systems are being certified, with certifiers who are engaged in performing systems certifications, and with organizational management to provide updates on program status.
- Reviewing documentation for quality control purposes, presenting these deliverables to supported organizations, and responding to customer comments and questions about the deliverables.
- Overseeing ongoing certification and accreditation efforts and spot-checking compliance.
- Acting as an intermediary for the system owner and supporting certifying agent to ensure that requirements are being accurately understood and organizational requirements for certification and activities are being met. The definition of boundaries between systems is a common issue that calls for the intercession of the program manager.

- Offering solutions for implementing the organization's certification and accreditation methodology or ruling on whether a particular planned approach will comply with policies and standards.
- Educating personnel on certification and accreditation practices and procedures. This may take the form of telephone discussions, one-on-one briefings to executive managers, presentations to small groups of managers, and formal training sessions presented to large groups of employees. These education sessions seek to educate recipients on what certification and accreditation is, to describe the program, to detail how the program is being implemented in the organization, and to define what roles and responsibilities for certification and accreditation are. Education responsibilities also usually include mentoring of personnel assigned to the certification and accreditation program staff.
- Justifying findings and recommendations detailed in certification documentation. The program manager must be able to work with systems owners, business unit managers, authorizing authorities, and senior management to explain the documentation, the methodology used, the weaknesses identified, and the corrective action recommended. The program manager must have total familiarity with these issues to provide assurance in the quality of work performed and their soundness as a basis for planning and decision making.
- Participating in system development activities. In this capacity the program manager serves as a subject matter expert to describe certification and accreditation objectives, methodologies, products, and, most important, how the security interfaces with the system development process. The program manager must be careful not to become overly involved in requirements definition and analysis and system design tasks. Failure to heed this advice can quickly outstrip the time the project manager has available. It is also better to maintain a certain degree of distance from the nuts and bolts of the system development project to be able to remain independent when it is time to certify the system.

Organizational Skills

Dealing with a large number of people on a multitude of systems issues requires that the certification and accreditation program manager be well organized and fully on his or her game regarding requirements, obligations, promises made, and discussions conducted. Therefore, the program manager must either have a photographic memory or be able to rely on meeting notes, records of conversations, and lists of things to do to stay organized. The volume of information that the program manager must be able to readily access mandates that well-thought-out filing systems for both electronic and hard-copy information be established and maintained. These systems need to allow recovery of information related to system-level and program-level activities for a period of at least three years. It is also particularly important to have e-mail files available to document decisions made, agreements reached, and work performed.

Organizational Placement of the Certification and Accreditation Function

There is one final issue to discuss relative to certification roles and responsibilities, and that is to establish the most effective organizational placement of the certification and accreditation function. To be most effective, responsibility for certification and accreditation should reside with the CISO. This places the responsibility for the program firmly in the hands of the senior security professional where it belongs. To ensure the program receives the management support, emphasis, and visibility it requires, the CISO should report directly to the chief operating officer or chief executive officer of the organization. This also permits the degree of independence the CISO needs to monitor and report on certification and accreditation activities enterprisewide.

Program relationships with other organizational elements are shown in Table 2.3, which lists and describes the relationships between various organizational functions and the certification and accreditation program.

Summary

As in most processes, employees are the most important components, and matching the right personality to the right role can mean the difference between success and failure of a certification and accreditation program. The program relies on five primary roles and their attendant responsibilities: the system owner, the authorizing official, the CISO, the ISSO, and the certifying agent. Each of these roles must be competently performed, and each role and responsibility must be documented so as to complement the other primary roles. Managers must make wise choices regarding the selection of personnel to fill these key positions, must motivate individuals in supporting secondary roles, and must mobilize the support of other organizational functions to ensure the program's success. Through the effective interplay between these various roles, both the efficiency of the certification and accreditation program and separation of critical functions can be assured.

Table 2.3 Functional Relationships to the Certification and Accreditation Program

Function	Relationship
Incident Response	Provide input for remediation plans
	Access for certification test plans and system security plans
	Review security documentation for impact of risks/vulnerabilities
	Trigger review of need for recertification
Security Awareness and Training	Provide input for the system security plan and certification test
	Draw on rules of behavior
	Review/track findings
Data Classification	Define data sensitivity for certification and accreditation inventory
	Provide input to system security plan
Risk Management	Support plan of action and milestones (POA&M) process
Compliance/ Enforcement	Support certification and accreditation assessment processes
	Provide input into POA&M process
	Monitor compliance of certification and accreditation processes with established policy and guidance
Contingency Planning	Provide input for system security plan and certification test
	Review/track findings
Auditing	Review findings during regular audits
	Oversee system inventory
	Validate security documentation
Resource Management	Obtain funding for certification and accreditation program management
	Obtain funding for system-level risk remediation
IT Security Oversight	Monitor certification and accreditation program goals and strategies
	Monitor POA&M process
Record Retention	Establish retention periods for certification and accreditation (C&A) documentation
Physical Security	Implement/maintain physical security controls
	Review/track findings
Facilities Management	Provide input for security plan and certification testing
	Review/track findings

Table 2.3   Functional Relationships to the Certification and Accreditation Program (Continued)

Function	Relationship
Supervision and Management Functions	Provide input for security plan and certification testing
	Enforce policies and procedures
	Report incidents
	Recommend disciplinary action
	Obtain security awareness
	Implement/maintain security controls and corrective actions
	Review/track findings
Departmental Management	Provide input for security plan and certification testing
	Enforce policies and procedures
	Review/track findings
Chief Privacy Officer	Provide privacy input into certification and accreditation inventory, system security plan, and certification testing
	Review/track privacy-related findings
	Perform privacy impact assessments
IT Services/ Operations	Review/track findings
	Respond to incidents
	Implement certification and accreditation–driven security architecture
	Implement controls
Human Resources	Review/track findings
	Implement/maintain personnel security controls (e.g., background screening)
	Oversee disciplinary action
	Hire, transfer, and terminate process ownership
Legal	Review memorandums of understanding/agreement (MOUs/MOAs)
	Review contracts
	Coordinate disciplinary actions
	Advise designated approving authorities (DAAs)
Contracting/ Purchasing	Review MOUs/MOAs
	Contract C&A support
	Review statement of work (SOW)
	Implement contract security clauses

Chapter 3

The Certification and Accreditation Life Cycle

In a perfect world, security would be a primary factor in considering the feasibility of developing a new system. Early in the planning stages the sensitivity of data would be defined, risks to processing would be identified, and security controls necessary to protect the system would be determined. When this happens, security becomes an integrated part of the project and controls are incorporated into the system design. Implementing security in this fashion saves money, time, and aggravation. Unfortunately, for a variety of reasons, this does not always happen and security considerations do not surface until well into the project when it is too late for them to be efficiently addressed, making them more difficult, more costly, and less practical to implement. In fact, systems often go fully into production without any formal identification of security requirements. Consequently, security employed in this manner almost always results in the security function being put in an adversarial role, giving it a reputation as an enforcement "heavy" as a result of this often seen scenario.

Certification and accreditation aims to rectify this state of affairs by providing an accepted, proven methodology for determining business needs for security and presenting a prescription for addressing them at the appropriate stage in the system's life cycle. The certification and accreditation framework can be effectively employed for new systems in development and implementation, for operational systems, for systems undergoing change, and for systems being retired. Most people are familiar with certification and accreditation of operational systems in which an owner of a legacy system that has been in production for years "gets religion" and decides the system needs to be certified and accredited. (This normally happens because he or she is directed to do this by someone higher in the food chain.) So, kicking-and-screaming certification and accreditation is initiated with little likelihood of a change in the system's authorization to process, except to document that it has been formally approved to process. The problem with this scenario is that management knows that the system is not going to be shut down if significant weaknesses are found, because the system has already been operating without negative consequences for a long time. This antisecurity bias points to a major obstacle in accrediting systems already in production.

A better alternative is to begin the certification and accreditation process parallel with system development to ensure certification and accreditation activities are performed at the appropriate time in the appropriate manner to the appropriate degree so that security and certification and accreditation can become a solution rather than a hindrance. The first step in making sure this happens must take place long before a development project is kicked off. It begins with education of project managers, system developers, and employees at large on the role of security, the importance of integrating security into information technology systems, and how certification and accreditation plays a role in system development. Unless program managers are aware of these things, the phone call inviting the information technology security staff to a meeting where managers will be informed about a new project will never be made. The information technology security team must make certification and accreditation a prominent part of its ongoing security awareness efforts to ensure that the security function is brought into the picture very early in the initiation phase. System developers should be aware of certification and accreditation procedures and requirements to allow them to understand the process and to permit them to address security requirements as they construct the system. Finally, employees must be aware of the program and what it is designed to achieve to prepare them for roles they may potentially play in certification and accreditation.

The services delivered through the certification and accreditation process are ideally suited to ensure that security is fully integrated into the system design, permitting the system to begin processing securely with full authority to process from management without having expended additional funds and resources to make that happen. Table 3.1, which follows, is taken from NIST SP 800-64, and it identifies various security activities according to where they are performed in the system development life cycle (SDLC).

Table 3.1   Information Technology Security Activities in the SDLC

Phase	SDLC Activities	Security Activities

Initiation	Needs determination
	Perception of a need
	Linkage of need to mission
	  and performance
	  objectives
	Assessment of alternatives
	  to capital assets
	Preparing for investment
	  review and budgeting
		Security categorization
		Preliminary risk assessment

Acquisition/
  Development
	Functional statement of
	  need
	Market research
	Feasibility study
	Requirements analysis
	Alternatives analysis
	Cost-benefit analysis
	Software conversion study
	Cost analysis
	Risk management plan
	Acquisition planning
		Risk assessment
		Security functional
		  requirements analysis
		Security assurance
		  requirements analysis
		Cost considerations and
		  reporting
		Security planning
		Security control
		  development
		Developmental security test
		  and evaluation
		Other planning components

Implementation	Installation Inspection Acceptance testing Initial user training Documentation	Inspection and acceptance System integration Security certification Security accreditation

Operations/
  Maintenance
	Performance measurement
	Contract modifications
	Operations
	Maintenance
		Configuration management
		  and control
		Continuous monitoring

Disposition	Appropriateness of
	  disposal
	Exchange and sale
	Internal organization
	  screening
	Transfer and donation
	Contract closeout
		Information preservation
		Media sanitization
		Hardware and software
		  disposal

Initiation Phase

The risk assessment when performed as part of the initiation phase provides a mechanism for documenting the sensitivity of the system, for identifying threats to the system and potential vulnerabilities, for calculating and ranking risks inherent to the system's operation, and for selecting controls necessary for protecting the system. Controls selection also addresses identification of controls necessary to implement established minimum security baselines and controls necessary to ensure compliance with statutory, legal, operational, and contractual obligations. It also allows the system owner to determine how the system will meet the organization's minimum security control standards and if those standards are stringent enough to protect system data. When done properly and at the right time, the results of the risk assessment can feed directly into the requirements analysis process and can allow them to go from being "security requirements" to simply being considered requirements. Ideally there will be no distinction of this type.

A plan of action and milestones is generated as a result of the risk assessment to document controls that must be implemented to address potential risks and any identified weaknesses. The remediation plan serves as an effective tool for managers to know what needs to be done relative to each risk-based control, what resources are necessary to accomplish the corrective action, the individual who is responsible for the task, and the schedule for implementing the control. Additionally, the risk assessment provides a risk ranking to each control recommended, allowing the project manager to prioritize how potentially limited resources can best be utilized.

As part of requirements definition, controls are defined in increasing detail and are further refined as the system progresses through development and implementation on into production.

Acquisition/Development Phase

The primary activities performed during this phase include analysis of security functional requirements, analysis of security assurance requirements, cost-benefit analysis of security controls, selection of security controls, and development of the system security plan. During this phase the system security plan is initiated to begin to document the system description, ownership, environment, technical architecture, interconnectivity, applicable directives and drivers, system sensitivity, and controls mapped to the minimum security baseline for the organization. Although begun during the acquisition/development phase, the security plan is revised and updated throughout the implementation and operation phases as well.

Certification test plan development begins with the acquisition/development phase when tests necessary for measuring the effectiveness of controls are documented in a certification test plan. All weaknesses identified during the risk assessment are included in the certification test plan as well as all other controls that may be categorized as implemented (although there are normally very few of these at this stage of the system's development). For each control a specific test is designed along with expected results and evidence required to substantiate that it meets requirements. This test development process is covered in Chapter 13.

Implementation Phase

Once the certification test plan has been developed it is then executed during the system implementation phase to ensure required controls are in place and are functioning properly. Because the information technology security function has been involved in the project from its inception, the certification test plan can be developed in time to be performed as part of acceptance testing, thereby reducing coordination time and execution costs. The results stemming from use of the certification test plan are recorded in the certification test plan results report, which becomes part of the certification and accreditation package for the system. Any controls that do not meet predefined standards are documented in an updated remediation plan for submission to the approving authority as part of the certifier's recommendations. The security plan is also updated to record the results of testing and to document whether controls either are in place or are planned.

Following this integrated approach, the approving authority will have all necessary documentation to make a decision authorizing the system to process prior to the system being approved to go into production, and as an element of the larger process for approving the system to operate based on both performance and security conditions being met. This is the ideal solution and is pure heaven for the CISO.

Operations/Maintenance Phase

Once operational, system owners must then ensure that the system stays secure. Owners must exercise controls that permit continuous monitoring of the security environment and review the system's security for the potential need for recertification and reaccreditation following certain types of incidents or situations, commonly known as significant events. Significant events include serious security incidents (an intrusion or severe virus/worm attack, for example); recognition of the potential for the introduction of new threats (terrorism) or low-frequency risks not previously considered (perhaps a tsunami); changes in the user community (additions due to an acquisition); changes in data sensitivity or system criticality; changes in system hardware and software components (a rehosting); a new interconnection with another system; occupation of new or upgraded facilities; or an expansion in system functionality. Prior to diving headlong into a full-blown recertification based on one or more of these conditions being met, a more reasonable approach is to first evaluate the need for recertification by first reviewing the impact of the change. This is best accomplished by means of a risk assessment.

During the operations phase the organization's configuration management process can be used to trigger recertification of systems. As the configuration control board addresses changes in the environment, connectivity, or other conditions of operation, the security representative (assuming there is one) then should evaluate the change to determine if recertification is warranted. A policy needs to be developed to provide guidance on what sorts of changes constitute grounds for recertification of a system and how this will be accomplished. The same principle applies to the incident response function. When an incident has an adverse impact on the data processed by a system or impairs or circumvents its controls, these new conditions should be evaluated in light of the existing certification and accreditation package to determine if recertification is necessary. Because a known set of controls has already been identified and a complete certification and accreditation package already exists, the recertification effort can normally be completed relatively quickly when compared to the initial effort.

Reaccreditation must also be performed at normal cycles, and for most systems a three-year cycle is adequate. However, highly sensitive systems may need to be reaccredited every two years or perhaps even more often.

The scope of the periodic reaccreditation should include a full review of all documentation in the certification and accreditation package for the system. Reaccreditation based on other events or situations need only focus on those elements of the initial package that are affected by the change.

Disposition Phase

Finally, the certification and accreditation package is the best starting point for addressing security requirements for systems in the disposal phase of their life cycle. It permits sound decisions to be made on disposal of sensitive data and documents controls to be employed to ensure data is purged from storage devices so as not to be disclosed to unauthorized individuals. Once it has been decided that a system is no longer useful and decommissioning is warranted, certification and accreditation activities should be addressed to provide assurance that system assets are properly disposed of, accounted for, and approved. Confidential data processed by the system in all its forms must be purged from hardware, destroyed if no longer needed, or shredded in the case of hard-copy reports and forms to ensure sensitive information is not disclosed. For historical purposes and potential future use, the integrity of the data must be ensured through proper archiving and storage techniques. Availability concerns must be addressed to ensure the future needs for system data can be met to include availability of storage media and hardware/software platforms to allow access to the media.

To address system disposal issues, a risk assessment of system confidentiality, integrity, and availability needs during this phase should be conducted and a remediation plan documenting required actions and milestones for ensuring protection of system resources needs to be developed. Once requirements have been identified in the remediation plan and required actions have been taken, verification by certification test plan can be performed to provide assurance that all assets have been accounted for and protected. A certifier who conducts this minicertification testing uses a certification statement to document these activities and to make recommendations to the approving authority regarding disposal-related security issues. The final step in the disposal is the decision of the approving authority declaring his or her decision to retire the system and addressing all reasonable risks to system resources. This decision should be documented in an approving authority statement.

It stands to reason that certification and accreditation activities performed during the disposal phase are scaled-down versions of the processes employed earlier in the system's life cycle. The risk assessment, remediation plan, and certification test plan follow the same process for the same purpose, but the scale of the activity is normally much reduced. However, organizationwide systems that are interconnected to many other systems are a notable exception because tracing these data links can be an imposing task.

Most often the retirement of one system is accompanied by the implementation of a replacement system. It makes sense to link the life-cycle activities of incoming and outgoing systems to ensure that security requirements for each are addressed simultaneously and comprehensively.

Another task that must be addressed as part of the disposal phase is the disposition of system hardware and software that can be reused with other systems. Additionally, disposition of documentation for hardware and software must be decided. Employees who are to be terminated or reassigned due to the system's retirement should be required to sign nondisclosure agreements to protect against the release of confidential information. Finally, the system needs to be formally removed from the organization's system inventory using the existing formal process, ensuring that the justification for the retirement is fully explained.

Challenges to Implementation

Many organizations either fail to develop mature SDLC methodologies or allow them to lapse into a coma because of the demands placed on rapid development and implementation of systems. The need to quickly speed the development cycle to meet pressing business needs (such as accelerating the development of an enhanced feature to match the release of one of your major competitors) overwhelms the ability of the SDLC model to keep pace. Too often in such situations, security becomes an afterthought if a thought at all, because of preconceived ideas that security impedes progress and is costly besides. It is difficult to implement a certification and accreditation process in a setting like this, but it can be done. A good strategy for addressing this assault on the viability of its certification and accreditation program is to establish a two-track certification methodology: one track is a full certification and accreditation track for systems being developed on a normal schedule in which the full SDLC methodology can be implemented, and the second track is an abbreviated certification and accreditation methodology in which time is an overriding concern and tight schedules must be adhered to. This latter track will lead to an interim certification that is more responsive to organizational needs while still providing some degree of assurance that security controls have been addressed in the design and have been implemented prior to going live. This abbreviated methodology is akin to the SCL-1 methodology described in Chapter 13 and should only apply in about 25 percent or less of an organization's development efforts. However, it is not a precise fit in that even systems with highly sensitive data may need to be certified using this abbreviated approach when the business situation demands expedited development.

As an alternative to a specialized "quick fix" methodology, an organization can fine-tune its standard certification and accreditation methodology so as to be fully responsive to any and all demands system development requirements place on it. When the methodology invariably takes six months to run its course, its utilization will be minimized. If, however, the methodology can lead to accreditation in two months or less, then it will be flexible enough to support even the most demanding

Table 3.2   Comparison of C&A Methodology Life-Cycle Phases

Methodology	Phase 1	Phase 2	Phase 3	Phase 4
NIST	Initiation	Security certification	Security accreditation	Continuous monitoring
NIACAP	Definition	Verification	Validation	Postaccreditation
DITSCAP	Definition	Verification	Validation	Postaccreditation

time-to-market scenarios. A responsive certification and accreditation program such as this will prove to be far less onerous than developers have come to expect and has a greater than average chance of being accepted and employed.

Not only can the certification and accreditation process support the system development methodology, but SDLC products can also support the implementation of an effective certification and accreditation program. The system concept, feasibility study, requirements document, system design, implementation plan, and test plan provide highly valuable information for determining data sensitivity, assessing risks, evaluating applicability of minimum security controls, and constructing a certification test plan for testing controls.

According to the most broadly used certification and accreditation methodologies, the certification and accreditation process has a life cycle of its own. It generally consists of four phases: the precertification phase, followed by validation, then accreditation, and finally postaccreditation. Table 3.2 shows the labels used in NIST SP 800-37, NIACAP, and DITSCAP methodologies, along with the primary activities associated with each of these four phases. To summarize this approach, the precertification phase comprises tasks performed in preparation for certifying a system; actions related to actual certification are performed in the validation phase; the accreditation phase addresses accreditation of the system; and, finally, actions performed after the system is accredited are covered during the postaccreditation phase. Although this taxonomy helps organize the certification and accreditation process, it is much more useful to connect specific certification and accreditation activities with the more broadly accepted system development methodology as shown in Table 3.1.

Integration of certification and accreditation into the SDLC is promoted by the consistency of the role of the project manager/system owner in each of the two processes. The project manager plays the lead role in the development project, and this is certainly not at odds with his or her responsibility that he or she is expected to exercise over implementing security for the system. In security certification and accreditation terms, the system development project manager performs the complementary role of system owner. In this case, the mapping between the two roles is direct.

Summary

Inclusion of certification and accreditation processes and products in an organization's system development methodology can substantially raise the visibility of a security program, particularly with management. Integration of security requirements at an early stage along with other system requirements makes them far less onerous. In fact, it helps define them more clearly and permits one to consider them in practical ways. It is far easier to convince a project manager during the design stage that encryption for the system is important than it is to convince him or her after the system has been operational for a year.

Chapter 4

Why Certification and Accreditation Programs Fail

Unfortunately, the history of certification and accreditation is marked by the frequent failure of well-intentioned programs. This chapter lists a number of reasons that programs fail. By studying the causes of these failures, we can perhaps discover the pitfalls to be avoided when designing and implementing an enterprise information technology certification and accreditation program.

Problems in Program Scope

Often programs are unsuccessful because they fail to effectively identify and inventory systems. When the program is not applied evenly across all organization information technology systems, controls are not comprehensively applied. Therefore, vulnerabilities in the enterprise processing environment open up and increase the potential for threats to exploit vulnerabilities in security controls that have been implemented.

Management must actively concentrate on the identification and inventory of all systems without exception. As stated earlier, failure to effectively make all of the organization's systems subject to the program will risk security gaps and uneven application of controls and resources. It is therefore important to ensure that all systems are identified, that a 100 percent inventory is conducted, and that the inventory is updated regularly (at least annually).

Assessment Focus

A program can also fail to mature and never advance beyond mere assessment of controls. This constitutes only half a program. Identification of security weaknesses, although essential, is only part of a comprehensive program. Assessment must be followed by remediation. Action to correct deficiencies is needed to complete the program. A mature program also provides mechanisms for an iterative process of assessment and remediation to ensure that, as systems change, controls change appropriately in response to vulnerabilities that accompany changes. An extension of the lack of program maturity failure is management's inability to connect certification and accreditation to budgeting for resources. As weaknesses are identified and corrective actions are prescribed, there has to be a process for providing the necessary resources to ensure these actions can be completed. Without the resources to take corrective action, the program is reduced to merely an emasculated assessment process.

Short-Term Thinking

In many cases, certification and accreditation programs fall prey to an organizational attitude that prevents a focus on long-term, strategic requirements, which prevents a certification and accreditation program from getting off the ground. Organizations in this category never get a glimpse of the future due to a concentration on present-day requirements. Such thinking leads to implementation of point solutions that cannot be integrated into an overall security architecture, because one does not exist. An organization that is buried in fixing short-term problems will never be able to get beyond that level of immaturity until strategic programs like certification and accreditation can be launched.

Long-Term Thinking

Conversely, an organization that focuses its energy at the strategic level alone usually fails in its efforts to implement an effective certification and accreditation program. A comprehensive, integrated security architecture is a thing of beauty once it has been developed. However, if the requirements identified in the security architecture cannot be translated down to the implementation level, it is similar to a bird without wings. A certification and accreditation program that emphasizes strategic solutions will eventually fail without resting on a foundation of system-level building blocks serving as entities through which security solutions are implemented.

Poor Planning

Certification and accreditation programs do not develop and implement themselves. It takes effort and resources to establish them, and they do not happen overnight. Failure to recognize the costs of establishing such programs can lead to a lack of follow-through on program requirements and can lead to the need to continually start over. The frustration of fits and starts of this nature will fray management confidence in the program, leading to its eventual scrapping before it ever gets off the ground. To avoid unpleasant surprises, the security manager cannot afford to be unrealistic about program costs. Other ways that inadequate planning diminishes a program's likelihood of success include:

- ■ Failure to ensure that program requirements are realistic, leading to waste of critical resources and loss of program credibility. Similarly, the failure to tailor certification and accreditation requirements to real organizational needs can cause weaknesses in program implementation.
- ■ Failure to assign responsibility to the most appropriate staff element or individual can greatly reduce chances for success. For example, the audit function is not in a good position to manage the certification and accreditation program because of its need to remain independent. Assignment of program responsibilities to the CISO is a better approach and a wiser decision.
- ■ Failure to integrate the certification and accreditation program with other processes can doom a program from the start — the effect of competition for time and resources.
- ■ Failure to train personnel in their certification and accreditation roles and responsibilities can put a drag on your program and keep it from achieving the level of professionalism it requires.
- ■ Failure to correctly identify assumptions can lead to misconceptions about the nature of the program. Organizations that fail to make sound assumptions about certification and accreditation programs may find themselves doomed by the effects of not preparing for the amount of time required, the costs associated in establishing and operating the program, or may assume unrealistic expectations

about what the program can actually achieve. On the other hand, organizations should not assume that the program is for government entities only or that it is not necessary in the organization's current circumstances.

■ Finally, failure to recognize the limitations of certification and accreditation can contribute to poor planning for implementation of the program. Planning must accurately set expectations for the program and its goals.

Lack of Responsibility

Programs also fail because they fail to fix responsibility at the system level and at the program level. There has to be balance and separation between these two levels. The program must distinguish program-level responsibilities that are applied enterprisewide from system-level responsibilities that apply to individual systems. In practical terms a single entity cannot perform both nor would you want them to. On the other hand, if the program does not fix responsibility at either level, it risks failure.

Too Much Paperwork

In other cases, history has shown that certification and accreditation programs have failed when they lost sight of their goals and became bogged down in bureaucracy. A slow choking death by paperwork in such cases is usually well deserved because such programs have clearly failed to deliver. One cannot expect program participants to embrace a program that buries them in paperwork that they perceive to be unwarranted, unnecessary, and onerous.

Lack of Enforcement

Failure to properly enforce certification and accreditation policy can kill an otherwise sound certification and accreditation program. Program requirements are necessary but plentiful, particularly at the system owner and ISSO levels. If there are not processes in place to enforce program requirements, the program will become inconsistent, ineffectual, and will fall into disuse once those with program responsibilities perceive or observe that accountability for system security improvements is lacking. A program that is inconsistent in its treatment of program participants, individuals, organizations, solutions, or processes leads to ineffectiveness eventually. The certification and accreditation program's failure to be evenhanded and consistent causes confusion in meeting requirements. Inconsistency in program management can also cause difficulties in performing review and audit tasks, uneven results due to a failure to provide consistent guidance. Programs in this category permit participants to shop for the answer they desire. Everyone must be onboard for the program to work on a consistent basis without favoritism. This is often caused by a failure to document program policies and procedures or by a failure to adhere to the established requirements. The level of enforcement can sometimes be driven by the program's failure to overcome strong personalities and forceful (negative) opinions. Such influences may be expressed in terms of support of favored point solutions and support of inadequate alternatives to the program (e.g., security around the perimeter only). These negative influences have to be confronted directly in an early test of management support for the program.

Lack of Foresight

Organizations that fail to adequately understand the benefit of a certification and accreditation program will never consider its implementation. Consequently, a program will never be initiated. Although this is not an outright failure, it is a failed opportunity. Organizations that do not have the foresight to study the benefits of a certification and accreditation program should seriously consider the need to conduct a cost-benefit analysis to assess the potential of the program in enhancing its information technology security program. Such a study could find that implementation of a program could result in increased visibility of the information technology security program, in enhanced tracking of security weakness and corrective actions, in quantifying resource requirements for security, in providing a vehicle for security oversight, and, finally, in measurement of security program success (or failure).

Poor Timing

A certification and accreditation program can also fail when the organization is simply not ready for it. Perhaps the company is not far enough along in its maturity, or perhaps a real need for the program has not yet evolved. Poor timing is also responsible for the failure of a program when it is established without the personnel and resources are simply not available due to other, more pressing business needs (i.e., product development).

Lack of Support

Perhaps the most significant obstacle to the implementation of a certification and accreditation program is the lack of support. This is observed in management's emphasis on the program and failure on the part of lower-level program participants to support the program. Program neglect can lead to its starvation in a short time. Management buy-in is necessary to ensure program success because the program can only survive if management stands fully behind efforts necessary to enforce program requirements. Committed management support is needed to ensure that program participants follow through on their obligations. Certification and accreditation programs that cannot force active participation and carry through on its requirements often end up in the dustbin of forgotten programs and initiatives. This is also the end result of programs where management fails to ensure that risks are mitigated, leaving systems excessively exposed to vulnerabilities. Finally, lack of management support can result in a failure to accredit or reaccredit the organization's information systems in a timely or efficient basis. Certification and accreditation program managers should keep management involved in the program through the use of scorecards and metrics coupled with regular and frequent program updates to force management to pay attention.

Those who are governed by the certification and accreditation program must be convinced that it has value for it to be effective. Of all the roles and responsibilities associated with a certification program, the role played by the system owner is unquestionably critical to its success. A program that cannot get system owners to recognize its value cannot succeed because of the reliance any program must place on owners' active involvement. A program that does not apply sufficient energy to obtaining system owner buy-in through training and education efforts and to maintain their involvement through close and continual communications is like expecting a body to function without a heart. Sometimes an effective tactic for gaining program support is fear. Fear of embarrassment by system owners can enhance their willingness to comply; fear of lawsuits can accomplish the same thing. Willing support can often be obtained when compliance is linked to project funding. Failing the acceptability and effectiveness of these approaches, using the management "stick" may be the only alternative for system owners who fail to comply.

Summary

As we have seen, there are several obstacles in implementing certification and accreditation programs. Consequently, many brilliant initiatives never quite deliver what they promise. Programs can falter due to poor planning, lack of support, and failure to understand what a certification and accreditation program can and should be able to deliver on. Security managers need to be aware of these pitfalls and need to design and manage their programs to avoid them. Also, they must continually track progress and performance to ensure that the ill effects of these problems do not derail their programs.

CERTIFICATION AND ACCREDITATION PROCESSES

Certification and accreditation is a comprehensive methodology that consists of a number of individual processes, most of which the reader will probably recognize. It is the combining of these related processes into a unified risk management approach that gives a certification and accreditation methodology its real value. Although there are many well-known approaches to implementing a risk management program, there is a need for a coherent methodology to manage risks at the individual system level. To meet this requirement, the risk management approach would need to be sufficiently integrated to provide for consistent inputs and outputs from each process in the methodology; on a micro level it would provide assurance that necessary controls are implemented at the lowest level of technology in each organizational element; and on the macro level it would serve the entire organization as a foundation for the enterprise information technology security program. The certification and accreditation approach to risk management ties these necessary security processes together to create a pathway to success. Figure II.1 shows how the certification and accreditation processes interrelate.

Section II will discuss each of these essential certification and accreditation processes and how each can be implemented by the security

Figure II.1   Interrelationships of certification and accreditation processes.

professional in practical ways as part of an overarching risk management program. The section will first detail how to plan for a certification and accreditation project from the perspective of a project manager. Detail of the establishment of a system inventory process and how systems are assessed for sensitivity and criticality will follow. The section will then outline the development of system security plans and the coordination of security for interconnected systems, followed by a description of the process of implementing minimum security baselines and principles for assessment of risks. The final five chapters of Section II will discuss the importance of security procedures, elements of certification testing, planning for remediation of identified weaknesses, creation of certification documentation, and, finally, documentation of the accreditation decision.

Chapter 5

Certification and Accreditation Project Planning

Certification and accreditation of a system is normally an effort that requires the accomplishment of many tasks and it affects many resources over a period of several weeks or months. Unless the certification and accreditation effort is properly coordinated, effectively organized, and closely managed, achieving a predetermined objective at a projected time will be a virtual accident. As shown in Chapter 4 there are myriad things that can go wrong and cause the effort to fail, and the only solution is effective (rather than lucky) project management. This chapter outlines the role and responsibilities of the individual charged with managing a certification and accreditation project for a single system or for a group of systems, with an emphasis on how managing a certification and accreditation project differs from the management of other types of projects.

Planning Factors

The project management is only completed when the project is finished, and it must be performed for the duration of the effort, hopefully by the same individual throughout. The project management function normally requires an additional 10 percent of the overall project labor effort. This project management surcharge provides a realistic guide for planning the number of man-hours that will be required to organize the effort, coordinate accomplishment of tasks, and oversee the performance of the project team. Using this planning factor, a six-week certification and accreditation project will require around three man-days of dedicated project management support. This factor increases as the number of systems in the scope of the project increases. Speaking in rough terms, a project comprising certification of ten systems will require a full-time project manager. For a single system, the system owner or ISSO may serve as his own project manager. The system owner's availability may limit his ability to perform this task, however, and he or she may choose to assign another staff member to perform the project management function as a collateral duty. For a highly sensitive system, a consultant may be called in to perform dedicated project management functions. Normally, an individual is sufficient for the project management role; however, an alternate who has knowledge of most aspects of the project should be available to step in and cover for the project manager when there is a scheduling conflict or during other times of nonavailability.

To be effective, project managers must be knowledgeable, personable, persistent, and involved. They must understand certification and accreditation objectives and methodologies, must have detailed knowledge of certification and accreditation tasks and tools, and must know how to successfully manage a project and the people performing it. The certification and accreditation project is people-centric and requires continual coordination and work toward achieving needed cooperation. It takes someone who can communicate well with others verbally and visually. The interpersonal skills of project managers cannot be stressed too much. Project managers must also be doggedly determined to ensure schedules are met and promises are kept. When someone agrees to do something, project managers should prod people into keeping their agreements and schedules. Finally, project managers must be immersed in the project. They must be continually aware of project schedules, status, risks, problems, and issues in order to foresee difficulties before they arise. This cannot be done from a distance and can present problems for those performing project management functions only on a part-time basis. Being a project manager is a hands-on exercise.

Dealing with People

Being a "people person" helps project managers understand the roles and responsibilities of individuals involved in the project, those they have control over (and those who control them), those they support, and those who support them. Project managers must not only identify but must also estimate and then solidify the expectations of those affected by the project: the approving authority, the organization staff, the system owner, the CIO, the CISO, the certifying official, the ISSO, certification team members, auditors, and quality control. Each views the project in a different way with different objectives and expectations. Project managers must understand these points of view and use them to improve the likelihood of success.

The first tasks that project managers must perform is identifying individuals involved in the project at several levels and defining project-related roles and responsibilities. This includes those both internal and external to the supported organization. A contact list should be constructed to at a minimum identify the approving authority, certifying official, team members, ISSO, system administrator, quality assurance personnel, and key management personnel.

Team Member Selection

Another people-related task required of project managers is selection of certification team members. Who makes up the team is a decision of the project manager and should be based on the knowledge, skills, abilities, experience, and integrity of the individual rather than simply determining who is not doing something else more important. Project managers should seek team members who can be critical, impartial, and fair; who have good people skills themselves; who are analytical; and who have sound writing capabilities. Team members should each have a good balance of technical and nontechnical skills. Of course, experience with certification and accreditation in general, and with significant certification and accreditation processes in particular, should be the overriding selection factor. Also, as much as possible, the project manager should evaluate each potential team member on the basis of his or her integrity, character, credibility, and trustworthiness. If project managers have an opportunity to review résumés to select potential members, they should list brief selection criteria and prioritize qualities desired in a candidate. Criteria should also include security clearance and background screening requirements demanded by the project.

Team members may be part of the organization and may be well known to the project manager. Or they may come from another organizational element and familiarity will not be ensured. When team members are provided by external entities under contract it is important to consider and arrange for logistical matters such as time accounting, travel authorization, expense claims, and disciplinary actions, etc. When contractors provide support by assuming responsibility for an aspect of the project in its entirety (i.e., certification testing), the project manager should ensure that there are no secrets regarding man-hours set aside for their slice of the project. Also, the project manager must review the methodology he or she intends to use to be sure it is in balance with other project objectives, work, and schedules. Appendix C contains a sample statement of work.

Scope Definition

The primary questions the project manager must ask when preparing for project initiation is how many systems are within the project scope, what types of systems they are, and how complex the systems are. The scope is also affected by the number of organizations involved and the level of cooperation (with interviews and documentation), the location of systems, the number of people who will be involved, the number of people available to assist with the project, the time available to perform the work, the certification level or levels of systems within the project scope, and, finally, what systems do not have to be certified.

Naturally, the more systems involved in the project provides opportunities for economies of scale and a reduction in per-system costs based on volume of work performed. But this is only really true because of similarities in the approach to the work. If the project comprises three systems, but there is little similarity between them, then little if any time can be saved. Similarly, time and savings can be achieved if the systems are somewhat alike in design, functionality, and location. In fact, such similarity may provide the potential for grouping tasks even on deliverables.

The biggest drivers in scoping a project besides the number, types, and complexity of systems involved are time and available resources. Time required for a project ranges from as little as one month for a single system to a year or more for multiple, complex systems at several certification levels. An average project will run from three to six months and will involve between five and fifty systems. Of course, when a project requires six months but deadlines dictate that the project be accomplished in three, then staffing of the project must be increased to meet the deadline. To properly scope a project, the project manager must know how long it takes to perform tasks for an average system. This normally is based on a high-level project work plan like the one shown in Appendix D, which documents the number of days normally required for standard certification and accreditation tasks. From this baseline project, work plan adjustments for system complexity factors are made to appropriately refine it to address the specifics of the project. From the updated project work plan a schedule of project activities, milestones, and deliverable targets can be established. For large projects involving multiple systems, a project management tool will help in tracking project performance, making scheduling changes, and supporting reporting requirements. The project work plan is the project manager's road map to success and his or her greatest aid.

The work plan should include a few key ingredients. The plan should clearly describe work in terms of activities, tasks and subtasks, each of which are identified through a coherent numbering scheme. The plan must record realistic start dates and end dates for each level of work. Included in the plan should be resources required to complete work at all levels, as well as dependencies between tasks. This helps identify critical work and potential bottlenecks.

One final and highly important issue is the phenomenon known as scope creep, or incremental changes in the scope of work. Although management requests that additional or different work be included in the project can be easily accommodated without difficulty, usually the additional work is insidious and can quite easily result in eventual delays in the project's completion. At the very least, the project manager is obligated to clearly inform management of estimates of the costs of changing the scope and the impact they will have on the project's completion.

Assumptions

Project managers seldom have all the information required to plan for the project. They have to speculate on certain aspects of the project that are not well defined, at least early on in the project. To deal with these uncertainties they must build assumptions into the project plan. These assumptions are about things like sufficient manpower to staff the project, sufficient time to complete necessary tasks, sufficient funds to permit travel and production of work products, and availability of key personnel for interviews and documentation for review. It is important to document these assumptions and work to validate them as much as possible. When they are considered assumptions, then they can be addressed with management to transform them from assumptions into known planning factors.

Risks

The project manager must also identify in the project plan risks that could potentially prevent the project from meeting its objectives. Lack of manpower risks the ability of the project team to be able to complete project tasks according to schedule or standard. Failure to complete data collection due to lack of cooperation also risks delays in meeting schedules. And failure to review and provide comments on draft deliverables risks achievement of work product finalization and submission. During the execution phase of the project, the project manager should continue to highlight these risks when reporting project status to management. Whenever possible, risks should be clearly quantified to facilitate their understanding by executive management.

Project Agreements

In the role of project manager, there is the inherent condition of being in a supporting role. The project is being performed in support of some individual or organization. To facilitate understanding between the supporting project team and the supported organization, there should be an agreement on who does what, when, how, etc. This project agreement sets the ground rules for the project and serves as the basis for setting expectations. It should accompany the project work plan and is normally drafted by the project manager. An example of a project agreement is provided in Table 5.1.

Project Team Guidelines

The project manager may find it necessary to develop guidelines for team members to ensure consistency of work performed. Policies and procedures internal to the project team should be published based on project agreements to give team members guidance on administrative matters like time reporting, work hours, appropriate attire, travel requests and authorizations, supplies, methodology-related guidance such as use of templates and checklists, lines of coordination and communication, conducting interviews, collecting and accounting for documentation, recording test results, using tools, performing vulnerability scans, and progress reporting requirements (weekly status reports and problem reporting). This guidance should be disseminated prior to the beginning of the project so that all project team members can be trained on them to achieve a common level-set. However, as the project progresses, adjustments usually need to be made and the guidelines have to be updated. Guidance should be firm and authorized and must be available to and followed by all team members. Posting guidelines in a shared directory is an ideal solution. Having comprehensive, clear, up-to-date guidance on how to do the work is instrumental when bringing on new team members after the project has begun, and it serves as a solid foundation for future projects as well, even though specifics of individual certification and accreditation projects will change.

Table 5.1   Project Agreement Outline

1   Document Information and Revision History
2   Project Agreement Approvals
3   Project Mission Statement
4   Project Background
5   Project Overview and Scope
6   Critical Success Factors
7   Project Team
8   Project Timing
9   Project Deliverables
10   Project Approach
    10.1   Phase 1: Project Initiation
        10.1.1   Time Frame and Deliverables for Phase 1
    10.2   Phase 2: Data Collection and Analysis
        10.2.1   Activity 1: Preparation
        10.2.2   Activity 2: Data Collection
        10.2.3   Activity 3: Data Analysis
        10.2.4   Time Frame and Deliverables for Phase 2
    10.3   Phase 3: Certification Testing
        10.3.1   Activity 1: Test Plan Development
        10.3.2   Activity 2: Test Execution
        10.3.3   Activity 3: Documentation of Test Results
        10.3.4   Time Frame and Deliverables for Phase 3
    10.4   Phase 4: Develop Certification Package
        10.4.1   Activity 1: Prepare Security Plan
        10.4.2   Activity 2: Prepare Risk Assessment
        10.4.3   Activity 3: Prepare Plan of Action and Milestones
        10.4.4   Activity 4: Prepare Certification and Accreditation Statements
        10.4.5   Activity 5: Prepare Final Deliverables
        10.4.6   Time Frame and Deliverables for Phase 4
11   Assumptions

Administrative Requirements

Project managers must anticipate and identify administrative requirements necessary for their team as well. This allows them to estimate requirements for funding where necessary and supplies as needed. Requirements for and costs of production materials like copy paper, binders, dividers, print cartridges, software tools, references, hardware, electronic media, etc., will surely need to be determined, budgeted for, ordered, and stockpiled. Workspace requirements including workstations, connectivity, communications, and physical access to facilities ideally should be settled on before the first team member is selected. Travel requirements need to be identified in detail, using realistic planning estimates for airfare, ground transportation, parking, meals, lodging, etc. This cannot be prepared until the scope is defined and the work plan is developed. It is the project manager's responsibility to efficiently manage travel by making adjustments to the project plan to pool travel requirements and consolidate trips as much as possible. Often it is advantageous to revise team assignments based on team members' availability to travel. Project managers should also anticipate modifications to the travel schedule because in the course of data collection the scope of the system may include components and operations at other locations, necessitating travel there for testing. Scope changes such as these may cause other changes to the project scope and project plan, particularly as related to milestones and delivery dates. Project managers should also establish and implement a process that accounts for all documentation received throughout the project. This ensures that it can be returned in full to the rightful owner once it is no longer needed.

Reporting

One key responsibility of the project manager is status reporting, which allows the project manager to monitor the progress of the project and to inform management. Reporting requirements need to be defined prior to the project to ensure consistency and to forecast and plan for the level of effort required to gather information for and to develop and provide status reports. Following a standard reporting format and procedures throughout the project is more efficient than frequently changing requirements after the project begins. The project manager should estimate reporting requirements, then stick with them within the constraints of meeting project needs. Also, member input should be kept to a minimum because reporting should be secondary to members' primary responsibility of performing project tasks and documenting results. No more than 5 to 10 percent of an analyst's time should be dedicated to progress reporting, as compared to the 25 to 30 percent of the project manager's time. Reporting consists of submission of routine ad hoc reports supplemented by face-to-face meetings to elaborate on submitted reports. This can be viewed as beneficial to both the project manager and to management, but often project managers disdain reporting as a necessary evil. To avoid this less than positive view of status reporting, the project manager must use it to his or her advantage. Reporting can improve support and cooperation rather than intrude on the manager's time. However, the project manager should avoid submitting overly detailed reports. They should be succinct, clear, and to the point, consisting of ideally one or two pages of bulleted items. The report should highlight what has been accomplished during the reporting period (weekly or monthly), what will be accomplished in the next reporting period, and should identify problems and impacts (risk). An example of a project report is Table 5.2.

Problem-related reporting and coordination is a special class that must be handled carefully. Problems at the lowest level possible should be worked up the management chain only when absolutely necessary. This approach allows the project manager to function as problem solver rather than problem maker. When low-priority issues are surfaced to top management first, this runs the risk of alienating those at lower levels, and it may jeopardize long-term cooperation at the expense of short-term gain. Give the system owner a chance to set up interviews and provide documentation first, then give him or her a second chance before reporting to his or her boss that the owner has been uncooperative. Good coordination also includes sharing and discussion of schedule changes with others involved in the project. The schedule that is presented to management at the weekly meeting must be synchronized with dates being used or reported by others involved in the project. Schedule discrepancies can be embarrassing and can quickly erode good relations that have been carefully built up over a long period of time. Finally, reporting by the project manager can be used to manage expectations of management and of supported organizations. By giving them frequent, candid, realistic, and up-to-date information on project status, they will become active participants in the project and build management support when it comes time to getting the accreditation signed. This also allows project managers to somewhat inoculate themselves from the effects of surprises. It is not reasonable to expect a manager to react positively when told two weeks before the projected completion date that the project is thirty days behind schedule. The project manager must take the initiative and initiate the reporting process, avoiding reliance on management to request updates. Because they are likely to assume that no news is good news because of the nature of their positions (where management by exception is their normal mode of operation), they may never request an update until someone other than the project manager reports to them that there are problems. This is never a good situation for the project manager. If there is bad news about the project, it needs to come from the project manager, not someone else. So, the project manager must be proactive.

How does the project manager avoid other pitfalls? Things like delays in meeting project timetables need to be addressed by anticipating them first. Extra time should be built into the project plan, and larger tasks should be broken into smaller pieces, with assigned due dates. This may only be necessary for team members or system owners who have demonstrated an inability to stay on track. Recalcitrance or a lack of partici-

Table 5.2   Project Report

Certification and Accreditation
Weekly Status Report
Week of February 19–February 25, 2004

Issues to be Resolved/Risks:
Technical: None
Cost: None
Performance: Tom Turner, who has been performing certifications for OST
systems has resigned and will depart on Mar. 12th. Interviews
for his replacement are now being coordinated.

Summary:

	Technical	Cost	Performance
Certification and Accreditation	GREEN	GREEN	GREEN

Work Status by Business Unit:
- **Administration:**
  - Concluded ST&Es of seven systems in San Diego; now anticipate delivery of draft C&A packages on Mar. 12th. ST&E of two remaining Admin systems rescheduled for week of Mar. 15th due to lack of scope definition (Diana System) and inadequate current security posture (Zeus).
  - Data collection for three Admin systems (Acme, Ajax, Mercury) behind schedule due to lack of receipt of input from system owner.
  - ST&E for Admin's Mars Web site delayed one week due to nonavailability of system owner. Will be completed on Feb. 27th. C&A package submission now anticipated for Mar. 12th.
  - Development of certification schedule for Admin Regional LANs, Jupiter, and Pluto systems pending receipt of feedback from system owner.
  - Development of Neptune and Venus LAN C&A packages delayed two weeks due to concentration of team on Admin ST&Es. Anticipate submission of both by Mar. 5th.
- **Manufacturing:** ST&E on three systems scheduled for Mar. 2nd. Expect delivery of draft C&A packages on Mar. 12th.
- **Sales:**
  - Saturn System C&A package on schedule for submission on Mar. 5th.
  - Schedule delayed for four systems due to lack of receipt of 800-26 input.
  - Sales resolved contractor cooperation issue with Apollo System.
- **Research:**
  - A C&A package for the Research LAN is on schedule for delivery on Mar. 5th.
  - Data collection for Research's private Web server on schedule.
- **Corporate Headquarters:**
  - Data collection for the Uranus System delayed pending receipt of input from system owner.

Table 5.2   Project Report (Continued)

— Certification of the Luna System delayed pending identification of point of contact.
— ST&E of Achilles Server on schedule for Feb. 26th.
— Titan System C&A Package completed and submitted on Feb. 24th.
— Ares System deleted from OST inventory.
— Notified that Athena will soon be ready to finish certification. Will coordinate ST&E.
— Certification responsibility for Hermes System still to be resolved.

System C&A Status by Business Unit
The number of systems reflected in the following table is based on information received directly from business units and may not as yet be reflected in the official systems inventory.

Business Unit	Total Number of Systems	Number of Systems Certified and Accredited Last Year		Number of Systems That Will Be Certified and Accredited This Year		Number of Systems Accredited to Date	
		No.	%	No.	%	No.	%
Headquarters	7	5	71.4%	2	100.00%	0	71.4%
Research	12	7	58.3%	5	100.00%	2	75.0%
Sales	8	6	75.0%	2	100.00%	0	75.0%
Manufacturing	5	3	60.0%	2	100.00%	0	60.0%
Administration	18	5	27.8%	13	100.00%	6	61.1%
Agency Total	**50**	**26**	**52.0%**	**24**	**100.00%**	**8**	**68.0%**

pation and cooperation is a matter to be reported to management. The thinking is that if system owners are not responsive to the project manager who they are equal or superior to, then perhaps owners will respond to someone who is in their supervisory chain.

Failure to provide support — time and resources — can be attributed to a lack of visibility or urgency on the part of management. The project manager must ensure that management has the facts through timely, regular reporting and by not pulling punches. Management must know the risks involved if the project fails.

Other Tasks

When documenting the project plan, the project manager must ensure that he or she builds in sufficient time for training of the project team. This should include training in the methodology that will be used, particular standards and regulations that apply to systems within the scope of the project, guidelines applicable to project team members, and reporting requirements. In the plan, the project manager must also include tasks for guidance development as well. Rules for conducting interviews, collecting documentation, recording findings and analysis, preparing deliverables, and providing status reports should be given. The plan must address reporting requirements, too, to ensure that the amount of time they will require is properly estimated and anticipated. Finally, the plan should allow sufficient time for preparing and presenting kickoff and closeout briefings for each system within the scope of the project.

Project Kickoff

The project manager is usually well served when he or she takes the time to prepare and schedule a kickoff meeting for those involved in the project. It is essential to provide a project briefing with management to give them feedback on the conception of the project's objective, definition, approach, scope, timetables, and resources, providing management an opportunity to get onboard with the project plan and to give them a chance to query the project manager about particulars. This solidifies management support for the project. It is also important for supported organizations to be given a project briefing for the same reasons. And, where possible, depending on the number of systems in the scope of the project, the project manager may want to provide a kickoff presentation to each system owner to demonstrate commitment to quality, cooperation, and support and to offer the system owner a line of communication for problem resolution should the need arise. A sample kickoff presentation is provided in Appendix E.

Wrap-Up

Likewise, the project manager should be prepared to present a wrap-up or closeout briefing when the project is concluded. This gives management a view of objectives achieved and the success (or failure) to achieve them, as well as summary findings, recommendations, and next steps. Additionally, the project manager may want to brief individual system owners as each system is certified to highlight findings and recommendations and to speed up the deliverable review process.

The information that is briefed to managers at the end of the project should be documented separately in a lesson learned report. This historical document summarizes the project with an aim to serve as a starting point for improving the probability of success in future projects. By documenting successes and failures experienced in the project, project managers of future projects will obviously benefit. The time required to prepare such a report (which does not have to be more than a few pages) and to collect project work papers will be more than made up for by the increased quality and efficiency of future certification and accreditation efforts. A sample wrap-up briefing is provided in Appendix F.

Summary

The prime responsibility of the certification and accreditation project manager is to ensure that the project is executed smoothly, on time, within budget, and is compliant with project guidance, objectives, and requirements. Success in a project generally means that the systems in the scope of the project will be professionally certified, allowing the accrediting authority to authorize processing. To achieve this goal the project manager must chart a course to avoid a wide range of certification and accreditation pitfalls that include delays in project performance, lack of support from personnel, lack of adequate documentation, lack of participation by key personnel, and loss of project visibility. Using sound planning techniques, interpersonal skills, and deep reserves of energy, the project manager can usually overcome problems and navigate the project to a successful conclusion.

Chapter 6

System Inventory Process

An effective system security program and workable certification and accreditation program rely on a sound process for identifying and inventorying all the information systems under the control of an organization. Anyone who participated in inventorying systems as part of the Y2K effort knows how imposing a task this can be. The difficulty in inventorying information technology assets is caused by the lack of understanding of what constitutes a system, the failure to distinguish between systems, the rapid rate of creation of new systems, and then the failure to monitor the information technology operating environment. Yet, it is important that a reliable and complete system inventory be created and maintained because it is one of the most important steps in certification and accreditation. The goal of the systems inventory process is to provide assurance that systems requiring protection have been identified and are included in security planning and oversight.

Unless systems are known and identified in a centralized, enterprise inventory process they cannot be protected with any degree of assurance. Managing systems accountability in a rapidly changing environment was previously addressed in Chapter 3. This chapter concentrates on the definition of systems and on identifying where one system stops and another begins. The chapter also addresses the need for monitoring the systems inventory through the use of automated tools to identify previously unknown applications and network servers for identification purposes, as well as to administer updates to the inventory.

Establishing and maintaining a centralized systems inventory program is not an easy task. Fortunately, the task gets easier once it has been established. To build an effective program there are three critical success factors: continuing management support, clearly documented guidance, and a well-constructed implementation plan.

- Management support for the effort is critical because lines of business at some point will question the need for the inventory process and will escalate their concerns as far up the chain as they are able. Committed management support will ensure that everyone plays the game according to the rules, will disallow invalid exceptions and waivers, and will provide the staying power necessary to see the project through to its conclusion. Management has to be sold on the benefit of establishing a system inventory process and this is the first crucial step. Security managers will not be able to proceed without management backing no matter how hard they try because they will never be able to use their own pleasing personalities to the extent necessary to earn the willing participation of systems owners. It takes muscle as well as personality. The proposal for presentation to the boss should be built around the fact that an information technology security program cannot function without knowing what needs to be protected, and that this must start with knowing what information technology systems the organization possesses.

- Once approval for the program has been gained, the CISO must document a basic policy on systems inventory. This will be prepared for an executive's signature and needs to be approved at the highest organizational level possible, preferably by the CEO. This is the document, written in "thou shalt" language, that requires systems owners to identify their systems using an established process. A sample system inventory policy is provided in Appendix G. Naturally, it must be supported by a description of the process to include roles and responsibilities, steps, schedules, formats, and rules for defining systems. Both the policy and procedures must pass through the organizational staffing chain to gain concurrence and support.

- Finally, once the policy and procedures have been completed, staffed, and approved, the CISO must develop and oversee the execution of an implementation plan for the initiative. The CISO must develop instructions for complying with policy and procedures including timetables, tasks, and activities and reporting requirements. Although it is difficult to account for exceptions, execution of the plan for a large organization should take 60 to 90 days, and for smaller organizations (less than 100 systems) it

Table 6.1   High-Level System Inventory Project Work Plan

Task One	Identify general support systems and applications
	Identify business functions
	Identify automated information resources
	Categorize automated information resources as GSS or application
Task Two	Classify GSS and applications
	Determine information sensitivity
	Determine mission criticality
Task Three	Identify major applications
	Determine applications that qualify as major applications
	Determine major application–general support system linkages
	Map nonmajor applications to general support systems
Task Four	Submit to CIO
	Business unit executive review
	CIO review
	Publish inventory

can be accomplished in about a month of diligent effort. A sample work plan for a system inventory project is provided in Table 6.1.

Responsibility

System owners will play the primary role in the inventory process. Their role along with all those involved in the inventory process needs to be defined in writing. System owners in the organization must be identified and must know and accept that they are the owners of the information systems in their area of responsibility. Further, system owners must be trained in the responsibilities inherent in that role. An ISSO needs to be appointed for each system to provide the system owner his or her primary point of contact for system security. The ISSO must also be trained in system security responsibilities. The third person in the inventory process is the line of business information technology security manager. This individual will play a key role in collecting system inventory information from system owners in his or her business unit. And, finally, the CISO as owner of the inventory process will play the largest role in collecting and consolidating inventory submission data and for keeping it up to date. All of the roles identified here require a degree of security expertise because this is a security process at its heart, even though it can support other business requirements as well. The data is collected primarily to meet security needs, using security terminology. Hence, the individuals selected for these roles must understand information technology security and preferably must have demonstrated experience in applying it. There are, however, others involved in the process that will have little if any security experience or interest. Business managers own the processes and help define business needs for security based on their knowledge of the importance of the system and the impact of its loss or degradation on the organization or mission. Although it is not necessary for each individual mentioned here to sign off on the inventory form, each should fully concur with the information contained in the submission.

System Identification

The system owner plays the primary role in the initial identification of information systems. He or she can obtain assistance in performing this task from information owners, the CIO, CISO, and others but has the primary responsibility for determining what collections of information resources should be identified as a system, either an application system that supports a tightly defined business process or a general support system that serves as the computing platform for multiple computer applications. When the system owner considers what constitutes a system, he or she may need to consider a wide variety of information technology hardware, software, and processes. The system owner may be responsible for stand-alone computers, applications, office automation systems, word processors, vendor-hosted systems, subscription services, manual processes, mainframe computers, mid-range computers, local area networks, and wide area networks. A useful and broadly accepted definition of a system comes from Office of Management and Budget Circular A-130, where we find that,

> The term "information system" means a discrete set of information resources organized for the collection, processing, maintenance, transmission, and dissemination of information, in accordance with defined procedures, whether automated or manual.

A-130 also gives us useful definitions for a general support system, which it says is "an interconnected set of information resources under the same direct management control that shares common functionality. It normally includes hardware, software, information, data, applications, communications, and people." It further defines a major application as "an application that requires special attention to security due to the risk and magnitude of harm resulting from the loss, misuse, or unauthorized access to or modification of the information in the application." These definitions help us to focus on the discrete elements of an organization's information resources that are most useful in determining what needs to be protected.

Small Systems

It is important to separate the assets that constitute general support systems or major applications to avoid placing emphasis where it is not needed. This can happen when other less significant applications are also included in the certification and accreditation inventory. Limited purpose applications developed to help a user or small number of users to do work more efficiently, such as databases and spreadsheets, fall into this category. These systems are also distinguished by their near total reliance on the general support system for their security, as opposed to a major application that has substantial technical controls built into its design. Although such applications also require attention to security because of the harm that can result from loss of confidentiality, integrity, or availability, for certification and accreditation purposes, they are normally addressed as part of the general support system through which they are accessed. This approach helps the organization limit the number of systems for which formal certification and accreditation is exercised, ensuring that visibility for security is apportioned appropriately without losing sight of minor applications.

Large Systems

Large, complex systems pose another difficulty to development of the system inventory. They are more difficult to certify and accredit not because they are difficult to define but because of their size and complexity. Large, complicated systems, such as corporate finance and accounting or personnel systems, contain multiple processes and subsystems that are combined into a single integrated major application. However, each of these components may in itself be larger than another major application the organization operates. This creates a disparity when it is time to certify the system because the level of effort is so much greater than an ordinary major application. Such systems may also have several different managers responsible for each of its component parts, which cloud the single ownership principle. For these large, complex systems, certification and accreditation is best approached through their subsystems. Breaking them into manageable chunks that support a larger whole is for practical purposes the only way to ensure the system is certified and accredited in a timely and cost-effective way.

Combining Systems

Another approach that can be used to streamline the certification and accreditation inventory is the grouping of similar systems. This reduces the amount of documentation that must be developed and maintained, and it is acceptable so long as certain conditions are met. First, systems can be grouped when all of the systems in the group fall under the responsibility of the same system owner. Second, each must process in the same operating environment (e.g., reside on the same server). And, third, each must be protected within a common security perimeter (e.g., are protected by the same set of management and operational controls). This loose set of criteria can be very helpful in ensuring that security is applied properly to all systems within the group while doing away with the need for creating superfluous security documentation.

Type accreditation and site accreditation are other certification and accreditation approaches that can be utilized to minimize the demands of creating security documentation without jeopardizing the loss of security visibility. Type accreditation relates to the common certification and accreditation of all systems of a given type that are secured in a like manner. This may apply to an application that is installed and used by multiple users throughout an organization. Although the security perimeter and processing environment of each are similar though not identical, ownership of the system varies greatly in that there are usually multiple system owners involved. On the other hand, with site accreditation, all the systems at a given location (i.e., computer room, data center, facility) are protected within the same security perimeter, have common but often different processing environments, and are certified and accredited under the ownership of the site manager, rather than by individual system owners. Both of these approaches are acceptable solutions for minimizing the number of systems requiring individual certification and accreditation.

Accreditation Boundaries

For the purpose of certification and accreditation, it is important to remember that everything must be certified. Consequently, there should be no dispute over the fact that every component of the organization's information system inventory has to undergo the same process. Hence, establishment of accreditation boundaries is more concerned with establishing responsibility for the accreditation of a given information resource, not on whether a system has to be certified. Accreditation boundaries are drawn between one or more general support systems or one or more major applications. It is best to proceed on the basis of business processes first, security perimeter second, and ownership last. All information resources related to the same business process (i.e., asset management) should naturally be grouped into the same major application. However, if one component supports two different processes (e.g., two applications reside on the same server), then server controls can either be addressed in each certification (effectively doubling the certification and accreditation burden on the server owner), or the server can preferably be certified as part of a general support system because it is within the same security perimeter. If the same manager functions as the system owner of these two applications, it is possible that they can be grouped into a single accreditation even though they do not support an identical business process because they have consistent ownership and both are within the same security perimeter. The owner of these two major applications can also argue that he or she should own the computing platform, making the case that it should be included in the same accreditation as well.

One principle also to be considered in assessing the security perimeter is to make boundaries as small as possible for systems with elevated levels of sensitivity to ensure that the cost-effectiveness of controls is maximized. For instance, it will be more effective to accredit the most sensitive components of a general support system (e.g., a remote access server) in a separate enclave rather than to attempt to accredit the entire general support system at the high level of sensitivity. Nor is it appropriate to accredit the high-sensitivity component at the moderate level of sensitivity of the general support system either.

The organization must clearly define the outer boundary of its security perimeter to ensure that security of all its assets is in place at this outermost extent. First, this is done by ensuring that devices that guard the perimeter (i.e., firewalls, routers) are defined as part of a specific system that is to be certified and accredited itself. Systems of this nature are more sensitive and controls protecting them should be subjected to more rigorous scrutiny. And, second, the perimeter must be defined through identification of interfaces and interconnections with systems lying outside the secure perimeter. This is done through coordination and negotiation with system owners of these external systems, which transmit data to and receive data from our organization. This process is detailed in Chapter 9. There is a great variety of ways to package information resources for accreditation purposes. This flexibility is permitted by the fact that the certification and accreditation program is all-encompassing and that the outer perimeter of the organization's information technology resources has been defined.

The Process

The system inventory process begins with the system owner, who identifies general support systems and major applications for which he or she is responsible. This is best achieved with the assistance of the business manager, who identifies business processes and then the information technology that supports them. A three-step approach identifies business functions, identifies supporting information technology resources, and then categorizes these resources as types of systems.

Next, systems are classified by determining their needs for protection on the basis of disclosure, modification, destruction, or denial. Further guidance on how this is achieved is in Chapter 7. From this step the sensitivity of the system is set. Then a system inventory form is completed for each general support system and major application (see below) and is submitted to the CIO, or CISO as his or her agent. Finally, the CIO approves the official system inventory for the entire organization.

Validation

The CISO should perform a sanity check on all submissions. For new inventory programs it may be helpful to interview each business unit point of contact and system owner to validate input to gain assurance about the accuracy of their submissions. This is best achieved in a short face-to-face meeting between them to ensure that they follow organizational guidance, use sensitivity rankings appropriately, ensure forms are completed correctly, and ensure they have understood terms and definitions and have applied them properly. They must also be able to justify their rankings regarding data sensitivity and system criticality. Additionally, the CISO must be sure to check that submitted information is consistent with previous years' submissions. Criticality information must be closely scrutinized because there is a temptation for each system owner to classify his or her system as mission critical. Although it is possible that all systems could be classified as mission critical, it is highly unlikely. Under normal conditions not everything can be critical, and not every security impact can be categorized at the highest levels of sensitivity. Actually, someone with a view of the big picture must decide on the criticality of organization systems. Similarly, someone with knowledge of security impacts must be the judge of systems sensitivity rankings.

The CISO must be careful not to punish the good guys or those who submit their inventory data on time, well ahead of the average. There may be a temptation to focus on inventory deficiencies of those who report their systems first, while paying progressively less attention to the information submitted by system owners late in the process. The CISO should maintain system owner cooperation. So those reporting first should be applauded for being diligent, and negative feedback should be apportioned equally, regardless of when inventory information is submitted.

Inventory Information

It may be tempting to collect a lot of information regarding the system using the system inventory form and process. However, to minimize the impact on system owners, the form should be used to capture only enough information to provide a snapshot of the system. Essential information that should be collected include the name of the system, abbreviated description of the system and its environment (no more than three to four sentences); the status of the system (operational or in development); a list of systems it is connected to; data sensitivity impacts; mission criticality ranking; and identification of system points of contact (owner, approving authority, and ISSO). The name of the individual authorizing the submission should also be indicated. Table 6.2 provides additional information on these essential data elements. An organization should also consider implementing a unique number or naming scheme for its systems to facilitate the identification process. Such a scheme should accommodate systems of varying types that belong to different business units at different stages of their life cycles, and its most important characteristic will be the fact that it is centrally issued and managed. A numbering system can also be used as a means for controlling the development and funding of systems. Without an official system designation, there will be no continued resources committed to the system.

Inventory Tools

Three tools are necessary for managing the inventory program: the inventory form, an inventory change form, and an organization inventory summary. These can be combined into an integrated inventory tool with controlled access, can be built using existing office automation software, or can even be based on the use of hard-copy forms. There does have to be centralized and controlled collection and validation of forms by a

Table 6.2   Inventory Data Requirements

System name	■ Official name ■ Approved abbreviation ■ Other cross-reference numbers
System description	■ Specify what the system is intended to do ■ Identify the business function it supports ■ Indicate data flows
System environment	■ Hardware ■ Software ■ Components ■ URLs ■ IP addresses
System status	■ Stage of the system's life cycle ■ Operational ■ Development
Dependencies and interconnectivity	■ Data flows ■ Hosting systems ■ Supporting systems ■ Supported systems
Sensitivity	■ Consider all data processed ■ Ensure knowledgeable personnel are involved ■ Justify all determinations ■ Consider consequences of over- and undercategorization
Criticality	■ Ensure the term criticality is understood ■ Ensure ramifications are understood, both positive and negative
Points of contact	■ Include system owner and system security officer
Approval	■ Management should sign off on each system inventory form

single authority. Templates for these forms are provided in Tables 6.3, 6.4, and 6.5.

Using the Inventory

The inventory process can be helpful in gaining support for and participation in security initiatives. As stated previously, funding can be tied to the process. This is probably the benefit with the greatest potential for the CISO. The program can be used to support periodic reporting requirements (like FISMA) as well. The program can be beneficial in supporting the information needs of the information technology security oversight board, enterprise architecture team, and other management groups tasked

Table 6.3   Sample Inventory Form

Owning Organization:	Office of Administration
Date:	April 1, 2005
Information System Name and Acronym:	General Disbursement System (GDS)
System Status:	☒ Operational ☐ Under Development
Accreditation Status:	☒ Yes ☐ No
	Date: <u>11/13/2003</u> Scheduled Completion Date: _____

Points of Contact:

Position	Name	Telephone
Information System Owner	John Brown	202-123-4567
Information Owner	John Brown	202-123-4567
Information Systems Security Officer	Tom Green	202-123-5678
Primary System Administrator	Jane Black	202-123-6789
Secondary System Administrator	Bill White	202-123-7890
Designated Approving Authority	Mary Blue	202-123-8901

Type of Automated Information Resource	☐ GSS (General Support System) ☒ MA (Major Application)
Associated URLs:	http://www.gds.xyz.com
Associated IP Addresses:	123.45.678.90
Technologies (i.e., Windows, Oracle, etc.):	Microsoft Windows 2003; Microsoft SQL Server; Microsoft IIS 6.0
Name(s) of System(s) the Information System is Interfaced, Interconnected, or Shares Data With:	Resides on corporate intranet general support system; interconnected to the financial management system
Description of Data and Business Function:	GBS data consists of financial information related to distribution of government funds. GBS is used to process disbursements of appropriated funds to state-level agencies
Mission Criticality:	☒ Critical ☐ Noncritical
Criticality Justification:	GDS is essential to the performance of corporate funds disbursement operations, which directly support one of the company's major missions

Information Sensitivity:

Protection Requirements	High	Medium	Low	Justification
Confidentiality		X		The application is used to process department financial information that must be safeguarded from public access.

Table 6.3   Sample Inventory Form (Continued)

Integrity	X		System information is used in the disbursement of government funds and must be accurate.
Availability		X	Users access the system during normal hours only, and manual processes are available for use when required. The system can be down for 7 days without significant disruption.

Comments: The General Billing System is currently scheduled for replacement by Universal Disbursement System within the next 12 months, at which time GBS will be retired.

Signature of Approving Official	Date

with managing information technology resources. Also, the program supports compliance review and audit functions. One should not discount the value of such a system in gaining management support by avoiding the risk of embarrassment and erosion of credibility.

Disputes involving the inventory are a near certainty. One can anticipate disagreements over what constitutes a system; why a system should be added to or deleted from the inventory; over ownership of and responsibility for systems; about criticality of systems, and responsibility for reporting. I have found that the system inventory shrinks proportionally to the number of requirements associated with identifying a system. Once system owners understand requirements, they are prone to deactivate systems outright if possible or combine them with others when feasible. The CISO stands in the middle of all these disagreements, but the inventory process can be used to assist in resolving them rather than simply causing them. Such disputes need to be surfaced and addressed rather than being left to fester while vulnerabilities are not addressed.

Maintenance

There needs to be a formalized, annual requirement to review, update, and authorize system inventory data. With an automated inventory system, input and registration can be continuous, reducing reliance on periodic data calls. This periodic review permits close scrutiny of changes to the inventory, which may affect total system count, number of critical systems, and identification of personnel and environment changes. It also can be used to trigger a review of security documentation like the system security

Table 6.4   Inventory Change Form

System Inventory Change Procedures
Background
Information recorded in the certification and accreditation system inventory
may change between scheduled inventories. Changes to the inventory may
surface due to changes in the type of the information processed,
software/hardware modification, or other changes to the processing
environment of the system. Awareness of these changes by the CIO is
necessary to permit maintenance of the appropriate level of security controls
for systems in the inventory.

Responsibilities
Business unit security managers will complete one of the following forms to
record system inventory changes and will submit it to the CISO for update
of the organization systems inventory. The CISO will track changes to systems
requiring certification and accreditation to ensure compliance with federal
guidelines.

Procedure
Business unit security managers will use the appropriate form (add, update,
or delete) included below to update system inventory for their business unit
and will forward it to the CISO for action.

Systems Inventory Form — System Addition
Business Unit:
Date:
Name of System:
Type of System: GSS or MA
Mission Critical: Yes or No
System Security Plan Date:
Risk Assessment Date:
ST&E Date:
Contingency Plan Date:
Security Certification Level (SCL): High, Moderate, or Low

System Inventory Form — Update System Information
Business Unit:
Date:
Name of System:
Nature of Change:
Reason for Change:

System Inventory Form — System Addition
Business Unit:

Table 6.4 Inventory Change Form (Continued)

Date:
Name of System:
Mission Critical: Yes or No
Reason for Deletion:

---

plan or risk assessment and contingency plan. Periodic review will only be effective if the program owner — the CISO — locks down and tightly controls the system change process. This will establish requirements for justifying changes to the inventory and prevent manipulation and churning. Keeping the inventory up to date will be a continual challenge and needs continuing management support to be effective. The inventory system must also be simple to use and be responsive to organizational needs. When possible the inventory process should be integrated into the system change management process. An inventory form should be submitted as part of the initiation phase of the system development life cycle, and inventory change forms should be updated as part of routine change management. All changes need to be fully approved on the submission side. The system owner needs to be informed as does the ISSO as a minimum. This ensures the form is properly documented with the approval of the responsible manager. Inventory data should be updated any time that information submitted in inventory forms changes. This means that the system owner needs to establish a process for identifying these changes and for submitting an updated inventory form whenever there are changes in the system name, operating status, environment, connectivity, sensitivity, criticality, or responsibilities. The CISO should have a corresponding process to review inventory data regularly to ensure there is close scrutiny of increases and decreases in the number of systems in inventory, particularly changes in the number of systems considered mission critical. Monitoring this information is important because of the potential impact on resources.

Summary

Unless there is an accurate assessment of what composes an organization's general support systems and major applications, it will be impossible to have any degree of assurance that its information resources have implemented appropriate security controls. Therefore, it is of utmost importance to know what the organization's information resources consist of. The most effective approach to identifying information technology assets is to

Table 6.5 Inventory Summary

No	Name of System	System Type GSS/ MA	Mission Critical Y/N	C&A Y/N	C&A Date (actual or planned) (MM/DD/YY)	System Security Plan Date (MM/DD/YY)	Risk Assessment Date (MM/DD/YY)	ST&E Date (MM/DD/YY)
1	NUTRIA	MA	N	N	09/30/03	05/06/03	05/06/03	06/11/03
2	APOLLO	MA	N	N	09/30/03	03/30/03	03/30/03	06/11/03
3	HERMES	MA	N	N	09/30/03	04/01/03	04/01/03	06/09/03
4	JUPITER	GSS	Y	Y	08/11/03	03/21/03	03/21/03	06/24/03
5	MERCURY	MA	N	N	09/30/03	03/26/03	03/26/03	06/11/03

identify systems. A systems inventory process can help an organization specify information technology security requirements at the appropriate level of sensitivity with the right amount of detail. From an enterprise perspective, a certification and accreditation program can only be effective when it has a comprehensive systems inventory as its foundation. Unless all information resources are identified, classified, and inventoried, the certification and accreditation program has no place to begin, and is certain to find a quick end.

Chapter 7

Assessing Data Sensitivity and Criticality

If it were not for the data that they process, information technology hardware and software could be secured like any other piece of high-value property. We could protect them just as we would safeguard tools, typewriters, merchandise, and other types of physical property. But in the case of an information technology system made up of hardware, software, and data, it is the data that places them in an altogether different category where protection against a distinct set of threats must be provided. And many of these threats (e.g., unauthorized access) do not pertain to other types of physical property. In terms of determining protection requirements, it is the sensitivity of data and the criticality of systems that are the primary drivers. This chapter will explore data sensitivity as it relates to information technology systems, and will also address the criticality or importance of computer systems to an organization's overall mission. It is imperative to determine data sensitivity and criticality in order to define requirements for protection of information.

Defining Sensitivity

It is the data that a system processes that makes an information technology system sensitive. Unlike other pieces of equipment, it is not the value of the hardware or software that governs sensitivity ranking of an information technology system. Requirements for security have to be addressed in the context of the business requirements. Similarly, implementation of security controls for a system has to be grounded in the context of the sensitivity of the data that the system is used to process, transmit, or store.

Sensitivity is often thought of being that quality that makes it necessary to protect data from being seen by those who do not have a need to see it. This view is based on the consideration of data as "confidential," "secret," and "top secret" in National Defense terms. However, this narrow view obscures the breadth of how we actually define sensitivity. Sensitivity is more than simply protecting the confidentiality of system data, although that is surely a key aspect of the definition of sensitivity and is perhaps the overriding factor in determining the sensitivity level of a large number of government and business systems. Rather, the sensitivity of a system must also be based on how prone system data is to risks to its integrity and to its availability.

This broader definition was first found in the Computer Security Act of 1987. This act, which has since been replaced by FISMA, established minimum acceptable security practices for federal computer systems that do not process National Defense (i.e., "classified") information. The act specifies that federal computer systems be protected against unauthorized modification or destruction, as well as unauthorized disclosure. The act therefore more broadly defines "sensitive" information, which is said to be

> any information, the loss, misuse, or unauthorized access to or modification of which could adversely affect the national interest or the conduct of federal programs, or the privacy to which individuals are entitled under section 552a of title 5, United States Code (the Privacy Act), but which has not been specifically authorized under criteria established by an Executive Order or an Act of Congress to be kept secret in the interest of national defense or foreign policy.

There is a common misconception that there exists a class of systems that is not sensitive on the basis of the nature of the data they process. However, the federal government's view is that all federal systems are inherently sensitive and require protection to a lesser or greater extent. According to the National Institute of Standards and Technology, the intent of the Computer Security Act was not to create two distinct categories of information: "sensitive" and "nonsensitive." Also, the act did not create a category of "nonsensitive systems" that do not require implementation of security controls. All federal systems are required to be protected by security controls that correspond with the actual importance of the information the system processes or to the government investment in the system. Office of Management and Budget Circular A-130, which implements the Computer Security Act, also defines sensitivity to include all three of these important components. This means that information that has no requirement for protection against unauthorized disclosure, such as information on a Web site intended for public access, can still be categorized as sensitive, because it may still need to be protected against modification and denial of service. In the federal sector there has been an unfortunate tendency toward using limited information technology security resources to determine which systems should be labeled "sensitive." This is not only wasteful but also unnecessary because all systems require some minimum level of protection and are therefore sensitive.

Data Sensitivity and System Sensitivity

The sensitivity of a system is based on the data that it processes. Simply stated, remove the data and the system is no longer sensitive. It may be of high value on the basis of what it would cost to replace it, but it will not be sensitive by definition. Even though systems themselves are often referred to as being sensitive, it is actually the data processed, stored, or transmitted by the system that makes it sensitive. It is possible to establish an overall sensitivity level for a system on the basis of the aggregated sensitivity levels of data by security objective (i.e., confidentiality, integrity, availability). Federal Information Processing Standard (FIPS) 199 refers to this as the "high water mark" that is to be used in defining the security category of an information system. This categorization represents the worst-case potential impact relating to the system.

Sensitivity Assessment Process

The most practical approach to determining sensitivity is by assessing the data by each of the three security concerns: confidentiality, integrity, and availability, in no particular order. This assessment should not only include a determination of the applicability of the security concern but should also result in a relative ranking of the sensitivity against a predetermined standard, as well as an overall ranking of sensitivity based on a view of the combined sensitivity in all three impact areas. The relative importance of the following three security objectives will depend on the nature of the system and the data it processes.

- *Confidentiality*: The sensitivity of data must be assessed on the basis of its need for protection against disclosure. One should identify the impact that unauthorized disclosure of the data would have on the organization. The level of confidentiality that data requires naturally depends on the nature of the information. The confidentiality of information that is widely available to the public requires no, or perhaps only minimal, protection from disclosure. On the other hand, protection against disclosure is a key consideration for personal information about employees or customers, trade secrets and other proprietary information, information regarding operational plans and procedures, or information that could otherwise result in a loss or embarrassment to the organization should it be disclosed. Of course, confidentiality is a primary consideration in the protection of National Defense information or data that is classified in nature. Confidentiality protection also includes protection of the privacy of those to which data processed by the system pertains.

■ *Integrity*: System data must be protected from the effects of unauthorized or inadvertent modification or alteration. This quality of data defines how severe a loss would be incurred if the data integrity was lost. Determining the appropriate level for data integrity requires consideration of the needs for protection of the information from unauthorized, unanticipated, or unintentional alteration or loss. The data integrity security objective also includes consideration of the security objectives of authenticity, nonrepudiation, and accountability, which are also sometimes used. For example, a system that processes financial information may result in it being targeted for unauthorized modification. Consideration should be given as to how the system is employed in a business process. For example, when system data is not the sole source of input for a business process, data integrity needs are generally less than when the business process fully relies on system data for its performance.

■ *Availability*: Data must be protected from adverse consequences of denial of its use or its destruction. Should system data not be available, how severe a loss would the organization suffer? To determine the appropriate system need for availability, one must consider the need for its data to be available to users on a timely basis in order to avoid substantial losses or to meet mission requirements. Protection requirements for availability need to be based on the period of operation during which the system is most critical to the business function it supports. For example, if the system is used only the last two weeks of each quarter, consider the availability requirement only for that period.

Ideally, early in the system development life cycle, the sensitivity of the data that the system will process will be determined. Because data sensitivity drives controls, this will permit the identification and employment of appropriate controls when it is most cost-effective. However, the system owner should continue to assess data sensitivity throughout the development/acquisition, implementation, and operations/maintenance phases to ensure that the adequacy of controls is maintained. Any change in the functionality of the system, in the user population, or in interfaces with other systems should trigger a review of system sensitivity.

Data Classification Approaches

The systematic definition of data sensitivity and protection needs normally results from the application of formal data classification schemes. FIPS 199 is one example of an approach required for the classification of U.S. government data. There is a common misconception that data classification schemes relate only to the need to protect data against unauthorized disclosure. Perhaps this is because use of the term "classification" is thought to relate only to classified (i.e., national security) information. However, a formal data classification process as used most currently addresses the three main system security objectives of integrity, availability, and confidentiality. A sample of a data classification scheme is provided in Table 7.1.

Table 7.1   Example of a Data Classification Scheme

Classification	Definition	Examples
Public	Information that can be disseminated to the public following management review	Marketing materials Public records
Internal use	Information related to the day-to-day operations of the company that is restricted to company employees and consultants only	Customer information Financial reports System configuration data Incident reports Personnel records
Restricted	Information that must be closely safeguarded and is restricted to use by less than 5 percent of employees of the company	Trade secrets Merger and acquisition information

Responsibility for Data Sensitivity Assessment

Because system owners are responsible for securing their information technology systems by defining and implementing necessary controls, it is the system owner who must be primarily interested in the sensitivity of the data the system processes. Many times, system owners are also responsible for defining the sensitivity of the data their system processes in terms of confidentiality, integrity and availability of the information, and performance of the functions of the data owner. However, in other cases systems process data that is the responsibility of another department or individual. Here system owners must rely on the judgment of a data owner as to the sensitivity of the data rather than making their own determination of the sensitivity of the data. For instance, the human resources department is in the best position to determine the sensitivity of an employee database, rather than the mailroom manager whose mail application uses information from that database to distribute benefits information to each employee's home address. The data sensitivity determination must be made by someone who has knowledge of the process for identifying the confidentiality, integrity, and availability impacts on the data. That individual must know what those terms mean and how they apply to specific sets of data. This means that there has to be a process for making data owners aware of their responsibility for designating data sensitivity and for educating them in how to do this. Consultants are often relied on to facilitate the data sensitivity designation because of their familiarity and expertise with these processes as well as their independence. Although this approach can ensure consistency, data owners, because of their familiarity with the data and the nature of its use, should consider the consultant's work simply as a recommendation and must continue to exercise ultimate responsibility for the data sensitivity designation to ensure it is accurate, applicable, and reasonable.

Where the system owner and the data owner are distinct entities, it is essential that they closely coordinate how the system processes the data to ensure that it is properly safeguarded. It's important to note that as the owner of the data, the data owner should review the system design and grant permission to the system owner to use or otherwise process data only when he or she is satisfied that the data is being properly protected. This is because once the data owner permits the data to be processed by the system, the data owner gives control over the protection of data to the system owner. In this case, the system owner becomes a custodian of the data.

Ranking Data Sensitivity

It is important to distinguish levels of sensitivity using well-defined categories. The most common means of expressing sensitivity is by use of such terms as "high," "moderate," and "low" or some similar scheme (e.g., red – amber – green; 1 – 2 – 3; etc.). The definitions for each sensitivity level need to be both clear and consistent for each security impact area. However, it is not enough to simply attach a ranking to the data. The data sensitivity assessment must document in writing the justification for ranking the data. Table 7.2 provides examples for describing various sensitivity rankings for a government system, which are taken from NIST Special Publication 800-18. Samples of assessment justifications by impact area and by category of information are provided in Table 7.3.

The basis for ranking sensitivity can be based on predefined criteria relating to the sensitivity of data according to category of information processed (i.e., public, national security, financial, personal, etc.). Sensitivity can be ranked according to operational, contractual, regulatory, and legal requirements relative to its use. In determining appropriate protection measures, it is important to bear in mind that requirements for the protection of particular types of information are often provided by statute or according to organizational decision. Information required to be protected under statute includes, for example, privacy information (protected under the Privacy Act), financial information (protected under the Federal Manager's Financial Integrity Act), taxpayer information, and census data. In other cases, an organization may establish security requirements according to specific types of information. For example, some organizations have created internal "restricted" or "official use only" labels for certain types of information that need to be protected from unauthorized disclosure. Table 7.4 provides a sample of information categories.

Criticality

Criticality is a term that is often confused with sensitivity; unfortunately, they are often used interchangeably. Criticality is similar to sensitivity in that it is used to determine the nature and types of security controls necessary to protect a system. It differs, however, in that it relates to a system as a whole, whereas sensitivity relates to the data that the system processes and more often is used to determine the priority for implementation of security controls according to the importance or criticality of a system. The key aspect of criticality that must be remembered is that criticality is a statement of the importance of a system to the organization it supports. Criticality answers the question of how valuable a system is to the performance of an organization's operational mission. Criticality most often relates to the amount of time that an organization can tolerate the nonavailability of the system, and therefore it is directly related to the availability objective of the system. Hence, the difference between sensitivity and criticality is one of breadth; sensitivity addresses all three security objectives, while criticality

Table 7.2   Examples of Sensitivity Ranking Descriptions

Ranking	Confidentiality	Integrity	Availability
High	The consequences of unauthorized disclosure or compromise of data or information in the system are unacceptable. Loss of confidentiality could be expected to adversely affect national-level interests, prevent mission accomplishment, or create unsafe conditions that may result in loss of life or other exceptional grave damage.	The consequences of corruption or unauthorized modification of data or information in the system are unacceptable. Loss of integrity could be expected to adversely affect national-level interests, prevent mission accomplishment, or create unsafe conditions that may result in loss of life or other exceptional grave damage.	The consequences of loss or disruption of access to system resources or to data or information in the system are unacceptable. Loss of availability could be expected to adversely affect national-level interests, prevent mission accomplishment, or create unsafe conditions that may result in loss of life or other exceptional grave damage.
Moderate	The consequences of unauthorized disclosure or compromise of data or information in the system are only marginally acceptable. Loss of confidentiality could be expected to adversely affect agency-level interests, degrade mission accomplishment, or create unsafe conditions that may result in injury or serious damage.	The consequences of corruption or unauthorized modification of data or information in the system are only marginally acceptable. Loss of integrity could be expected to adversely affect agency-level interests, degrade mission accomplishment, or create unsafe conditions that may result in injury or serious damage.	The consequences of loss or disruption of access to system resources or to data or information in the system are only marginally acceptable. Loss of availability could be expected to adversely affect agency-level interests, degrade mission accomplishment, or create unsafe conditions that may result in injury or serious damage.
Low	The consequences of unauthorized disclosure or compromise of data or information in the system are generally acceptable. Loss of confidentiality could be expected to minimally affect agency-level interests and have little to no impact on mission accomplishment.	The consequences of corruption or unauthorized modification of data or information in the system are generally acceptable. Loss of integrity could be expected to minimally affect agency-level interests and have little to no impact on mission accomplishment.	The consequences of loss or disruption of access to system resources or to data or information in the system are generally acceptable. Loss of availability could be expected to minimally affect agency-level interests and have little to no impact on mission accomplishment.

Table 7.3   Examples of Justifications by Impact Area and Category of Information

Information Category	Confidentiality	Integrity	Availability
Personal information	Some groups within the institution collect private citizens' contact data concerning certain ongoing research projects. Departmental contact lists with addresses and phone numbers are also stored within the system. This information needs to be guarded against unauthorized access.	The integrity of contact information stored on the systems is important to ensure the ability to follow up with individuals.	The data is not time-sensitive in most circumstances. Current operations require the ability to retrieve any lost or corrupt data within 72 hours.
Research and development information	Certain institutional servers contain information concerning ongoing tests and results of statistical research. This data is expected to be kept confidential until final results are released to appropriate parties.	Any unauthorized modification of R&D data would affect the reliability of institutional reporting and affect the institution's reputation in the research community.	R&D data is not time-sensitive. An event that causes the data to be unavailable for two days or less would not affect the institution's mission.

generally places emphasis on system availability. However, it should be noted that criticality does not have to relate to availability only. For instance, it is possible that a critical system that is used to submit a consolidated report to Congress on a quarterly basis would be judged as low sensitivity for availability, but because of the need for assurance of the integrity of submitted data, it would still qualify as a critical system but on the basis of data integrity and its importance to the organization.

Criticality Assessment

Definition of mission or business criticality is an approach to determining the importance of a given information system to the organization. A

Table 7.4 Examples of Information Categories

Category	Explanation and Examples
Personal	Information that is related to the identity of a person (i.e., human resources, medical, and similar data). Includes all information covered by the Privacy Act of 1974.
Financial	Information related to the financial operations of an organization. Includes budgeting and accounting records.
Proprietary and trade secret	Commercial information received in confidence or trade secrets (i.e., contract bidding information, proprietary, and sensitive patent information).
Administrative	Information related to the internal administration of the organization that requires protection against disclosure. Category includes policies, procedures, guidelines, internal memoranda and messages, management decisions, and advance information concerning procurement actions.
Procurement-sensitive	Advance information concerning procurement actions to include selection criteria, assessments of vendor qualifications, etc.
Investigative, intelligence, and security-related	Information related to law enforcement investigations; intelligence-related information that is confidential; and security documentation to include security plans, contingency plans, emergency operations plans, incident reports, reports of investigations, risk or vulnerability assessments, certification reports.
Business partner information	Information, the protection of which is required by agreement or statute, which has come from another business partner and requires release approval by the owning organization.
Controlled research and development	Information related to novel technology; scientific information that is prohibited from disclosure to designated foreign governments or that may require an export license.
Mission critical	Information designated as critical to the organization mission and includes vital statistics information for emergency operations.
Operational information	Information that requires protection during operations; usually time-critical information.
Life critical	Information in which loss of integrity, availability, or confidentiality could result in loss of human life.

Table 7.4 Examples of Information Categories (Continued)

Category	Explanation and Examples
System configuration	Information related to the configuration and functioning of an information technology system. This includes network management information protocols, network and device addresses, implemented system and protocol addressing schemes, network information packets, device and system passwords, and device and system configuration information.
Public	Information that has been cleared for public release by official company authorities. This category includes information contained in official press releases and information posted on publicly accessible World Wide Web (WWW) sites.

mission-critical system is a system that would have a "debilitating" impact on the mission of the overall organization if it is lost. Mission criticality defines how integral the general support system or major application is to carrying out the mission of the organization and must also be considered as part of the sensitivity assessment. Systems should be evaluated to be either mission critical or non–mission critical using the definitions provided below. As part of the assessment it should be recognized that the criticality of some systems may vary according to peak processing periods of operation. The mission criticality of such systems should be based on the period of operation when it is most essential for the supported business function to be performed.

- *Mission Critical*: A mission-critical system is one that is used or operated by an organization or by an agent of the organization that meets one or more of the following three characteristics:
  - Classified as a national security system under section 5142 of the Clinger–Cohen Act of 1996 (40 U.S.C. 1452); or
  - Used to process information classified by an executive order or an Act of Congress in the interest of national defense or foreign policy; or
  - Processes any information, the loss, misuse, disclosure or unauthorized access to or modification of would have a debilitating impact on the mission of an agency.
- *Non–Mission Critical*: A non–mission-critical system is one that does not fit under any of the conditions for a mission-critical system defined above and whose failure would not prevent the owning

or using organization from accomplishing critical business operations. However, such a loss might result in either a short- or long-term impact on the efficiency of routine business operations.

In determining whether or not a system is mission critical, an important question to ask is whether or not the business process supported by the system can be accomplished through manual means, even if less efficient, or what the extent of the impact of the system being unavailable for thirty days or more would be. Another consideration in this determination is that if a major application has been determined to be mission critical and resides on a general support system, then the general support system must also be identified as mission critical. Conversely, a major application does not automatically qualify as mission critical simply by residing on a mission-critical general support system.

Criticality in the View of the System Owner

System owners tend to think their system is the most critical. When asked, they will almost always say that the continued survival of the organization depends on the availability of their system. Accordingly, their system is critical to the performance of the mission of the entire organization, not just their office. The problem is, in the grand scheme of things, not every system can be the most critical. Not every system can be restored first because recovery resources are limited and priorities for restoration have to be established. Criticality definitions are important for making such decisions. Criticality is a matter of perspective and an objective entity needs to be the honest broker to make fair assessment of the relative criticality between systems. This will be someone with higher perspective who has an objectively broad view of the whole organization, its mission, and its operations. This typically is not the system owner.

Ranking Criticality

Ranking of systems by criticality can be based on several key factors, each related to the importance of the system in terms of its impact on the overall mission of the organization. Criticality can be judged on factors such as:

■ The *financial* impact, or the dollar loss, that can accrue if the system is at risk or harmed, such as falling behind in a production schedule.

- The *operational* importance of the system (e.g., the system is critical to paying employees in a timely fashion).
- The importance of the system based on *health, life, safety* considerations (for example, the system is necessary to control airline traffic).
- The *breadth/scope* of impact/value/importance of the system is also useful in ranking criticality. For example, on the basis of breadth of use, an employee time accounting system that supports the entire organization is more critical than a time accounting system used by a single business unit.

The business impact analysis is the methodology normally used to quantify the criticality of systems on the basis of the amount of time that an organization can tolerate the nonavailability of a system. The business impact analysis process supports both disaster recovery/contingency planning requirements as well as certification and accreditation needs. Therefore, it is a well-suited approach for conducting the criticality analysis. A sample business impact analysis is provided in Appendix H.

The findings of the criticality assessment should document the criticality of the system in relation to other systems in the organization. Most often criticality will be expressed in two or more criticality tiers. These can be labeled as high, moderate, and low criticality categories. Alternatively, systems may simply be defined as either critical or noncritical.

Changes in Criticality and Sensitivity

System criticality is based on how a system is used by an organization. Of course, this can change over time, and the utility of this categorization is not set in stone. When the scope, data, business process supported, or user population served change, for example, the criticality of the system is likely to change accordingly. There must be a process for ensuring that system criticality is considered when changes to the system's environment occur. There are three good ways to ensure that the criticality of a system is evaluated either on a periodic basis or when changes to the system occur. First, a criticality review should be a part of an annual review of the security plan for the system. Second, the change management program should be in tune with the need to evaluate system criticality when changes take place, too. Third, assessment of system criticality should also be integrated into the system inventory processes, which review all systems annually. An annual criticality review should be conducted by an official with a more objective view of systems criticality, and the CISO is well situated to perform an objective reassessment of criticality.

When similar changes result in changes to data sensitivity, the system owner must update the system security plan and also make changes in system inventory. Changes in sensitivity should trigger a reevaluation of security controls. For instance, NIST SP 800-53 employs enhanced controls for more sensitive systems. Hence, changes in sensitivity can lead to additional vulnerabilities, which warrant consideration of reassessment of risks to the system. Also, the system owner should define processes that measure the impact of changes in system design, use, operations, and interfaces.

Summary

Sensitivity and criticality assessments are essential processes in determining specific controls that are to be implemented to protect system data and in the prioritization of resources. Definition of data and system sensitivity permits the organization to identify protection requirements based on the nature of data that the system processes, and then it permits mapping of the system to predefined controls sets or minimum security baselines (as addressed in Chapter 10). The criticality assessment allows the organization to define the relative priority of importance of information systems to permit efficient apportionment of protection resources. The determination of system criticality is a matter of perspective and must be done with an objective eye because decisions relating to funding, priority for support, restoration and recovery operations, application of controls, and crisis management are affected by the system's criticality ranking.

Chapter 8

System Security Plans

Security plans are necessary because they provide a single reference for defining how a system needs to be secured and how it is secured. A good security plan facilitates the review of system security controls to determine its current security posture. The security plan permits the identification of resources required to secure the system. And the plan documents controls that work as well as those that do not. All this information needs to be identified in writing rather than being stored in someone's head as is often the case. Well-written security plans support oversight, planning, budgeting, and compliance requirements for the system. However, security plans addressed in this chapter relate to information technology systems, and these plans should not be confused with program-level plans that are often mistakenly referred to by the same name.

Applicability

In the federal government, security plans are required. But does the fact that they predominate in government circles translate to them being impractical for nongovernment systems? As you might expect, my answer is no. Security plans both inside and outside government can be helpful in implementing controls at the system level to form a coherent security architecture. They can also be used to drive development efforts, and finally in both public and private sectors security plans serve to integrate controls not only enterprisewide but also at the system level where integration is necessary to ensure there are no gaps in controls boundaries.

OMB Circular A-130's categorization of system-level controls into management, operational, and technical controls categories is practical for application with all systems, making this approach useful to the masses.

Responsibility

Now that I have stated my case that security plans are useful and important, the next issue to resolve is who should develop them. Obviously, it should be someone who is familiar with the system — what it is designed to do, how it operates, how it is constructed, and how it is secured. The system owner, like with everything else related to the system, is responsible for security planning, which includes documenting the plan. However, the owner may want to delegate this task to his or her ISSO, assuming that an ISSO has been appointed for the system. The plan will take both time to prepare and detailed information gathering, and the ISSO will probably be more available to perform such duties. The system owner may want to consider using contractors to develop the security plan, particularly if he or she requires them for multiple systems. This ensures consistency. However, the time necessary to train contractor personnel and to familiarize them with the system(s) will extend the duration of the initiative as will the effort required to approve their methodologies, to supervise them, and to review their work.

Plan Contents

A well-written security plan provides all the information necessary to describe the security posture of a system against a set of controls requirements. The contents of the security plan normally must include the following categories of information related to the design, operation, and security of an information system.

- *System Description:* The security plan describes what the system does and the business process it supports. It defines the system environment in a clear and understandable way, using both text and graphics as necessary. This will include a listing of system hardware components and software products that make up the system and how they are configured. The plan will document data flows into and out of the system and interconnections with other systems. The system description will include a description of the organization and user community that is supported. This will identify the locations and sites where the components and users are situated.

Means of access must be described such as dial-up, VPN, wireless, dedicated connection, etc. The system description should specify the operational status of the system and planned changes to the system environment. Process flow charts can be helpful in defining data input and output. The type of data processed by the system should also be included in the plan. Components and products whose primary function is to protect system data should be given emphasis in the system description. Firewalls, secure gateways, anti-virus products, intrusion detection systems, and vulnerability scanning tools need to be highlighted. For the user community, the clearance level, category of clearance, and need-to-know levels should be defined. Facilities where equipment and users are located should be described from a security perspective, too.

■ *Description of Controls*: The purpose of a good system description is to allow all necessary controls to be described in the plan. Controls can be taken from a number of sources such as NIST Special Publications 800-18, 800-26, 800-53, and ISO 17799. These are addressed in Chapter 10. The controls description must include controls requirements and the implementation status of each control. Details for each control should identify if controls are fully in place or not. Controls that have not been implemented need to be justified in full, and plans for future implementation need to be stipulated. When using a standard set of controls to format the plan, controls that are not applicable to the system should be specified as such and should be identified with a justification of why the control does not apply. This is superior to merely deleting the nonapplicable control. Once again, the control must be described in terms of the system to include the "who," "what," "why," "where," "when," and "how." For example, it is not adequate to state that changes to an operational system will be documented. Rather, the security plan should specify that the system administrator will record all changes in operating system software as specified in the system's change control procedures document. Security control documentation contained in the system security plan need not be quantified. That is, it is normally unnecessary to state that the control is green, amber, or red, or that there is a high, medium, or low degree of compliance. The standard for the control is either met or not met. Controls that have not been implemented should be categorized as planned and should strictly map to remedial actions identified in the plan of action and milestones (Chapter 14).

■ *System Security Roles and Responsibilities*: The plan is used to document the roles and responsibilities for security of the system.

The name, title, office, major organization, address, phone number, and e-mail address for each individual named in this section of the plan must be provided. Ideally, the plan will identify the system owner, security officer, system administrator, line of business security manager, database administrator, approving authority, user population, and developer involved in the maintenance of the system. Other roles referred to in Chapter 2 should be considered for inclusion in the security plan.

- *Security-Related Business Drivers*: The plan should include a section that identifies external requirements that drive security controls. This section should identify all legal, operational, contractual, regulatory, and statutory requirements that call for protection of the system or its data. When necessary, the specific requirements should be annotated for each source. For example, the security plan of a system that processes data that is governed by the Privacy Act of 1974 should cite not only that reference, but should also specify that the confidentiality of such data will be protected by output labeling controls.

- *Information Categories*: All categories of information processed by the system should be included in the plan following the guidance provided in Chapter 7. For each category a brief description of the severity of impacts should be documented. Associated with the category of information is the sensitivity of information, which must be specified in the plan. This information is drawn from the system inventory (Chapter 6) and from the system sensitivity review (Chapter 7). The security plan should fully document why the system needs to be protected in terms of its confidentiality, integrity, and availability requirements.

- *Interconnectivity*: Next, the plan needs to document the system's interconnectivity and dependencies with respect to other systems. The plan should explain data input and output flows (both automated and manual), whether they are one-way or two-way flows, trust relationships, types of connections, and the status of formal agreements between connected systems. Whenever possible, these data flows should be graphically depicted. Refer to Chapter 9 for a discussion of coordinating security for interconnected systems. For general support systems a listing of applications that are hosted on the system should be provided.

- *System Certification Level*: The security plan should also be used to document decisions made regarding the certification level of effort that is necessary to provide adequate assurance of security controls. Although this will have to be determined prior to conducting the security test and evaluation, the security plan as the document of record in the certification process should also contain this information. This decision will be based primarily on the sensitivity of the system, but also may be based on internal and external exposures to threats. External exposures include the means of user access, the nature of back-end connections, and the number of users. Internal exposures include user clearance level access approval, and need to know for information processed on the system. Internal exposures are only a concern when dealing with information that is highly sensitive to disclosure. Table 8.1 provides a sample for documenting the certification level of effort to match assurance level to the sensitivity and criticality of the system.

■ *Rules of Behavior*: Rules of behavior were mandated by OMB A-130, and they are a good way for ensuring that users of all types acknowledge their responsibilities for securing the system. Hence, they are normally signed and dated by a user and are maintained on file as long as the user's account is active. Automated acknowledgement is an efficient alternative to signed, hard-copy documents as long as an audit trail exists. The rules of behavior serve as a basis for security awareness training and provide a basis for disciplinary action when rules are violated. The rules must be specific to the system to address all responsibilities that apply. Likewise, they need to be specific to the actual role the individual plays with regard to system operations. These rules of behavior can be considered agreements between the user and the system owner regarding proper use of the system. When a user understands his or her role in the protection of the system he or she will be more likely to exercise security responsibilities. And, because users are one of the primary sources of threats to information systems, rules of behavior establish ground rules that can minimize many of the threats users pose. Appendixes I and J provide sample rules of behavior for a general support system and for a major application respectively.

■ *Plan Development Information*: The security plan should document details regarding who developed the plan, when it was developed, the methodology used in its development, the duration of the project to develop the plan, who provided input for the plan's development, source documentation used in developing the plan, and the authority for developing the plan. This information serves as a historical reference point for future evaluation of the plan, update activities, and related efforts.

To demonstrate how the information that forms the security plan is normally presented, a sample security plan in outline form is provided in Appendix K.

Table 8.1 Example of Security Level of Effort Matrix

Concern	Ranking	Justification
Data Sensitivity		
Confidentiality	Low	The consequences of unauthorized disclosure or compromise of data are generally acceptable. The loss of confidentiality could be expected to affect company-level interests and have some negative impact on business operations.
Integrity	Moderate	The consequences of corruption or unauthorized modification of data are only marginally acceptable. Loss of integrity could be expected to adversely affect company-level interests and degrade business operations
Availability	Low	The consequences of loss or disruption of access to system resources or to data are generally acceptable. The loss of availability could be expected to affect company-level interests and have some negative impact on business operations.
Certification Level		
Certification Level (based on sensitivity "high water mark")	Moderate	Moderate intensity, demonstration-based, independent assessment that includes: ■ Demonstrations to verify security control correctness and effectiveness ■ Functional testing ■ Penetration testing ■ Regression analysis and regression testing ■ Low certification level verification techniques

What a Security Plan Is Not

One common misconception relating to security plans is that they are meant to serve as the repository for all security-related information for a system. They become gigantic in scale while becoming ever more difficult to create and impossible to use in the process. The purpose of the plan is not to prove the existence of controls. The plan should be brief and usable. It should not become a repository for security procedures or similar documentation. This is the purpose of the security handbook. The plan should merely cross-reference procedures, not include them or duplicate them. Consider using hyperlinks for such documents. On the other hand, controls must be completely described relative to the system. Only the controls of the simplest systems should be described in yes/no responses to a questionnaire like NIST SP 800-26. Complete answers should be documented to fully describe how the control has been implemented for the system. Who is responsible for it? When is it used? How is it implemented? What is its purpose? These questions should be answered for each and every control protecting the system or that is planned for implementation.

The purpose of the system security plan is to provide an overview of the security posture of the system. It is important to remember that the plan is a summary, or else it can evolve into a security procedures manual developed by an overzealous contractor. On the other hand it needs to provide enough information to describe controls to allow one to understand how requirements are being met (or are failing to be met). A lack of time or emphasis is not a good excuse for a plan that does not meet this standard.

Plan Initiation

The security plan can be initiated at almost any time in the certification and accreditation process, but it certainly needs to be finalized before the accreditation decision is made. However, remedial action should not be closely tied to completion of the plan. If vulnerabilities are identified they should be addressed immediately rather than waiting for the plan to be finalized. Vulnerabilities can be uncovered at any time during the process: when preparing the security plan, conducting a baseline security assessment, or during a security test and evaluation. There is nothing to be gained in waiting on security documentation to be completed before proceeding with corrective action, and a plan of action and milestones is not a prerequisite for remediation. Through this we see that the security plan is related to all the other documentation in the certification and accreditation process. It should be considered a summary or overview document that brings together information from these other documents: risk information from the risk assessment, controls data from the security test and evaluation, and remediation information from the plan of action and milestones.

When a security plan is prepared as part of certification, it may be necessary to prepare a draft plan very early during the certification effort to define security controls, then perform interim updates following the risk assessment, and then again after the certification test is performed.

However, this could result in extra, unnecessary effort and could become confusing and easily forgotten. As an alternative, it may be far more practical to wait until the conclusion of the certification process to prepare the plan. That way one is not burdened with the need to continually update the plan at major milestones in the project.

Information Sources

As we have seen, information necessary to complete the security plan is derived from several processes completed at various stages of the entire certification methodology. Therefore, the security plan should be completed as one of the final steps in certification, or at least finalization of the plan should occur late in the process. When the plan is completed near the end of certification, then its construction should take no more than a few man-hours to consolidate the required information in a desired format. This act of consolidation and formatting should be performed by an individual who has been involved with the certification of the system and who is familiar with the information. Usually the ISSO, system owner, or a dedicated analyst fulfills this role and prepares the system security plan. If the plan is developed apart from an overall certification process, then data collection for the effort can be expected to require from as little as two days for a simple system to several weeks for a complex one. A work plan for such a project is included in Table 8.2. Security plan data collection is primarily the responsibility of the system owner, who often delegates this task to the ISSO for the system or to a contractor charged with developing or updating the plan. The information necessary for the development of the plan is identified in the paragraphs above. This information is most often recorded in existing system and organization documentation such as requirements and design documents, system administration guides, technical architecture documentation, user guides, facility management documentation (i.e., evacuation plans, maintenance procedures), recovery plans, backup procedures, in-/out-processing procedures, etc. When documentation such as this is not available, those charged with developing the plan must identify individuals who have knowledge of the system, its design, operations, and security, and should then schedule and conduct interviews with these individuals to obtain the information.

Security Plan Development Tools

The security plan development process can be expedited through the use of automated tools. Such tools can facilitate the collection and organization

Table 8.2   Example of a Work Plan for Security Plan Development Project

Activity/Task	Duration	Start Date	End Date
Project Preparation	5 days	Jan. 20, 2003	Jan. 24, 2003
Prepare Data Collection Tools	2 days	Jan. 20, 2003	Jan. 21, 2003
Locate Existing Documentation	3 days	Jan. 22, 2003	Jan. 24, 2003
Data Collection and Analysis	15 days	Jan. 20, 2003	Feb. 7, 2003
Schedule Interviews	2 days	Jan. 20, 2003	Jan. 21, 2003
Conduct Interviews	5 days	Jan. 27, 2003	Jan. 31, 2003
Conduct Min. Security Baseline Assessment	5 days	Jan. 27, 2003	Jan. 31, 2003
Collect Follow-Up Information	2 days	Feb. 3, 2003	Feb. 4, 2003
Data Analysis	3 days	Feb. 5, 2003	Feb. 7, 2003
Documentation	7 days	Feb. 10, 2003	Feb. 18, 2003
Prepare and Submit Inventory Forms	1 day	Feb. 10, 2003	Feb. 10, 2003
Prepare Draft System Security Plan	4 days	Feb. 11, 2003	Feb. 14, 2003
Prepare Min. Security Baseline Assessment	2 days	Feb. 17, 2003	Feb. 18, 2003
Security Plan Submission	0 days	Mar. 19, 2003	Mar. 19, 2003
Receive Comments to Draft Security Plan	5 days	Mar. 19, 2003	Mar. 25, 2003
Develop Final Security Plan	4 days	Mar. 25, 2003	Mar. 28, 2003
Address Comments	2 days	Mar. 25, 2003	Mar. 26, 2003
Prepare Final Security Plan	2 days	Mar. 27, 2003	Mar. 28, 2003
Submit Final Security Plan for Signature	0 days	Mar. 28, 2003	Mar. 28, 2003
Security Plan Approval	0 days	Mar. 31, 2003	Mar. 31, 2003

of data related to system environment, operational status, data sensitivity, and controls status in particular. Whatever tool is chosen it must provide the user the flexibility to modify its parameters to suit the particular needs of the system and preferences of the preparer of the plan. The result must drive the tool, rather than the tool driving the result.

Many times a boilerplate template, sample plan, or plan from a similar system may be used to create an initial system security plan. This can save time and may ensure completeness. It can, however, lead to inaccuracies and can limit thoughtful consideration of system controls and the system's environment. When using such helper documents, care must be taken to remove superfluous facts contained in the sample or template, and careful proofreading and review for inaccuracies is essential. The information in the plan must be precisely tailored to the system. This ensures it is not overly vague and generic. Wherever possible, individuals responsible for the control should be identified by position, the steps involved in operating the control should be listed, and details of when and where the control is employed should be provided. For example, the description of a control that calls for periodic review of audit trails should specify that the ISSO conduct a review of operating system audit records on a weekly basis to identify security-related events.

Plan Format

There is nothing wrong with having several formats for security plans depending on the nature of the system for which the plan is written. In fact, NIST guidance calls for differences between plans for general support systems and major applications. However, the organizations should define formats that are permissible for use. Formats should be somewhat flexible, but plan contents should not be (see Appendix K). Minimum requirements for information required to be included in the plan must also be clearly defined in organization certification and accreditation guidelines.

Plan Approval

The approval of the plan should begin with the signature of the individual who prepared the plan. At times this will be the certification agent acting at the behest of the system owner. The system security officer should then review and approve the plan before it goes to the system owner. Because it will be part of the certification and accreditation package, accreditation will result in the designated approval authority's approval of the plan.

Plan Maintenance

The security plan is a living document and effort should be made to update it throughout the certification and accreditation process and during the effective life cycle of the system. The plan should be constructed before the system goes into production to aid in the documentation of protection requirements during system design and implementation. Meeting certification and accreditation requirements throughout a system's life cycle is addressed in Chapter 3. After the system goes live, the plan needs to be reviewed yearly to ensure it is current. Changes in the system's

Table 8.3   Security Plan Approval Sheet

System Owner:

_____   _____   _____
Name: Signature   Date

Security Officer:

_____   _____   _____
Name: Signature   Date

Security Reviewer:

_____   _____   _____
Name: Signature   Date

operating environment, changes in risks to the system, and changes in controls protecting the system should be cause for updating the plan. The annual review should seek to evaluate all such changes to determine if a plan update is warranted. The reviewer, normally the ISSO, should document in the plan that a review has been performed and should indicate the date of the review. If changes are necessary, they can be written in with pen with the initials of the individual authorizing the change. This works well as long as the changes are fairly minor in nature. For more significant changes, new pages should be inserted with each page bearing the date of the change. In addition, a change information page in the front of the security plan should be annotated to document the date, purpose, and page numbers of all changes for both minor and major changes.

Because the security plan is so critical and so tied to other report inputs, care must be taken to ensure it is kept up to date in response to system changes and to updates in associated documentation. This can be facilitated by including the date on each page, as well as by including in the plan format an approval page, a review page, and a change information page. The approval page provides a place to record the signatures of the ISSO, system owner, and perhaps the approving authority upon initial development of the plan. The review page allows the security reviewer to record when the plan was reviewed for currency. The change page is used to record the date and nature of changes made to the document. Examples of these pages are included in Tables 8.3, 8.4, and 8.5.

Table 8.4   Security Plan Review Page

This security plan has been updated and approved on the following dates to account for the latest changes. This plan must be reviewed annually.

Approval Date	Name of Security Officer	Signature of Security Officer

Table 8.5   Security Plan Change Information Page

Issue	Date	Pages Affected	Description

Plan Security

Because security plans document the status of security controls protecting a system, it allows one to see "warts and all." Consequently, plans need to be closely safeguarded. Access to electronic versions of the security plan should be limited on the basis of need to know, as is access to printed copies of the plan and associated working papers. Though it may be desirous to display security plans prominently on a bookshelf because of the effort that went into them, this practice should be avoided in the interest of confidentiality. Sensitivity labeling should be used copiously, and a good rule of thumb is that, once they are prepared, do not let plans out of your building. Armed with a copy of your well-written security plan, a bad guy will have more than enough information to successfully penetrate your system's security controls.

Plan Metrics

In establishing a program for security planning it is important to know how to measure its effectiveness. Security planning is effective if the following criteria are achieved:

- *Documented Plans*: Plans are documented for each system rather than being merely concepts in someone's mind or being unwritten practices routinely performed off the top of one's head.
- *Use of Defined Formats*: Security plans are documented following a prescribed format that makes it easy to determine their completeness and the security posture of the system. Basic information requirements are most easily established and enforced through reliance on the development and use of standard security plan templates.
- *Approved Plans*: Security plans have been provided to those entities that they affect, are approved by those responsible for the security of the system, and have been reviewed and appropriately updated within the past year.
- *Consistent Plans*: Security plans relate to, support, and complement other documentation for the system. The information they present directly maps to risk assessment, certification testing, remediation planning, and contingency planning documents that relate to the system. For example, the sensitivity rankings the plan reflects are consistent with those documented in the system inventory and risk assessment.
- *Documented Implementation Planning:* Plans are constructed so as to serve as a basis for improving security controls. That is, the plan clearly identifies controls that need to be added or how controls need to be upgraded to reduce residual risks. The plan will accurately describe actions to be taken to address deficiencies, identify responsibilities for those actions, and provide milestones for completion of actions.

Resistance to Security Plans

Given the advantages that security plans provide system owners, one must ask why they are not prepared more reliably or why their use is not more widespread. The primary reason is a failure by system owners to give priority to documentation tasks in general. This may be due to shortage of manpower or skills or because of more pressing issues that occur day to day that prevent the system owner from focusing on strategic initiatives like security planning. However, without resolving strategic issues such as this, resolution of tactical issues may not be possible either. In other words, security planning operates on both strategic and tactical levels.

Summary

This chapter has sought to convince you that you need to learn to love security plans. A well-constructed security plan provides the security manager an effective instrument for meeting security oversight, planning, budgeting, and compliance requirements. Because these requirements can be applied to all systems, security plans are both feasible and practical for commercial and government systems alike. The management, operational, and technical controls taxonomy that has been effectively applied in the federal government is a workable approach for categorizing controls for nongovernment systems as well. Additionally, as discussed in Chapter 3, security plans can serve as effective mechanisms for integrating security into system development efforts. The security plan provides a path for implementing an organization's security architecture, in that a security planning process implemented across the breadth of an organization can produce mutually supporting system-level plans that integrate security controls across multiple systems.

Chapter 9

Coordinating Security for Interconnected Systems

Certification would be a much simpler process if there were no interconnections between systems to worry about. In the days of centralized mainframe processing it was an easy task to determine certification scope and the boundaries of the security perimeter. Since those days, however, the definition of what is to be certified has become clouded by the increasing interconnectivity between an increasing number of systems. Because these systems share sensitive information, system owners have to be concerned about them and about how security controls are implemented to protect their data. It is nearly always impractical to draw the scope large enough to include these interconnected systems into a single certification. Therefore, an alternative approach must be identified.

The Solution

The response to the problem of certifying the protection of data that passes from one system to the next has come to be addressed through the process of establishing memoranda of agreement between system owners to address the responsibilities and roles of each. First, a formal approach is necessary to ensure that the controls of a connecting system are equal to or exceed those established for the system to which it will be connected. Because system owners surrender direct control over data when data leaves the confines of their systems' security perimeters, security agreements provide system owners some assurance that owners of inter-connected systems will provide a known level of protection to their data. Second, certification and accreditation of an information system is a formal process that demands documentation of requirements and the implementation of corresponding controls. The development of formal agreements between system owners satisfies this need for documentation to provide assurance of protection.

Agreements in the Certification and Accreditation Process

Certification and accreditation provides a commonly accepted standard for security that can facilitate the process of interconnecting systems. The owner of an accredited system should ensure that all interconnected systems have also been accredited. This includes accreditation for all data-sharing relationships (other than the exceptions listed below) to ensure requirements for protecting data that is passed between systems are established and that these standards are being met. The process used to certify and accredit interconnected systems should meet or exceed the standards in effect for the system they are connected to. The system owner evaluating the security posture of the connecting system should review all certification and accreditation documentation with a concentration on protection of data to ensure it is being protected at the same level as that of his or her own system.

Interconnectivity agreements between system owners are key elements of the system certification and accreditation process that are considered at several times during the process. The minimum security baseline review assesses the effectiveness of controls over data transmitted between con-nected systems. The risk assessment documents the value of assets asso-ciated with these incoming and outgoing data flows, identifies threats to this data, pairs identified vulnerabilities with the threats, and calculates corresponding risks. The certification test assesses controls designed to provide protection to this data. And the remediation plan documents the weaknesses and provides mitigating controls for shortfalls in protective measures. The system security plan identifies memoranda of agreement and existing documents and planned controls that relate to developing and maintaining agreements for interconnected systems. Without address-ing the security of data introduced into the system and transmitted out of it, the certification is incomplete. Therefore, it is important to identify all data flows with other systems as part of the risk assessment and to identify the sensitivity of the data, how it is being used, and how it needs to be protected. This information is best gleaned from the use of discovery tools, network diagrams, interviews, design documents, and from review of existing memoranda of agreement, memoranda of understanding, service-level agreements, and contracts with other system owners and vendors. Once there is a full picture of where data comes from and where it is transmitted, a complete picture of control requirements can be established.

Trust Relationships

Trust relationships between systems that share data should be based on full knowledge of how the gaining system intends to use and protect that data. Trust relationships need to be based on a mutually beneficial agreement between owners of the two systems. This is normally an agreement between equals, with neither having a superior or inferior position relative to the other. However, system owners may in fact both be part of a common organization in a supporting or supported relationship. The trust relationship may also be between supporting vendors and supported customers.

Initiation

The agreement may be sought by either party, but under normal conditions it is initiated by the system owner who desires access to data processed by another system. The requesting owner must meet any requirements established by the owner of the system from which the data is to flow. The data owner normally makes the call on what security requirements must be met to protect the data. If the system has been previously accredited then this is a relatively easy process. If not, then data protection requirements need to be established by some alternative process. Ideally this will be based on a minimum security baseline assessment or risk assessment that is part of an established certification and accreditation process.

A memorandum of agreement documents at a high level terms and conditions for the interconnection of two systems. This governs both one-way and two-way connectivity. The memorandum of agreement must then be supplemented with a more specific interconnection security agreement, which is used to detail security controls and procedures required relative to the agreement (e.g., incident response and reporting requirements). The memorandum of agreement is a formal contractual document and both parties must concur with it, and it must meet the standards each organization normally applies to formal agreements. A sample memorandum of agreement is provided in Appendix L, and a sample interconnection security agreement is included in Appendix M.

Memoranda of agreement and interconnection security agreements are critical documents to be reviewed in the certification and accreditation process, whether for the system being certified or for systems it connects with. Many times memoranda of agreement and interconnection security agreements will be made with system owners in other organizations of the federal government, or even in the same department where both systems must meet common certification and accreditation requirements as well as controls requirements. In such cases it may be tempting to merely seek the accreditation date for an interconnected system under the assumption that because the system has been accredited, this substantiates that that system can and should be fully trusted. This may not be the case, and both memoranda of agreement and interconnection security agreements as well as the actual certification and accreditation packages for these accredited systems should be reviewed in detail to ensure that the data will be or is being adequately protected.

Time Issues

Getting memoranda of agreement and interconnection security agreements drafted, approved, and signed takes a great deal of time and effort. This is because they are legal documents, which obligate two parties in a contractual arrangement. The agreements must undergo detailed legal review by the general consuls of both organizations. Also, much prior coordination and negotiation must take place before the two organizations can agree on what controls will be provided and the details of the interconnection security agreement can be worked out. There are several things that can be done to speed up the process for implementing security agreements. First, a system must have its security in order before a request to connect with another system is initiated. The system should have already undergone certification and be accredited or have it fully planned prior to starting the process. This way, it is known what is required to protect the system's data and there is a foundation for knowing what controls need to be considered for the system about to be interconnected. It is much simpler to begin with a written set of requirements that can be substantiated as accurate and complete through a comprehensive certification and accreditation process that produces coherent supporting documentation.

System owners must ensure that agreements are in place before an interconnection is made. The owner of the system to which the request is made is in the best position to ensure that this takes place. Requiring a finalized agreement prior to connection not only prevents exposure to potential security risks, but it also provides a clearly defined benchmark that both parties can work toward. Once systems have been informally interconnected, it becomes much more difficult to formalize that arrangement. Should there be an urgent necessity to interconnect the systems, and there is insufficient time to adequately finalize an interconnection agreement, a documented interim agreement should be created to establish responsibilities and timetables for finalizing the interconnection agreement and conditions for terminating the connection should the agreement be broken. Review and approval of memoranda of agreement and interconnection security agreements should follow established organizational processes, which normally include legal review by the general consul and contractual review by the procurement officer. Additionally, information technology operations and the CISO should review all interconnection-related documentation. At a minimum, agreements should be signed by the system owner and also preferably by the accrediting official for all systems concerned.

There are several steps that can be taken to facilitate the agreement process to ensure that systems are able to retrieve critical data when they need it. Communications between the requesting owner of the system requesting the connection and the owner receiving the request should be mutually open and can be expedited through face-to-face meetings to set expectations, avoid misunderstandings, and speed up the process. Wording of interconnection agreements should be simplified as much as possible to promote clarity, and involvement of the legal and contracting functions early in the process will promote the identification of requirements early in negotiations when they can still be effectively resolved. Ideally, agreements should be initiated during development whenever possible to permit integration of requirements for interconnection into the system development methodology employed by the organization. This allows for the systematic establishment of milestones for development, coordination, review, and approval of the agreement prior to placing the system into production.

The wording used in formal agreements should define the nature of the interconnection and of the data involved and should establish minimum standards for protective controls and for complying with these requirements. To ensure that these provisions are met, the agreement should include provisions for reporting on status of security controls and for the right to inspect operations to ensure compliance. Because it is not possible to foresee all future developments, on-site validation of the security posture of interconnected systems should be included, even though there may be no real intent to exercise them at the time the agreement goes into effect. The agreement should also establish requirements for timely notification in the event of a security breach that could put the connected system at risk. Finally, there should be provisions for cancellation of the agreement for cause when its provisions have not been met.

Exceptions

The need for formal agreements between system owners is not warranted when individual users of a particular organization have been granted access to a system. In such a case, these users are governed by existing user-level rules (i.e., system access, incident reporting, etc.), and the agreement is between the individual user and the system owner rather than between organizations. Here established rules of behavior suffice for communication of security requirements to protect system data.

Security rules need to be established and documented for all back-end connections, maintenance hooks, modem use, telecommuters, and other means of remote access to the system. However, the use of formal agreements between organizations solely for this purpose is seldom necessary. Instead, agreements with individual users in the form of rules of behavior or identification of security controls and rules in existing maintenance agreements, service-level agreements, etc., are easier to maintain, and they monitor and serve the purpose.

In addition, major applications that reside on a general support system do not normally need to have a formal memorandum of agreement and interconnection security agreement. This is because in most cases both the owner of the major application and the general support system owner are in the same organization. Any service-level agreement establishing this relationship needs to specify security requirements that the general support system will provide to the major application.

Maintaining Agreements

One of the most difficult problems to be surmounted by system owners is keeping up not only with changes to their own systems but also having to keep up with changes of interconnected systems, too. Those changes may be of equal or greater importance to the security of their own data and consequently must be assessed for their impact by the owning system. This is the most difficult aspect of maintaining the security of interconnected systems. Any time there is an incident or breach of security controls in System A, then the owner of System B needs to know about it so that he or she can assess the extent his or her own system had been affected. Language must be included in the memorandum of agreement to ensure that changes to connected systems and incidents affecting security controls are shared in each direction.

Agreements should be periodically reviewed to ensure their validity. However, as formal contracting documents, they should be written to expire when their conditions are no longer valid rather than on a specified anniversary date. This approach will prevent an unnecessary administrative burden for periodic renewal. Provisions should also be included in the agreement to permit either party to opt out should conditions for the interconnection change.

From the perspective of the CISO, the need for maintaining visibility of interconnected systems is a great concern since it is difficult to achieve and maintain. A process for mapping interconnected systems graphically will help the security manager visualize data flows across the enterprise and understand the potential impact of a security incident.

Summary

Interconnectivity agreements are essential in providing assurance that system data is adequately protected once it leaves the protective perimeter controlled by the system owner. Once system owners transmit data beyond their secure environment, they no longer have control over its protection. Formal agreements with interconnected systems help to ensure that the data is being protected beyond the limits of the system owner's direct control. Likewise, the agreements provide reasonable assurance that the information that is being introduced into the system owner's system from outside the security perimeter has originated from a trustworthy system.

Chapter 10

Minimum Security Baselines and Best Practices

A practical approach to securing information technology assets that an organization can take is the establishment of a minimum security baseline (MSB) and best practices for security configurations of its information technology platforms and devices. Here, the organization draws a line in the sand and says, "All of our systems will implement this basic set of security controls." Other controls may be necessary, but at least these minimum security baseline controls will be in place. Through this baseline the organization establishes a point of reference from which it can determine its security posture through compliance with minimum controls implementation. It also provides the organization a starting point for assessing the validity of this control set for a given system through the risk assessment process, which is used to enhance controls requirements, eliminate nonapplicable controls, or recommend alternative controls for each system. In short, a minimum security baseline is a set of standards that are applied enterprisewide to ensure a consistent level of compliance.

Levels of Controls

A single set of controls in minimum security baseline form is not normally the answer for most organizations because of variables in system type (general support system or major application) and system sensitivity. Controls applicable to a general support system will be different for a major application and vice versa. Although management level controls will be identical for both, as will many operational controls, many controls like incident response, integrity controls, and technical controls will vary substantially. Because the minimum security baseline set is system non-specific, it must be augmented by baseline security configuration standards for all technology components that make up the system. A separate set of technology-specific controls need to be developed to ensure that industry-accepted leading security practices are employed as an extension of the minimum security baseline. These must exist for operating systems, databases, web servers, networks, and routers among others. Table 10.1 provides an example of platform security configuration standards.

Organizations may want to consider additional sets of security controls for more sensitive systems to provide a greater degree of protection and security in depth. Although this approach tailors control requirements to the elevated need for security a system may have, it creates additional complexity that must be considered and managed. NIST SP 800-53 provides a good example of the application of controls according to system sensitivity. For instance, the three levels of controls pertaining to countering malicious code in NIST SP 800-53 according to system sensitivity are:

- *Low Sensitivity*: The information system implements malicious code protection that includes a capability for automatic updates.
- *Moderate Sensitivity*: The information system implements malicious code protection that includes a capability for automatic updates. The organization centrally manages virus protection mechanisms.
- *High Sensitivity*: The information system implements malicious code protection that includes a capability for automatic updates. The information system automatically updates virus protection mechanisms.

Selecting Baseline Controls

The sources of minimum security baselines are not as important as the organization's acceptance of them and adoption of them as its own. However, minimum security baselines have to be realistic. An organization should not create minimum security baselines for the sake of creating minimum security baselines. They should be grounded in actual business needs based on a systematic review of risks to an organization's resources

Table 10.1   Example Best Practice Security Configuration

Test	SITE: Corporate Headquarters	DATE: February 6, 2004

Number: 3

Test Name: SQL Servers

Resources Required:	All SQL servers.
Personnel Required:	Users with database administrator privileges for the network to be tested and a network security administrator.
Objectives:	To determine if the database servers are configured correctly and securely.
Procedure Description: (Summary)	Review system settings on the SQL servers. Interview database administrators and network security administrators.

Step #	NIST 800-26 Element ID	Procedure Description	Expected Results	Actual Results	Pass/ Fail/NA
1	3.1.6	Verify all SQL patches, service packs, and hotfixes have been identified, installed, and tracked for each server.	All patches and service packs are up to date.	On both servers auto update is used to install hotfixes. SQL versions are 8.00.760, which is current.	P
2	16.2.2	Is Secure Sockets Layer (SSL) or Transport Layer Security protocol (TLS) used for sensitive communications between servers and clients?	SSL or TLS is used for secure communication between the server and client.	SSL and TLS are not used because confidentiality is rated as low.	N/A
3	1.2.3	Ensure the "sa" and "probe" (SQL 6.5) accounts are secured with strong passwords and that the passwords are stored in a secure location. Note: The probe account is used for performance analysis and distributed transactions. Assigning a password to this account can break functionality when used in standard security mode.	The "sa" and "probe" accounts are secured with strong passwords and the passwords are stored in a secure location.	On both servers the "sa" account has a strong password, and the password is stored in a secure location. The probe account does not exist.	P

Table 10.2   Example of a Minimum Security Baseline

Production Input/Output Controls

8.1 Is there user support?

 8.1.1   Is there a help desk or group that offers advice? (NIST SP 800-18)

8.2 Are there media controls?

 8.2.1   Are there processes to ensure that unauthorized individuals cannot read, copy, alter, or steal printed or electronic information? (NIST SP 800-18)

 8.2.2   Are there processes for ensuring that only authorized users pick up, receive, or deliver input and output information and media? (NIST SP 800-18)

 8.2.3   Are audit trails used for receipt of sensitive inputs/outputs? (NIST SP 800-18)

 8.2.4   Are controls in place for transporting or mailing media or printed output? (NIST SP 800-18)

 8.2.5   Is there internal/external labeling for sensitivity? (NIST SP 800-18)

 8.2.6   Is there external labeling with special handling instructions? (NIST SP 800-18)

 8.2.7   Are audit trails kept for inventory management? (NIST SP 800-18)

 8.2.8   Is media sanitized for reuse? (FISCAM AC-3.4, NIST SP 800-18)

 8.2.9   Is damaged media stored or destroyed? (NIST SP 800-18)

 8.2.10 Is hard-copy media shredded or destroyed when no longer needed? (NIST SP 800-18)

through a high-level risk assessment and as identified over an extended period of time (several years of operation). An initial high-level, enterprisewide risk assessment will determine what assets need to be protected, what they need to be protected from, and to what degree the assets should be protected. This initial review should serve as the basis for selecting an industry-accepted minimum security baseline set in its entirety, in creating a wholly new set for the organization, or in customizing an existing minimum security baseline for use within the organization.

Minimum security baselines can be developed from external sources, such as ISO 17799, GASSP, NIST SP 800-26, NIST SP 800-53, etc. For example, NIST SP 800-26 is employed as one accepted minimum security baseline standard. An extract from NIST SP 800-26 is provided in Table 10.2. SP 800-53 expands on this approach by offering additional controls for more sensitive systems. All of these provide a comprehensive, integrated set of controls that is accepted by large numbers of organizations for use in setting standards for themselves. Because organizations are responsible for determining the appropriate level of security for their systems, they may consider developing minimum security baselines entirely on their own. In such cases, one of these common standards should be used as the starting point for developing a hybrid organization-specific set of minimum security baselines; or at least a review of the hybrid set should be made against at least two of the common standards. Any generally accepted minimum security baseline should be modified to incorporate business needs stemming from various other sources. This would include incorporation of controls mandated by regulatory require-ments such as HIPAA and GLBA. Minimum baseline controls should take into account organization policies, management statements and strategies, contracts, laws, operational rules, legal obligations, and regulations. The authority for the minimum security baseline set is an important consider-ation. When they have been approved by the highest management levels in the organization, which have directed their implementation, then they are far less likely to be questioned when the cost of implementing minimum controls is discovered. Management acceptance of the controls provides stronger justification for requesting resources for corrective actions. Additionally, external auditors are more prone to accept minimum security baselines fully underwritten by management as adequate, and which have been developed based on industry-accepted best practices.

The complexity and comprehensiveness of the controls set should be driven by the organization's ability to implement them and its commitment to enforcing compliance with them. Defining the minimum security base-line set too stringently will lead to the organization wasting resources in a quest to achieve unrealistic security goals. If the organization sets its control requirements too low, then the minimum security baseline approach will fail because the controls will not provide sufficient protec-tion against common threats to its resources. If the organization establishes a program requiring a set of stringent controls, which looks good on paper but fails to build an accompanying enforcement mechanism, the effects likely will be worse than having done nothing at all because a false sense of security on the part of management and a disregard of security by system owners will be the likely outcomes. Minimum security baselines need to be sufficiently detailed to allow their application across the entire organization and also must be specific enough to be clearly understood by those charged with their implementation. For cases where a system owner considers the baseline to be inapplicable to his or her system (perhaps the system has already been certified under a more stringent set of standards), a formal exception process should be available to document and approve noncompliance with the baseline standard. However, this process only applies to application for exemption of com-pliance with the minimum security baseline set in its entirety. Addressing nonapplicability of individual baseline controls is part of the normal certification process described below.

To ensure that a set of controls is identified that can adequately protect the largest proportion of its systems, an enterprise risk assessment needs to be conducted. This broad-based approach will provide a solid foundation for constructing the right set of minimum security baselines. At a high level the risk assessment will assess the assets to be protected and probable threats that may have an impact on the resources. The assessment should then focus on identification of the controls that will provide protection to organization assets, irrespective of existing, in-place controls. Although the application of minimum security baselines is assessed as part of the certification of each system, the minimum security baseline set must be continually evaluated and updated on an enterprisewide basis. Significant changes in the organization's processing environment, user community, business operations, or operating locations may very well necessitate changes in the minimum security baselines. The enterprise information security function should also review all system-level certification and accreditation documentation to identify trends that may affect the minimum security baseline set. For example, findings that show numerous privileged users have not been screened to the appropriate level of trust will indicate that a reassessment of the organization's standards for personnel security is warranted; review of certification results may show that systems in development are not ready to be placed into production due to lack of system security controls and this makes it likely that a lack of integration of security into the system development life-cycle methodology exists. Perhaps there will be recommendations for updating the organization's minimum security baseline on the basis of reviews of remediation plans over several review cycles. The minimum security baseline must be adjusted over a period of time — perhaps two to three years, in which incidents are measured and the threat list is updated to provide a current picture for controls implementation.

Minimum security baselines must be developed to ensure that the controls requirements for the organization are specified across the entire controls spectrum. They must address management controls, operational controls, and technical controls. The importance of minimum security baseline cross-reference numbers must be emphasized because they form the basis for the identification of controls and weaknesses in other certification and accreditation documentation.

Use of the Minimum Security Baseline Set

When performing a minimum security baseline assessment, it is important to use the baseline set in its entirety in order to record the system's compliance with the entire breadth of controls. Elimination of an entire section because it is not applicable to the system will merely give rise to questions that will have to be answered later. A better approach is to regard the minimum security baseline set as an inviolate whole. Individual controls that are not applicable to the system should be marked as such and a justification of why they are not applicable should be given. And controls that are not achievable and for which the risk of not implementing it is being accepted also need to be fully justified.

Summary

The employment of minimum security baselines provides an organization with a mechanism for ensuring that a minimally acceptable security posture is established. They provide a benchmark for system owners to aim to achieve. However, minimum security baselines are only a starting point, and their effectiveness can only be assured if they are tailored to the specific needs of an information system. As long as this condition can be met, and as long as they can be applied to the entire organization, adoption of minimum security baselines is a viable part of the certification and accreditation process. Establishment of minimum security baselines, which have as their foundation generally accepted security practices, provide a convincing argument that the organization has exercised due diligence in the implementation of security controls to protect its information systems.

Chapter 11

Assessing Risk

The objective of this chapter is to describe risk assessment as part of an overall certification and accreditation process. It is therefore not intended to be an in-depth exploration of risk assessment. In the context of the overall certification and accreditation process, risk assessment determines or verifies requirements for minimizing risks to the system. These requirements are expressed as controls, and risks are expressed in terms of vulnerabilities paired with threats.

Risk assessment of information technology systems involves the systematic identification and prioritization of risks to information technology resources. This analysis includes the valuation of assets; identification of threats to those assets; assessment of vulnerabilities in controls protecting these assets against identified threats; calculation of risks; and identification of cost-effective controls to mitigate risks. Risk assessment can range from highly complex efforts resulting in very precise quantitative results to a simple exercise conducted by a lone, knowledgeable individual. Normally, the complexity of the risk assessment is driven by the time it requires and by the resources available to perform it. However, the primary driver should actually be the level of precision demanded by the system being analyzed.

Background

In judging how risk assessment can be effectively integrated into an enterprise certification and accreditation program, it's a good idea to first look at issues that have hampered full-scale acceptance of risk assessment for information technology systems over the years.

■ *Scalability*: In the past, risk assessment came in one size, one flavor — big. Although there may have been an appetite for a sundae, only a banana split could be ordered. And an expensive banana split at that. Every system that was thought for various reasons to need risk assessment received the banana split treatment. For systems that were not considered to be worthy of the banana split treatment, they were simply not subjected to risk assessment at all. One size fit all, and it was expensive. Because security budgets were small, risk assessment efforts normally incorporated only a small number of systems each year and made little provision for updating these assessments once they were initially completed. Of course in a centralized, mainframe-based processing environment, focusing on the primary information technology resources generally worked fine because all systems processed in the same environment. However, with decentralization, all bets were off. Risk assessment methodology needed to change to accommodate the move away from centralized processing. But for a long time it did not and still to some degree has not. In many circles a risk assessment methodology most appropriate for a data center or enterprisewide application is still being shoehorned into use for an office automation system, LAN, or an application with limited functionality and applicability. A more cost-effective and practical approach tailors the risk assessment level of effort to the sensitivity of the system is called for.

■ *Terminology*: Another problem with old school risk assessments is that no one could understand them other than who wrote them. Their use of odd terminology (ALE, SLE, etc.), their complicated formulas, and their heft convinced managers that risk assessment was more magic than science. This led them to discount the usefulness of risk assessment reports, and if used at all, managers would only make use of the safeguard recommendations that they understood and had resources to address. So, nothing ever happened other than being able to say that a risk assessment of the system had been conducted.

■ *Automated Tools*: Tools were developed to support the laborious task of analyzing risk and they greatly eased the process. However, most organizations were unable to really take ownership of the automated process either because a great deal of knowledge of information technology security theory and practice was required to use them, and paid consultants were most often called on to use the tools. With the coming of the Facilitated Risk Assessment

Process (FRAP) and other approaches that aimed at ease of application, many organizations got risk assessment religion once again because these new methodologies offered practical approaches to assessing information technology systems in an understandable way. Although these methodologies still required outside help to learn how to perform them, they proved to be relatively inexpensive and led to more systems being assessed than before their advent.

Risk Assessment in Certification and Accreditation

The level of effort required to conduct a risk assessment of a given system must fit the situation. Because this has not always been the case with certification and accreditation, a new approach is warranted. Certification and accreditation has traditionally been hindered or at least has not been effectively supported by realistic risk assessment efforts and methodologies. The risk assessment must present a realistic and concise picture of what needs to be protected, what events threaten those assets, what vulnerabilities in security controls are of concern, and what safeguards should be considered for implementation. The risk assessment must successfully unveil these things clearly; if it cannot, the results of the risk assessment will be discounted and the effort will have failed.

As part of a certification and accreditation process that emphasizes tailoring effort to need (i.e., matching supply to demand) to be cost effective, the risk assessment must be cleanly integrated into the overall certification and accreditation process to be worthwhile. Asset identification must be tied to the system description and environment definition; vulnerability assessment must be connected to minimum security baselines as a start; and safeguard recommendations must match remediation plans.

When implemented as part of a comprehensive certification and accreditation process, the primary purpose of the risk assessment is to refine minimum security baseline controls to fit the need for the system's protection. This means that the relationship between system assets, threats, and vulnerabilities is used to tailor the initial set of controls established for the system to ensure it provides adequate protection for system resources. The risk assessment in this context looks for minimum security baseline controls that are applicable, and it identifies and justifies additional or alternative controls necessary above those called for in the minimum security baseline. For instance, the system may be subject to federal directives that call for controls that are not in the standard minimum security baseline. Using this approach the risk assessment serves as the foundation for defining how the system should be protected. It can also be used to document risks that management should accept so that corrective action is not wasted on the mitigation of costly risks that have little realistic impact on the system. The results of the risk assessment must identify and justify recommendations for risks that should be accepted, and the certification and accreditation process must ensure that these are carried forward into the plan of action and milestones.

Risk Assessment Process

The risk assessment process consists of five steps: asset identification, threat identification, vulnerability assessment, risk calculation, and safeguard identification. Each step depends on the results of the previous step. Each step in the risk assessment process is defined in the following paragraphs.

Asset Identification

The first step in the risk assessment process is asset identification. Once the system has been defined and the scope of the risk assessment has been established (general support system, major application, enterprise, facility, business unit, process, etc.), then system assets such as hardware, software, data, facilities, and people related to the operation of the system must be identified. Asset identification is actually the starting point of the certification and accreditation process in that it is the central element of the scoping exercise and system inventory process. Mainframes, servers, workstations, devices, and peripherals that make up the system need to be documented in the process — if not in the risk assessment itself, then in the security plan.

Operating system software, application programs, databases, and utilities must be considered in asset identification. The particular data files processed by the system as well as input and output data in all forms need to be addressed. The physical facilities where processing and system use takes place need to be included as system resources, as does the user population — internal, external, and system administration. Other asset groups that should not be overlooked are intangibles such as organization or product reputation and credibility. The primary groups of information technology system assets that the risk assessment must consider are identified in Table 11.1.

Threat Identification

Threat identification should document all threats that realistically apply to the system. For example, if the system does not process confidential

Table 11.1   Examples of Asset Groups

- Application software
- Data
- Database programs
- Documentation (plans, procedures, hardware/software documentation)
- Environmental systems (fire detection/suppression, temperature/humidity controls, drainage systems)
- Facilities
- Hardware and equipment
- Intangibles (credibility, reputation, trust)
- Operating system software
- Personnel
- Security software
- Security systems (badge system, access control systems, closed-circuit TV systems)
- Telecommunications equipment (cabling, routers, switches, gateways, bridges, etc.)
- Utility programs

information, then threats related to the disclosure of information will not apply. To make the threat identification process easier to perform, categorizing threats can be helpful. Normally threats are labeled as environmental or human, internal or external, and intentional or accidental. The methodology must include a master list of threats that can be pared down to fit the system's environment. Table 11.2 provides an example of a threat list. Threat identification includes determining the likelihood of the threat's occurrence and the impact of the threat should it occur. Likelihood and impact can be expressed in either quantitative or qualitative terms. For most systems it will be sufficient to use "high," "medium," and "low" terminology relative to each security impact category (confidentiality, integrity, availability). On the most sensitive systems actual frequencies by measurement of increments of time (i.e., annual expectancy) and impact in potential dollar loss may be necessary.

Vulnerability Assessment

The threat assessment is only useful in the context of vulnerabilities to the system. Pairing realistic threats to actual vulnerabilities results in identification of risks that management needs to address. Vulnerabilities are determined by assessment of security controls first against the mini-

Table 11.2 Example of a Threat List

Threat Classification	Specific Threat	Primary Impacts		
		Confidentiality	Integrity	Availability
Natural	Aircraft accident			✓
	Earthquake			✓
	Electrical interference/disruption			✓
	Extreme temperatures			✓
	Fire			✓
	Flood			✓
	Hurricane			✓
	Lightning			✓
	Tornado			✓
	Windstorms			✓
	Winter storm			✓
Environmental	Hazardous material incident			✓
	HVAC failure			✓
	Hardware/software failure	✓	✓	✓
	Illness/epidemic			✓
	Power outage/failure			✓
	Radiological incident			✓
	Rodent/insect infestation			✓

Structural fire	✓		✓
Substance abuse	✓		✓
Transportation accident	✓		✓
Administrative error	✓	✓	
Bomb threat	✓	✓	
Computer virus	✓		✓
Disgruntled employee or citizen incident	✓	✓	✓
Errors/omissions (user)		✓	✓
Industrial espionage		✓	✓
Intentional modification of data	✓	✓	✓
Management error/omission	✓	✓	✓
Sabotage/terrorist attack	✓	✓	✓
Theft of assets	✓		✓
Unauthorized access to client facilities	✓	✓	✓
Unauthorized access to client system/data		✓	✓

Man-Made

mum security baseline, and then against existing controls paired with identified threats. These include weaknesses in management, operational, and technical controls. Any control that does not provide protection in the manner for and to the extent to which it was designed is classified as a vulnerability, and if it can be paired with a realistic threat, then it is also a risk. The minimum security baseline or some other set of controls requirements serves as a reference point for judging the effectiveness of controls. This can show the weakness of and the lack of controls. Vulnerability scanning tools provide additional data on controls effectiveness and should be used as well. Where the minimum security baseline lacks detail, industry-standard best practices can be used to identify and evaluate technology-specific vulnerabilities. This ensures that the risk assessment identifies vulnerabilities in controls that exceed the minimum security baseline. Additionally, findings from previous risk assessments and system or organization audits can also highlight vulnerabilities applicable to the system.

Risk Calculation

As stated, a risk consists of a vulnerability that can be exploited by a realistic threat to adversely affect a system asset. How does one go about determining these pairings? There are a number of good sources from which to start this exercise, but the key is to be consistent. There may be multiple pairings for each threat and for each vulnerability. For instance, a breech in the wall of a server room causes a physical access vulnerability as well as an increased vulnerability to fire and smoke penetration of the room. Risk should be calculated for each threat/vulnerability pair by assessing the impact and likelihood of losses to data confidentiality, integrity, and availability. NIST SP 800-30 details a risk assessment process, which assigns a numerical score for high, moderate, and low impacts and the probability of occurrence for each of these three security components. Potential scores for each threat/vulnerability pair range from 0 to 300 with scores below 100 considered to be low risks, scores over 200 to be high risks, and all scores in between judged to be moderate risks. This is one very practical approach that can be performed by a system owner without difficulty (if he or she has a few hours to concentrate on the task without the phone ringing). Such an approach easily lends itself also to automation. Use of this approach allows one to readily identify the most significant risks to the system as starting points for safeguard selection and implementation of corrective actions. A sample risk matrix is provided in Table 11.3.

Table 11.3   Example of a Risk Matrix

Question	Vulnerability	Threat	Status I, P, NI, Accept Risk	Availability (Denial of Service)		Integrity (Destruction and Modification)		Confidentiality (Disclosure)		Risk Factor High (201–300) Med (101–200) Low (1–100)	Risk
				Likelihood High = 1 Med = 0.5 Low = .1	Impact High = 100 Med = 50 Low = 10	Likelihood High = 1 Med = 0.5 Low = 0.1	Impact High = 100 Med = 50 Low = 10	Likelihood High = 1 Med = 0.5 Low = 0.1	Impact High = 100 Med = 50 Low = 10		
166	11.2.4 Integrity verification programs are not used by the application to look for evidence of data tampering, errors, and omissions (NIST SP 800-18)	Data integrity loss/ modification	NI	0.1	50	1	100	0.1	50	110	Moderate
170	11.2.8 Penetration testing is not performed on the system (NIST SP 800-18)	Hacking/ social engineering	NI	0.5	50	0.5	100	0.5	100	125	Moderate
177	12.1.5 There are no software and hardware testing procedures and results (NIST SP 800-18)	Data integrity loss/ modification	NI	1	100	1	100	0.5	100	250	High
178	12.1.6 There are no standard operating procedures for all the topic areas covered in this document (NIST SP 800-18)	Human threats	NI	0.5	50	0.5	50	0.1	50	55	Low
190	13.1.2 Employee training and professional development is not documented and monitored (FISCAM SP-4.2)	User errors/ omissions	NI	0.5	50	0.1	10	0.1	10	27	Low

Safeguard Identification

The risk assessment should recommend appropriate controls that are needed to protect the system. The trick is to know what is appropriate. Recommendations must be specific to the system, detailed enough to allow them to be understood, and practical enough to make them cost-effective. In cases where controls are too costly, hamper system use, or do not provide adequate return on investment, the recommendation should consider management's role in accepting risk. Cost-effectiveness of controls should be a key consideration in the selection process, but one cannot forget the overriding principle of asset protection in the process. Because the use of a minimum security baseline is the foundation of the certification and accreditation process described in this volume, the primary focus of the risk assessment is to verify the adequacy of minimum security baseline controls, and to recommend changes: either additional controls, alternative controls, or decreased controls. Even in this context, risk assessment continues to perform its traditional role of determining controls requirements through safeguard selection. That is, risks serve as the primary drivers for safeguard recommendations.

The results of safeguard identification are documented in the security plan as either in place or planned for implementation. Safeguard identification also quantifying controls costs in either qualitative (e.g., high, moderate, or low) or quantitative terms (i.e., dollars and man-hours).

Risk Assessment Execution

The risk assessment team should include members of the organization who have knowledge of the value of information technology assets, threats to them, the posture of and vulnerabilities in security controls, and the information technology security program and operations. These personnel can provide the most current data necessary to calculate risks to the system. The involvement of these individuals is particularly important when outside consultants are engaged to perform the risk assessment. The use of consultants can be beneficial when the organization lacks risk assessment expertise or when it cannot afford to dedicate its own experts to the effort. Consultants can also provide a degree of independence that organizational personnel cannot, and on those grounds their recommendations may be easier for management to accept.

A successful risk assessment effort depends on current and reliable data. This is done by asking the right questions of the right people, by being aware of the most current sources of information, and from having knowledge of the system being assessed. The most valuable information is gained from personnel using the system from organization management, from reports generated by the system, from audits and incident reports, and with external data from local, regional, and national sources. The user community of the system is most familiar with current practices, system operations, system security features, and weaknesses in controls. System management personnel who are most aware of the sensitivity of the system can provide a historical view of incidents, threats, and vulnerabilities. Of course, personnel can only be valuable sources of risk-related information if the right questions are asked by risk assessment team members skilled in interview techniques. The team should prepare an interview matrix that identifies first the type of information needed mapped to the general identification of who can best provide this information. A sample interview matrix is provided in Table 11.4. In coordination with the system owner, this matrix can be fleshed out to include the names of specific personnel that need to be interviewed. For each type of information sought a standard interview questionnaire should be prepared to guide the interviewer, particularly if the person conducting the interview is not overly familiar with the system being analyzed. However, this should only be a guide, and interviewers must know the meaning of the questions they are asking and must have general knowledge of the system to be able to relate the questions to the specific system being analyzed. Advance knowledge of the system should be based on a review of documentation requested early in the risk assessment effort. System descriptions, data descriptions, design documents, policies and procedures, user manuals, organization charts, building layouts, audits and inspections, process flows, hardware/software inventories, and network diagrams should be requested in advance to allow the risk assessment team to familiarize itself before interviews begin. In addition to interview results, this documentation will provide the primary information for system description, asset identification, and system connectivity descriptions. It is critical that risk assessment team members have access to and make use of such data. Otherwise, organization personnel being interviewed will have to take longer than necessary to describe the system, wasting valuable time and lengthening the disruption of their work. Team members must understand the importance of limiting disruption of normal activities only within reason. To limit the amount of time required for data collection, facilitation can be effectively employed. The FRAP approach greatly speeds up the collection of good risk assessment data and minimizes the impact of the collection effort on the hosting organization.

It may be impossible to obtain all information helpful in analyzing risk to the system. It is important to know, however, when enough information has been obtained to avoid a prolonged effort chasing peripheral information with little value to the primary objective at hand. Therefore, the

Table 11.4   Example of an Interview Matrix

Position	Interview Topics
System owner	■ System description ■ System sensitivity ■ System criticality ■ System interconnectivity ■ Security drivers ■ Security incidents ■ Threats/vulnerabilities ■ Management controls ■ Operational controls
System administrator	■ Security incidents ■ Threats/vulnerabilities ■ Operational controls ■ Technical controls
ISSO	■ Threats/vulnerabilities ■ System sensitivity ■ Security incidents ■ Management controls ■ Operational controls ■ Technical controls
Database administrator	■ Operational controls
Application programmer	■ Operational controls ■ Technical controls
Facility manager/Physical security	■ Operational controls ■ Technical controls
User	■ Operational controls ■ Technical controls
Personnel security officer	■ Operational controls
Executive management	■ System criticality ■ Threats/vulnerabilities

team needs to know what information is essential and cannot be omitted in the interest of time, lack of cooperation of personnel, or paucity of documentation. The minimum essential information for the risk assessment relates to asset, threat, and vulnerability identification. The data gathering effort should focus on those three main areas of information as the basis for further analysis. The team should not cease data collection activities until it has enough data to understand what the system is designed to do, the kind of data it processes, how it works, system inputs and outputs, hardware software components, the user community, and facilities where the system resides and is used. Historical threat–related data is essential for determining threat impacts and likelihood. In all likelihood this will be obtained through interviews. Finally, a complete inventory of vulnerabilities in security controls should be considered essential to the data collection effort.

Often it is not possible to collect all information needed during the scheduled data collection period, and follow-up telephone coordination must be conducted after the fact. However, a face-to-face interview is far more effective and fruitful because it permits the analyst to probe into initial answers to identify associated issues, and every effort should be made to try to obtain information firsthand. For instance, when the person being interviewed nervously states that system security controls are reviewed "periodically," follow-up probing may reveal that the most recent review was conducted 18 months previously. Only in a personal interview can the impact of nonverbal communications be assessed.

When conducting risk assessments of large and complex systems, the use of automated tools can ease the effort substantially. Tools such as OCTAVE® and RiskWatch® standardize data collection, automate the risk assessments described above, and produce reliable quantitative results.

Risk Categorization

Depending on the needs the user may have, risks can be categorized according to the assets to which they relate, by related threat, by vulnerability, by associated safeguard, by threat impact, or by threat frequency. The only limitation is the ease with which the collected risk assessment data can be generated into lists. Housing risk assessment data in a relational database provides the greatest degree of flexibility in categorizing risks.

Documenting Risk Assessment Results

The risk assessment report documents all activities performed during the risk assessment. The report should not be so complex that it cannot be easily understood by a reader not familiar with the system. It should define terms and definitions as well as the methodology used in conducting the assessment. The level of detail contained in the report needs to correspond to the sensitivity of the system. The report should allow the results to be used by management in selecting controls that are most appropriate to the sensitivity of and risks to the system, allowing implementation of controls that are cost-effective. Therefore, risks must be ranked specific to the system according to their severity to allow the most cost-effective controls to be chosen. Because executive management is the target audience of the report, the report should make extensive use of risk summary information and graphics to highlight information. A sample risk assessment format is provided in Appendix N.

Summary

For the purpose of certification and accreditation, risk assessment must validate the applicability of the minimum set of security controls chosen for the system to determine if they are appropriate. The results should therefore substantiate the need for additional controls, alternative controls, or fewer controls. The findings of the risk assessment allow prioritization of corrective actions recorded in the remediation plan to allow resources to be applied to mitigate the highest risk weaknesses cost-effectively. Performance of risk assessment as a part of an integrated certification and accreditation allows the definition of how and in what order it will be performed and allows its results to be cleanly incorporated into other security documentation. These features permit the risk assessment to serve as a practical process rather than black art.

Chapter 12

Security Procedures

Security procedures play a prominent part in the minimum security baseline set. They are an important type of control that documents the security practices and processes that have been implemented to protect the system. Although system-level security procedures can be regarded as another type of security control, their development is key to the successful implementation of a certification and accreditation program. This is because the program can foster the development of critical controls by not only identifying and increasing the visibility of the need for documented procedures, but also by providing tools and techniques to aid in their development. This chapter addresses security procedures specific to individual systems, as well as those considered to be common controls that are applicable to multiple systems at either the business unit or enterprise level.

Purpose

Procedures are important to the security of information technology systems because they serve as the connection between people (who protect) and assets (that are protected). It has been said that the greatest risk to an information system is the people that are authorized to use it. Security procedures reduce the risk posed by people by providing users instructions in how to use the system securely, how to perform security-related tasks and functions correctly, and how to administer security controls properly. This allows secure practices to be repeatable over time and to be passed on from one user to the next, permitting alternates to be able to step in and assume the duties when necessary. Security procedures also provide a basis for training in the secure use of the system and they ensure that security policies and standards that are applicable to the system are translated and applied to the system. An additional benefit from the perspective of the security manager is that security procedures allow measurement of the level of compliance with and the adequacy of security. Reviewing compliance with security procedures demonstrates the degree to which system users and managers perform security-specific tasks.

The Problem with Procedures

The lack of security procedures is one of the more persistent problems in implementation of security at the system level. System administrators are busy, with much competition for their time. Security is but one of these competitors. Consequently, system administrators do not place much emphasis on documentation, particularly on the processes they already know how to do, because they do them routinely with their eyes closed. System administrators are "doers" by nature and specialize in knowing how to do things. For many, doing does not include putting down in writing the steps involved in doing something. This mind-set fails to give credence to needs for continuity of operations, cross-training of replacements and backups, and compliance measurement goals. Management must understand the importance of security procedures and be forceful in ensuring that procedures specific to its systems are developed and maintained.

Responsibility

The system owner is normally the official responsible for developing and approving system-specific procedures. This is because system owners have the most knowledge of the system and know what procedures are needed and what they need to address. However, the owner may need to call on someone like a system administrator to actually draft the procedures due to the administrator's more intimate knowledge of the process to be documented (i.e., backing up system data). Also, the system owner is in the best position to create procedures because they must apply to all users of the system irrespective of their location, business unit or organization, position, rank or status. Because procedures are considered mandatory in nature and noncompliance should be grounds for disciplinary action, users should be required to acknowledge their understanding and acceptance of them as a condition of use. This can be enforced through the use of an initial system access request approval process, which includes an acknowledgment form for the user's signature. Key procedures or elements of procedures that warrant emphasis and reinforcement through stricter oversight can be integrated into the rules of behavior for the system.

Procedure Templates

Management can facilitate the creation of security procedures by being proactive and developing approved procedures templates for system owners to use in developing their procedures for their systems. Table 12.1 provides a sample of procedures that should be prepared for each system. It should be pointed out that care must be exercised in the use of "canned" procedures of this sort to ensure that they are properly modified to fit the organization's environment and do not establish overly complex processes that have no prospect of being followed. The creation of a security procedures library can assist the entire organization in complying with minimum security requirements. NIST SP 800-26 and 800-53 minimum security baselines require a large number of procedures for both general support systems and major applications. An organization will be well served to create templates that permit system owners to tailor them to their own needs. The easiest way to build such a library is for the CISO to collect, review, and sanitize procedures drafted by system owners across the organization. This also permits the development of procedure templates for different types of systems by function, by business unit, and by level of protection necessary.

The Procedure Development Process

The organization should establish a standard approach for creating procedures to ensure standardization of content and format. Steps involved in this process ensure that requirements for procedures are routinely identified; that responsibilities for their development are assigned; that new procedures are reviewed and approved by appropriate operational and security personnel; that a procedure is disseminated to those charged with its implementation and compliance; and that procedures are maintained. Table 12.2 depicts the steps involved in the development of security procedures.

Style

Procedures may be several pages in length or may only be a few sentences. Generally, procedures should be written to be as concise as possible

Table 12.1 Sample Procedures List

Procedure	Type of Procedure
Account set-up	System-specific
Account termination	System-specific
Audit trail retention and storage	System-specific
Audit trail review	System-specific
Authorization to process (certification and accreditation)	Common
Configuration management and change control	Common
Contingency planning and testing	Common
Data backup	System-specific
Data entry/integrity/validation controls	System-specific
Emergency evacuation	Common
Incident response	Common
Interconnecting systems	Common
Malicious software prevention	Common
Media protection	Common
Nondisclosure of information/confidentiality	Common
Password compromise	System-specific
Password issuance	System-specific
Password reset	System-specific
Personally owned computers and software	Common
Personnel background screening	Common
Personnel in-processing	Common
Personnel sanctions	Common
Personnel termination and transfer	Common
Physical access authorization	Common
Portable computers/controlling laptops	Common
Position sensitivity designation	Common
Privacy impact assessment	Common
Property accountability	Common
Remote access	System-specific
Risk assessment	Common
Risk management (plan of action and milestones)	Common
Security awareness and training	Common
Security controls review	Common
Security planning	Common
System maintenance	Common
Third-party security	Common
User accounts review	System-specific
Visitor controls	Common
Vulnerability scanning	Common

Table 12.2 Procedure Development Process

Task 1	Identify the need for a new or updated security procedure as a result of an audit, the system certification process, or through routine self-assessment.
Task 2	Create or update the procedure by the organizational element responsible for performing the process being documented in the procedure.
Task 3	Review of the procedure by the task lead who supervises the element, creating/updating the procedure. The task lead ensures the procedure accurately documents the process in its entirety and reflects the manner in which it should be performed. If additional content or corrections are required, the task lead returns the material for corrective action.
Task 4	The information system security officer (ISSO) responsible for the performance of the procedures reviews the updated or newly created procedure to ensure adequate security controls are included in the procedure. If additional security-related content or corrections are required, the ISSO returns it to the prior task lead for corrective action.
Task 5	The updated or newly created procedure is reviewed by the organizational information system security staff to ensure adequate security controls are included in the procedure. If additional security-related content or corrections are needed, it is returned to the ISSO for action.
Task 6	The updated or newly created procedure is reviewed by the system owner. If the system owner desires changes, he or she contacts the ISS for action.
Task 7	Once the system owner approves the procedure, it is maintained by the division that created it. Any updates to the approved procedure should follow this approval process.

because use and maintenance of extensive, complex, and overly wordy procedures can be problematic. It is clearly possible to go overboard with procedures by thinking that more is better. But breadth is more important than heft. Ideally, system-specific procedures should be grouped into a consolidated security manual to make it easier to access and use them when needed and to facilitate updating individual procedures as necessary. Therefore, such a handbook should be constructed in a modular fashion with the authority, date of release, applicability, and scope of each clearly indicated on each individual procedure. Ideally, posting individual procedures on Web pages indexed by topic is the best solution because this facilitates ease of use as well as ease of updating.

Many organizations use the system security plan as the repository for security-related procedures, applying the principle that all security-related information should be consolidated into a single document. Although in principle this makes sense on the basis of ease of use, from a practical standpoint the approach diminishes the usability of the security plan and weakens the plan's ability to meet its primary purpose: documenting the security posture of a system. When detailed procedures are included in the plan, the overall status of system security is obscured. This is an unnatural blending of operational information with management information that is difficult to maintain. An additional reason for avoiding this practice is that it is an unnecessary addition to the certification package and is difficult to include, and this risks delays in the development of the certification and accreditation package. The security plan should merely make reference to individual security procedures as it addresses specific plan topics, but there is little value in including the procedures as part of the plan.

Formatting

First of all, procedures need to be documented. For the reasons stated above, it is not sufficient for the system administrator or other user to "have them in their head." If procedures are not written down, they do not exist (particularly from an auditor's perspective). The formatting of the procedures should be fully consistent with organizational standards to link them to the authority of organizational management, as well as to ensure consistency and comprehensiveness. A sample security procedure is provided in Appendix O. As stated above, procedures should be developed individually according to topic. The format of each procedure should include the subject or title of the procedure and should address the purpose of or justification for the procedure; its scope (what does it apply to); responsibility (who must implement, enforce, and comply with it); applicability (what individuals or organizational elements does it apply to); when it is to be employed (routinely, periodically, occasionally, as required, or during emergencies); and the process itself. Each procedure should be affixed with a date and should bear the signature of the individual responsible for the procedure, usually the system owner. The content of the procedure should permit the reader to understand how to do something. To promote this level of understanding, maximum use of bullet lists of tasks and activities to be performed, steps, graphs, figures, tips, and reminders is warranted. Screen shots of system-based processes should be incorporated into the procedures to promote clarity as well as brevity.

Access

It does no good to spend countless hours developing, coordinating, publishing, and updating an intricate set of security procedures if they are not available when they are needed by those who need them. To ensure that they will be available when they are needed they should be backed up, and a copy should be stored at an off-site location. It might be good for those to whom the procedures pertain to be required to maintain a copy at home as long as copies can be kept secure. Although there may be a need for some users to have procedures in printed form (e.g., data entry personnel), this should be discouraged because of the difficulty of updating the procedures. A better solution is to post the procedures in a protected format on a shared directory on the network or on the company intranet. The CISO should establish a procedures library to serve as a repository for various security procedures developed by system owners. This will provide examples for organizations that are in the process of developing their own system-specific procedures.

Maintenance

Procedures should be reviewed annually to determine if they are current. The process for conducting such a review itself should be documented. Update of procedures should be built into the change management process, the incident response process, and in any other process that may result in changes to how things are done. Procedures update is enhanced when a change information sheet as depicted in Chapter 8 is included as a part of the procedure and is used to record the date and a brief description of each change. The identification of the approver of each of the changes should also be recorded. Users should be encouraged to submit requests for changes when they are observed, and such requests should themselves be subject to the change management process. This ensures that each change is fully documented for historical purposes and approval is recorded.

Common Procedures

System owners should not have to be responsible for developing procedures relating to controls that are outside of their area of responsibility; they have enough to do already. Instead, procedures that are common to several systems in a business unit should be addressed at the business-unit level, and at the enterprise level for controls that apply to all or most systems in the organization. Controls in the areas of facility physical security, environmental protection, personnel security, incident response, and security awareness and training should generally be addressed as common controls, and those functions should be responsible for developing procedures for them. However, this does not take the system owner entirely off the hook. Simply because there is an enterprise procedure, there may still be a need to write a system-specific procedure. The common procedure has to be made specific to the information technology system by identifying who is responsible for implementing, complying, and using it at the system level. This system-level augmentation must describe how the procedure is implemented on the system and under what conditions it must be followed. Table 12.1 identifies both common and system-specific procedures generally applicable to information technology systems.

Procedures in the Certification and Accreditation Process

Security procedures fall into the category of security controls, and they directly impact the security of a system and indirectly impact the overall certification and accreditation program. The ways that procedures affect certification and accreditation processes and documents is that:

- They are established as requirements in the minimum security baseline for an organization.
- The existence/nonexistence of procedures is to be documented in the system security plan.
- Vulnerabilities related to lack of or failure to comply with procedures are included in the risk assessment.
- They are evaluated as part of security testing.
- Weaknesses relating to security procedures are documented and tracked in the remediation plan.

These various certification and accreditation processes and documentation are designed to record the need for, existence of, effectiveness of, and weaknesses in security procedures just as with all controls necessary for the system's protection.

Summary

The purpose of security procedures is to describe tasks to be performed and actions to be taken in securing a system. Procedures provide the detailed steps, assign specific responsibilities, and provide aids in the implementation and maintenance of security controls. The consequences to the system owner of not having documented procedures is a lack of consistency in controls implementation and maintenance, a lack of repeatability in their administration by system users, and the risk of failure to comply with minimum controls requirements. Additionally, the documented procedures ensure that there is no major loss of knowledge when a key user is absent. Procedures are the primary means for the system owner to address the significant threat of user errors and omissions affecting his or her system in that they translate controls requirements into specific user tasks that can be performed, measured, enforced, and taught.

Chapter 13

Certification Testing

Testing is necessary to provide assurance that implemented controls meet a predetermined set of standards. Testing as part of the system certification process seeks to answer the question, "Are controls doing what they are intended to do?" Also, certification testing determines if required controls are in place. The objective of certification testing is not to record quality of protection but to merely express if a requirement is being met or is not being met. Finally, certification testing provides assurance that information recorded in security plans, risk assessments, contingency plans, and elsewhere is accurate and complete.

Scope

The scope of certification testing should be driven by the entire range of controls requirements applicable to the system. These requirements as described in earlier chapters stem from minimum security baselines adopted by organizations and from adjustments in controls determined by means of a risk assessment process. Normally, controls requirements that are documented in the security plan for the system will comprise the scope of certification testing. As stated in Chapter 8, the security plan documents the broad range of controls protecting the system, both those that have been implemented as well as those planned for future implementation. That plan also identifies weaknesses in controls. Using the security plan as a start, a test plan is developed by the certification test team to validate that controls in the plan are in place as specified, to validate areas of weakness described in the plan, to identify additional areas of weakness, to document the status of planned controls, and to validate that controls identified as not applicable do not in fact apply. Additionally, certification testing validates controls for which management has accepted risk to determine if cause still exists to warrant continuation of this acceptance.

Level of Effort

When considering needs for and approaches to certification testing, system owners need to consider the sensitivity and criticality of the system. The organization may create a specific methodology based on the criticality of systems or a combination of factors that include need for integrity, availability, and confidentiality along with exposure the system's environment presents. It is important to tailor the level of effort of certification testing to the needs of the system to ensure testing is cost-effective. The level of effort established will drive the size of the testing team, the rigor of the testing, and the amount of documentation required. A comparison of levels of effort for systems categorized at three levels of risk is provided in Table 13.1.

Independence

The level of effort determination may also drive the decision on the level of independence required for the certification team. The certification team must normally be independent of the system owner. How independent must it be? Certification testing is different from the routine self-assessments conducted by the system owner on a regular basis. Certification testing is different in that it is not performed as often, is more rigorous, and is conducted by an independent entity. For our purposes, independence requirements call for testers to be independent of the influence of the system owner. A practical approach will be to permit testing of low-risk systems by personnel assigned to the approving authority's organization but not from the system owner's; for moderate-risk systems, by personnel assigned to the organization but not to the approving authority's organization; and for high-risk systems, by personnel from outside the organization. It is nearly impossible to achieve perfect independence because testers have to have some familiarity with the system and must be funded by the organization in some manner. Application of the common-sense test can avoid extended and pointless discussions about the relative existence of independence of a certification team. Independence can also

Table 13.1   Certification Levels of Effort

Certification Level	Elements of Testing
Low	Low-intensity, checklist-based, independent security review that includes: ■ Interview of personnel ■ Review of system-related security policies, procedures, documents ■ Observation of system operations and security controls
Moderate	Moderate-intensity, demonstration-based, independent assessment that includes: ■ Low certification level verification techniques (if appropriate) ■ Functional testing ■ Regression analysis and regression testing ■ Penetration testing (optional) ■ Demonstrations to verify security control correctness and effectiveness
High	High-intensity, exercise-based, independent assessment that includes: ■ Low and moderate certification level verification techniques (if appropriate) ■ System design analysis ■ Functional testing with coverage analysis ■ Regression analysis and regression testing ■ Penetration testing (Red Team optional) ■ Demonstrations and exercises to verify security control correctness and effectiveness

be achieved by using internal or external auditors; however, their use in this fashion should not be allowed to conflict with their primary auditing responsibilities to the organization.

Independence is most often achieved through the use of independent contractors skilled and experienced in certification testing or security testing and evaluation (ST&E) procedures. And, in many cases, certification testing will be performed by contractors who have been engaged to perform certification testing for the system or a group of systems. In some cases these contractors are tasked to perform all certification tasks relating to the system and prepare or update all documentation including the security plan, risk assessment, and certification report. Although this approach has the advantage of achieving consistency in project execution and work products, it presents a disadvantage in that the same team

Table 13.2 Planning Estimates for Testing

Certification Level	Duration of Testing
Low	One to two days
Moderate	Three to five days
High	Five to ten days

completes all tasks, lessening the opportunity for independent oversight of their work.

The team performing certification testing should be composed of the test director, the host, and test team members. The test director is responsible for coordinating requirements for the team to include testing methodology, tools, travel, support requirements, and documentation. Much of this coordination needs to be made with the host who is a representative of the system owner. Test team members are selected by the test director and are responsible to him for performance of testing functions. These functions include preparation of the test plan, performance of testing, and documentation of test results. The number of test team members is dependent on the size and complexity of the system being tested, as well as the amount of time available to perform testing and the methodology being used. Table 13.2 provides planning estimates for various levels of testing. With few exceptions, testing should be performed by a minimum of two analysts. This permits comparison of findings, ensures full coverage of controls requirements, and allows an additional perspective to be brought into play. In simple systems that are well known to the tester, a second analyst may be dispensed with in the interest of minimizing costs.

Team members need to be fully knowledgeable of the system, its processes, its functions, its purpose, and its user community. Additionally, team members need to have specialized skills in the technologies that make up the system to include operating system, database, and application software and other platforms as necessary (i.e., firewalls, switches, routers, etc.). When tools are used in support of testing, team members should be skilled in their use, know their limitations, and must be able to understand their output sufficiently to permit identification of false positives. They must have not only these technical skills but people skills as well because they will have to work very closely with hosting personnel throughout the duration of testing. Finally, they must have the requisite credentials to perform the tests. Security clearance, access, background screening, and professional certifications fall into this category. The test director should ensure that the host approves the qualifications and credentials of all team members before testing is initiated.

Developing the Test Plan

In planning for the certification testing task, the test director must consider a multitude of tasks, requirements, and issues that affect successful completion of testing. These should be documented in a certification test plan. Table 13.3 provides an outline of a certification test or ST&E plan. The plan serves to guide all involved in the test to include those performing

Table 13.3   Certification Test Plan Outline

Section	Description
Purpose	Describes the purpose of the test plan
Objectives	Describes the objectives of certification testing
Memoranda of Understanding	Specifies all memoranda of understanding with interconnected, hosting, or hosted systems
Responsible Organizations/ Personnel	Identifies the host organization and host personnel
Assumptions	Specifies any assumptions on which the test plan is based
Scope	Defines the scope of testing (i.e., components, locations, etc.)
Testing Requirements	Provides a high-level description of areas that testing will focus on (i.e., categories of controls to be tested)
Testing Approach	Provides an overview of how testing will be performed
Tests to Be Used	Makes reference to the specific tests that will be used to test each control that are found in the appendix
Schedule	Identifies the proposed start and end dates and times that testing will be performed
Test Team Composition	Identifies the names and positions of personnel assigned to the certification test team
Test Team Roles and Responsibilities	Specifies the roles and responsibilities for each test team member
Other Supporting Organizations	Identifies the role that will be played by other elements in support of testing
Remediation Plan	Describes the process for managing the correction of weaknesses identified through certification testing
Appendix: Controls and Tests	For each control applicable to the system, a specific protocol for testing is stipulated

testing and those supporting testing. Therefore, to effect coordination and to ensure optimum cooperation the plan should be prepared well in advance and be forwarded to all who will be performing a role in the certification test. It should be stressed that all controls are subject to testing, not just technical controls. Naturally, the types of tests to be performed and the types of evidence required will vary greatly between technical, operational, and management controls. Nevertheless, test standards and procedures should be prepared for all controls within the scope of the certification. Assumptions applicable to the certification test also need to be included in the test plan. Assumptions may address general issues, like availability of personnel to assist in testing, or specific concerns, such as the availability of a particular platform for testing in light of a planned deployment schedule.

The plan must include a detailed description of the testing methodology that will be used. It must address the support that is required from the hosting organization. It must clearly state the roles and responsibilities of those involved and must specify personnel to be involved in the exercise, if not by name then at least by position. This includes individuals to be interviewed, those required to demonstrate system controls, and those to provide documentation. If the team needs access to the system or its components, this should be specified in the plan so that it can be coordinated by the host in advance. Also, documentation necessary to perform testing (i.e., configuration standards, records of changes, system access lists, training records, etc.) should be identified in the plan to allow the host sufficient opportunity to locate and gather them prior to the initiation of testing. Identify particular facilities that will need to be accessed in the plan as well. If only a sampling of servers, workstations, wiring closets, or storage rooms will be selected for testing, provide the host the approximate number, type, IP address range, etc., to allow adequate preparation. The plan should detail the testing schedule and allow sufficient time for test preparation, actual test execution, and post-test feedback. If automated tools are to be used, they need to be identified in advance, and the plan should document requirements and coordination for their use. The plan should also detail administrative, logistics, and travel requirements. Finally, and most important, the plan must specify the scope of what will be tested, how it will be tested, and the results expected from testing for each control.

The plan must address testing of all controls within the scope of the project and must map directly to the previously developed scope statement. The plan should be jointly developed by the system owner and the test director to the maximum extent possible to ensure openness and facilitate efficient performance of controls testing. This is aided by providing the plan to the host as far in advance as possible and by gaining early agreement on the plan. For each control to be tested, the specific standard that is to be met must be documented. This should be written in the form of "expected results" and should make specific reference to a regulatory requirement or to a best practice. Additionally, the plan should establish the type of evidence required to prove findings (i.e., scan result, screen shot, documentary evidence, etc.). If special tools are required to test the control they should also be specified in the plan. Examples of certification test plan entries are provided in Table 13.4 and Table 13.5.

Procedures employed to test individual controls need to be comprehensive and complex enough to determine if the control meets the test standard and thereby determine if there are vulnerabilities in system controls. The types of testing that can be considered for employment in certification testing include:

- *Inspection*: Inspection is the physical review or examination of a control, such as review of a security setting or software version number
- *Demonstration*: Demonstration includes evaluation through operation, movement, or adjustment under specific conditions to determine the controls capability of satisfying a stated requirement
- *Test*: A test is the collection, analysis, and evaluation of controls by means of hands-on measurement under specified test conditions

Documenting specific steps to be followed in testing each control ensures the test adequately if the control standard is being met, aids the test team in test execution, permits the host to know in advance how the control will be tested, and provides historical data to allow understanding of testing procedures after testing has been concluded. These test scripts may have to be very detailed, down to the keystroke level, in the case of technical controls.

The plan should also document procedures for addressing findings that require immediate resolution such as discovery of malicious software, identification of child pornography, or other evidence of criminal wrongdoing. Provisions should be made to suspend testing pending resolution of issues such as these. It should be stipulated in the plan that incidents of this nature will be reported in accordance with policies and following procedures of the owning organization. Also, it is a good idea for the testing team to work with the owning organization to correct weaknesses on the spot whenever possible. This practice not only builds goodwill but it also limits the need for follow-up monitoring in the remediation plan. There is little for the test team to gain from playing "gotcha" during certification testing. Therefore, provisions for correcting weaknesses as they are discovered need to be recorded in the plan to assure the system

Table 13.4 Sample Certification Test Plan Entry

Question	Vulnerability	ST&E Actions	Expected Results	P/F	Actual Results Summary	Document Reference
Personnel Security						
64	6.1 Are duties separated to ensure least privilege and individual accountability?					
65	6.1.1 Are all positions reviewed for sensitivity level? (FISCAM SD-1.2, NIST SP 800-18)	Verify by inspection and interview with management that the system-related positions are reviewed for sensitivity level on an annual basis. (FISCAM SD-1.2)	All positions are reviewed by the system owner for sensitivity level annually.			

66	6.1.2 Are there documented job descriptions that accurately reflect assigned duties and responsibilities and that segregate duties? (FISCAM SD-1.2)	Review several job requirements and descriptions and interview management and personnel regarding system support and user positions. (FISCAM SD 1.2)	All reviewed job descriptions are accurately documented to reflect assigned security-related duties and responsibilities.
67	6.1.3 Are sensitive functions divided among different individuals? (OMB Circular A-130, III, FISCAM SD-1, NIST SP 800-18)	Determine if multiple steps in the process or key functions are performed by the same individual. For example: data entry and data validation, or data entry and supervisory authorization. Observe tasks performed by SA and security administrator.	Sensitive functions are divided between at least two different individuals.

Table 13.5   Sample Certification Test Entry

Question	Vulnerability	ST&E Actions	Expected Results	Pass/ Fail	Actual Results Summary	Document Reference
73	6.2 Is appropriate background screening for assigned positions completed prior to granting access?					
74	6.2.1 Are individuals who are authorized to bypass significant technical and operational controls screened prior to access and periodically thereafter? (OMB Circular A-130, III, FISCAM SP-4.1)	Review personnel security records for a minimum of two system administrators and security administrators to ensure that their records were screened prior to their access being granted.	Background screenings for assigned positions are completed prior to granting access and periodically thereafter.	P	A review of the records of four Nutria System users revealed that all four have undergone SF86 Public Trust investigations.	Interview with Personnel Security Officer; personnel records of four system users. These were: H. Snow, B. Crow, D. Glow, and R. Roe.

75	6.2.2 Are confidentiality or security agreements required for employees assigned to work with sensitive information? (FISCAM SP-4.1)	Verify personnel records of at least five system users to ensure that confidentiality agreements have been signed.	Nondisclosure agreements for all records of personnel reviewed are signed and maintained on file.	P	A review of five user files maintained by the office of primary responsibility revealed that all five users had signed confidentiality agreements.	Review of five personnel records maintained by the office of primary responsibility. These were: J. Doe, H. Snow, B. Crow, D. Glow, and R. Roe.
76	6.2.3 When controls cannot adequately protect the information, are individuals screened prior to access? (OMB Circular A-130, III)	Review records of background screening for at least three users with elevated system privileges and user access dates to determine if screening was concluded prior to their being granted access.	Individuals (i.e., system administration personnel) are screened prior to being granted access when controls cannot adequately protect the information.	P	All Nutria System users checked were found to have been screened prior to being granted access to the system.	Review of five personnel records and user access files pertaining to B. Crow, D. Glow, and R. Roe maintained by the office of primary responsibility.

owner that the team will play fair and does in fact seek the improvement of the system's security controls.

The test plan as developed and submitted to the host for approval must be constructed to permit its use in that same format for documenting the results of testing. That is to say the test team should initiate testing with the same test plan that the host has approved and should actually use it for the duration of the certification test. The plan should therefore provide adequate space for documenting the actual test results. For controls that meet standards the results must document how standards have been met, and for controls that do not meet standards, the results must record how or why they failed. An additional column for recording whether the control passed or failed allows the reader to quickly see which controls were lacking. When evidence of testing is required, the plan must specify the type of evidence that is necessary and the format for documenting it. This includes written procedures, screen shots, tool-generated output, etc. Normally, such documentary evidence is best presented as an appendix to the test report once it has been compiled. Also, the test plan must provide space for recording information about when individual or groups of controls are tested, who conducted the testing, where they were tested, and what components were involved.

The Role of the Host

The hosting organization is responsible for ensuring that certification testing is performed in a timely and efficient manner. This is done by making arrangements to have required personnel available to supplement the test team when they are needed. Requirements for personnel that have been documented in the test plan will be coordinated with the test director. Personnel necessary for interviews, for assisting with performing tests, for running test scripts, for demonstrating practices, and for escorting test team members must be identified in advance and personnel must be instructed about what is expected of them. The system owner should provide the test plan to all personnel involved to ensure they are aware of their roles in the test. The host should make a concerted effort to collect in advance all documentation required by the test team that has been specified in the test plan to avoid causing delays once the test team begins testing. The host is responsible for providing logistical support to the test team for the duration of testing. Network access, access to a phone and fax machine, reproduction support, and meeting rooms all fall into this category. Finally, access to facilities where testing will be conducted requires prior coordination between the test team and the hosting organization to ensure test team members can get to where they need to be without difficulty. However, testing should not require special access to be granted, and the host should ensure that normal access rules are followed in processing physical access for the team. Unescorted access should be arranged only when it is warranted and has been justified by the test team director. The host should also be involved in daily coordination meetings held while testing is under way.

Test Execution

Using the prepared and approved plan, the test team conducts the test. Results of testing should be immediately recorded into the plan as tests are performed one after the other. Deviation from conditions specified in the plan should be documented as they are observed. If specific components cannot be tested, this fact should be explained, and any exceptions should be clearly noted. Individuals involved in the testing should be specified by name, including those who provided assistance to the testing team.

It is useful to rank findings according to risk. This can be handled by including a column in the test results table that maps to risk assessment findings or by addressing it elsewhere in the results report such as an executive summary. The report should include charts to summarize findings by risk level and by control type. The process for ranking findings must be fully described in the results report too. Results should be ranked as either meeting standards (pass) or not meeting standards (fail). There is little value in ranking the degree to which a control passes or fails. Rather, the ranking should be based on the degree of risk attaching to the control.

When technical controls are tested it is advisable to have an authorized system user from the owning organization that has been approved by the host to enter commands to execute test scripts. This avoids having to grant the member of the certification test team access to the system, protects the owning organization against inadvertent errors, and protects the team members from claims that they have caused damage to the system. If this is not possible, a second team member along with someone from the owning organization should be present as witnesses. This helps achieve one of the main objectives of testing: the avoidance of disruption of normal operations. System crashes, accidental disclosures, and data integrity losses can be avoided or at least limited through thorough preparation and coordination. Knowledge of the system and of tools used will help achieve this objective. Resources and operations that are off-limits must be known to the team in advance. And system management must be aware of any plans to use social engineering, vulnerability scanning tools, or physical or logical penetration techniques. Assessing blame for problems can quickly deteriorate to a condition where testing can no longer be continued. To avoid this, escalation procedures must be established to provide a controlled process for identifying and resolving problems quickly and completely to allow testing to get back on track.

Conducting testing after normal hours of operation should be considered very carefully and must be well coordinated in advance. Testing during normal operating hours is preferable because the capability to respond to unexpected problems is greater, and the organization's staff is normally better prepared to respond to issues that may arise. They also have more depth and can better afford to accommodate testing during normal hours of operation, whereas after operating hours, testing can more easily lead to crippling disruptions of service. After-hours testing can also place additional stress on the staff of the owning organization, which may hamper its cooperation with the test team.

It is always a good idea to provide interim results to permit system owners to get a head start on remediating problems whenever possible. The certification testing team should conduct a briefing immediately following the conclusion of testing to provide system management/operations personnel an opportunity to know their security posture and to take immediate action. Additionally, if a "war-stopper" is encountered (e.g., evidence of criminal activity), testing should be halted until the issue is resolved. Should testing cause a system crash or other adverse effect on the production environment, all testing should be terminated immediately and should not be resumed until the situation has been stabilized, investigated, and resolved. The certification test team chief should immediately brief management on the incident.

Automated scanning tools can benefit the testing effort because they can detect evidence of the most currently identified vulnerabilities; also, they are easy to use, save time, and standardize output. The certification team must take sufficient time to ensure that vulnerability scanning results are integrated seamlessly into the test results report and are consistent with other report findings. Scan findings should map to individual controls requirements specified in the minimum security baseline and to the certification test plan. If this is not possible, then a new control requirement must be added. This will necessitate an update of the risk assessment to determine threat paring, the security (i.e., confidentiality, integrity, availability) impact and probability, and the risk factor. Once this has been done the results of the scan can be clearly documented in the plan of action and milestones and in the security plan.

There are normally controls that the system owner will identify in advance as being not in place for any number of reasons. It is not necessary to conduct testing on controls of this nature. There is no need to prove to the system owner that controls are really and truly not in place; he or she already knows this, and the methodology is not designed to qualitatively measure how well or how poorly controls have been implemented. However, these preidentified, failing controls must be documented in the test results report, for this report will serve as the basis for the remediation plan, and it needs to include all controls weaknesses, whether they have undergone testing or not.

As a general principle, the scope of certification testing should include all controls that are defined in the system security plan. Of course, this assumes that all controls that are necessary for the system have been documented in the security plan. If that is not the case, additional controls found in the risk assessment need to be tested even though they are not documented in the security plan. However, as stated previously, there is little need to test controls that the system owner has reported as not being in place. Controls of this nature are not tested, permitting more time to be spent on testing other system controls that actually need testing. Although they will not undergo testing, controls that have not been implemented still need to be recorded in the certification test results report as failing, so that they can be included in the remediation plan.

Documenting Test Results

Once certification testing has been completed, the test team should collectively record the results of testing. This should be done by completing the previously submitted and approved test plan. Raw data collected during testing should be transformed into documented test results immediately following the conclusion of testing while it is still fresh and while test team members are still available. The team should coordinate closely to compare observations and validate their individual findings. Scan results should be reviewed and integrated into the test results by the responsible test member. According to the test plan, each control should be annotated as either pass or fail, the actual findings recorded in detail, and sources and processes used to validate the status of the control. A sample certification test results matrix is provided in Appendix P.

The test results report should include an additional section that describes who conducted testing (i.e., the names of team members); who assisted in testing (from the hosting organization); where testing was conducted (an overview of locations, platforms, components, and subsystems included in the scope of testing); a summary of the process for conducting testing; and starting and ending times of the test. Additionally, the test results report should detail any case where deviations from the test plan took place. For instance, if a particular server could not be tested or a procedure could not be demonstrated, this should be documented with a recommendation that follow-up testing be conducted. In this case, if the functionality of a control cannot be verified, it must be recorded as a failure. Testing may also reveal that a listed control is not applicable to the system or that there are other controls not in the test plan that are required to secure the system. These deviations to the test plan should be recorded, and recommendations for additional controls should be emphasized.

Also, the test results report should rank test results (i.e., prioritize the significance of each control that failed to meet standards) and describe the process for ranking weaknesses found. This is most effective when based on risk assessment findings, rather than on the subjective view of the test team. The report should be written so as to map findings to specific risks previously identified in the risk assessment report, using the same ranking definitions. The report also needs to summarize, perhaps in an executive summary, a high-level view of testing results. This provides a snapshot of areas of concern, the most significant findings, and, for benchmarking purposes, the security of the system relative to other like systems, connected systems, or similar organizations.

Summary

Certification testing is the crown jewel of the certification and accreditation process. Because of its importance in the overall certification and accreditation program, certification testing must be well planned, conducted by knowledgeable professionals, and well documented. The certification test determines if all technical and nontechnical controls designed to protect the system have been implemented and meet a predetermined set of standards. Certification testing identifies weaknesses in a system's controls from an objective point of view and serves as the basis for remediation efforts. The certification test also serves as a quality control process to validate the results of other security processes such as the security plan, risk assessment, and contingency plan. Most important, certification testing serves as the basis for the decision by the accrediting official to authorize or not authorize the system. The documented results of the certification test along with the recommendations of the certifying agent provide the accrediting authority assurance of the effectiveness of security controls and all other information that he or she needs to make this decision.

Chapter 14

Remediation Planning

Certification and accreditation is more than merely an exercise in documenting security controls and assessing security weaknesses. The purpose of an effective certification and accreditation program is to ensure that sensitive information resources are being protected and to point out shortfalls when they are not. As stated earlier, certification is an assessment exercise rather than a mitigation activity. However, one must understand that certification does not stand alone and that mitigation of risks is essential to the success of the entire certification and accreditation process. What is needed following assessment is a plan for mitigation of risks. A risk remediation plan is necessary to provide a consolidated, easy-to-use road map for correcting security weaknesses. Also known as a plan of action and milestones (POA&M), risk mitigation plan, remediation plan, or system risk management plan, the risk remediation plan provides a source document for tracking the correction of deficiencies and improving a system's security. The development of a risk remediation plan assumes that an assessment has been completed, at least temporarily, and that deficiencies in security controls have been adequately documented.

There are two perspectives to be taken in addressing remediation plans: that of the system owner who is only concerned in mitigating risks to one system, and that of the approving authority or upper management, who must be concerned about risk to multiple systems. To aid the system owner in his or her task of mitigating risks, the risk remediation plan must classify corrective action by risk level and resources required. This allows him or her to focus remediation efforts first on those risks that are the most severe and second on those that can be fixed with relatively little effort ("low-hanging fruit"). This narrow perspective of these two factors fully supports the needs of the system owner who normally does not have to be concerned with competition between systems for resources.

Contrast this with the perspective of the executive manager who is responsible for corrective actions for many systems across the entire organization, all of which compete for resources necessary to get well. Because of this, upper-level managers must have an additional qualifier that tells them the relative importance of systems or criticality (see Chapter 7). If managers know that the accounts receivable system is more critical than the property inventory system, then they can emphasize the mitigation effort toward the more critical system, giving it priority for resources. Therefore, each risk remediation plan should reflect the criticality of the system to permit management of the risk mitigation effort at a high level across multiple systems. A simple high, medium, or low categorization is sufficient for this purpose or perhaps a binary approach where a system is critical or it is not.

Applicability of the Remediation Plan

It is indeed a rare occasion when at the conclusion of a certification a system is found to have no security weaknesses. Normally, there are between 10 and 50 issues to be resolved, ranging from the severe (malicious software found to be present) to the relatively mundane (time that a visitor departed the server room not recorded in the visitor log). This being the case, practically every system then needs a risk remediation plan to correct these weaknesses.

Responsibility for the Plan

System owners have ultimate responsibility for mitigating risks to their systems and must plan for the correction of deficiencies in security controls. This is achieved by developing a usable plan that guides implementation of new controls or improvement of existing controls over time. Although many others may use the plan to guide corrective action or monitor progress in improving system security, system owners need to initially develop and maintain ownership of the plan. Often system owners will delegate this responsibility to the ISSO or another worker, and this is fine so long as system owners understand that they are the official ultimately accountable for implementing corrective action to improve the security of the system.

Whoever is assigned responsibility for maintaining the risk remediation plan must be careful not to update the plan based on inaccurate or incomplete information. He or she should accept updated information only from bona fide sources, preferably only from the individual assigned responsibility for implementing the corrective action, always being sure that the individual is held accountable for the status information provided. And, the system owner as owner of the mitigation effort must be sure to hold the risk remediation plan gatekeeper accountable as well.

Risk Remediation Plan Scope

The risk remediation plan should include all vulnerabilities that have been identified during certification testing of the system. Additionally, other weaknesses that have been identified from other sources (i.e., financial audit, IG inspection, privacy impact assessment, prior material weaknesses that relate to the system) should also be included in the plan. It should provide a comprehensive list of all vulnerabilities irrespective of vulnerability, threat, or safeguard category or risk level. Management controls should be included alongside technical controls alongside operational controls. Vulnerabilities ranked as high risk should be identified along with those ranked lower. The primary principle is that they all are included in a single plan to make corrective action easier to manage. They may vary, however, in the level of detail offered for each. For instance, it may be worthwhile to group types of vulnerabilities together if it makes them easier to manage. Low-severity vulnerabilities identified during a vulnerability scan may be easier to manage as a single risk remediation plan issue as long as details relating to their description and remediation are readily available, preferably as an attachment to the certification test. Risks that have been or are likely to be accepted by the approving authority should also be included in the risk remediation plan so that they can be tracked.

Plan Format

The risk remediation plan at a minimum must identify a weakness, a fix, a milestone, and a responsible person for each identified risk to the system. Though one could have a plan without them, without these four elements the plan would not identify what the problem to be solved is, how the problem can be solved, who will solve it, and the deadline for solving the problem. These are the essential data fields and are depicted in Table 14.1. Additional information, while not essential, can make the plan a more useful tool. When determining what information should be included

Table 14.1   Remediation Plan Contents

ID	Weakness	POC	Resources Required	Scheduled Completion Date	Milestones with Completion Dates	Status	Comments	Risk Ranking
1	1.2.3 Log-ons are cached on security-sensitive servers.	J. Doe	24 man-hours		Prevent log-ons from being cached on sensitive servers.	Ongoing		Low
2	2.1.5 Security alerts and security incidents are not analyzed and remedial actions are not taken. (FISCAM SP 3-4, NIST SP 800-18)	G. Cross	8 man-hours	5/30/2004	Develop a process for analyzing alerts and security incidents and for taking appropriate remedial action.	Ongoing		Moderate
4	6.1.3 Sensitive functions are not divided among different individuals. (OMB Circular A-130, III; FISCAM SD-1; NIST SP 800-18)	G. Cross	4 man-hours	9/30/2004	Develop a process for ensuring that sensitive functions are divided between different individuals.	Completed	Procedure # 27-A finalized on 4/15/2004	Low

#	Finding		Effort	Date	Corrective Action	Status	Comments	Risk
7	10.1.4 The system boot time is not set to zero seconds.	J. Doe	8 man-hours	9/30/2004	Set system boot time to zero seconds.	Ongoing		Low
8	15.1.7 Password complexity has not been enabled.	J. Doe	2 man-hours	9/30/2004	Modify the system to only accept passwords that contain case-sensitive alphanumeric and special characters.	Completed	System modified to enforce password complexity on 4/11/2004	Low
9	16.1.3 Access to security software is not restricted to security administrators. (FISCAM AC-3.2)	J. Doe	4 man-hours	5/30/2004	Restrict access to security software to security administrators only.	Completed	System modified on 4/12/2004 to limit access to security administrators	Moderate
10	17.1.1 The audit trail does not provide a trace of user actions. (NIST SP 800-18)	J. Doe	4 man-hours	4/30/2004	Modify audit trail to ensure that provides a trace of user log-ons, log-offs, password changes, and file deletions.	Completed	Audit trail modified to record recommended events on 4/12/2004	High

in the plan, do not lose sight of the requirement for the plan to be usable. Following is a discussion of the types of information that should be included in the risk remediation plan.

- *Cross-Reference Numbering*: A simple cross-reference numbering system helps identify the plan entry and serves as a sort of shorthand to facilitate identification. Ideally, this number would map to entries in the risk assessment, security testing, and in the security plan. A reference can be included along with each weakness to answer the question of why there is a vulnerability. Inclusion of a NIST SP 800-26, 800-53, FISCAM, ISO 17799, etc., controls cross-reference numbers, for example or perhaps an organization policy or procedure number provides a basis for better understanding both the vulnerability and the corrective action. The responsibility column can be expanded to record both the primary and secondary players as well as both direct and indirect responsibilities. For example, the plan can specify that the system owner will be responsible for reviewing the facility access list (a direct responsibility), while the facility manager (who is only indirectly related to system operations) will be responsible for updating the access list once he or she receives an update from the system owner.
- *Risk Ranking*: It is helpful if the risk ranking for each weakness is also included for each weakness listed in the plan so that the relative need for corrective action can be readily noted. Additionally, sorting the risk remediation plan by risk further aids in the effort to emphasize those corrective actions that have the greatest need for attention. The ranking reflected in the risk remediation plan is obtained from the risk assessment (Chapter 11). The ranking must be specific to the system, must be relative to the nature of the system depending on its sensitivity and criticality, and must not be established simply on the basis of a generic template. One challenge for the security manager is to determine the risk ranking of weaknesses that are added to the remediation plan from external audits, reviews, and inspections. To achieve this, the weakness should be mapped to the control to which it is most closely associated and should assume the risk ranking of that control.
- *Corrective Actions*: Corrective actions can be broken down into more detailed subtasks that have their own responsible individuals and milestones. This will facilitate completion of mitigation activities by showing dependencies and fixing responsibility more clearly. Resources necessary for implementing corrective actions can also be identified in the plan to help estimate costs and manpower. Costs to purchase or license software, buy hardware,

and the man-hours required for their implementation and operation or to develop policies, plans, and procedures can be detailed in this resources column. Finally, the plan should provide space to record the status of corrective action, which allows the document to be current.

■ *Responsibility for Corrective Action*: The risk remediation plan should be very specific when it comes to responsibilities for corrective action. Rather than identifying an organization, the plan should state the name of an individual. And a name is better than just entering a generic position title or job title. It will be easier to determine who has responsibility for corrective action if you can read "Joe, the system administrator" rather than simply "system administrator." It is much easier to hold people accountable if you identify them by name because by nature individuals are more responsive if they are identified in the plan by name. In fact, the first fight in coordinating the plan will be defending the decision to choose particular individuals as responsible for corrective actions specified in the plan. Early on it may be difficult to identify a specific person for each task or milestone, but that should be the end goal. As the plan matures with use, these identities should become known and should be documented into the plan.

■ *Milestone Dates*: Likewise, milestone dates may be difficult to project in the initial version of the plan. However, as the plan matures, milestone dates should become increasingly more specific and realistic. From "within the next six months" should evolve into "no later than June 30th." Once again, it is easier to keep mitigation on schedule when precise dates are established. Measuring success is easier with fixed dates as well. The CISO should provide basic guidance on milestone dates. For instance, high-risk weaknesses have to be corrected within 30 days, those ranked as moderate in 60 days, and low risks to be completed within 90 days or when resources are available. Although the CISO can provide a framework for corrective action dates such as these, it should always be the system owner who decides the actual milestone date. This is because the system owner has the best idea of resources available, knowledge of competing priorities, knowledge of the system, and primary accountability for the security of the system. Within reason, the system owner should be given free reign to determine when the corrective action must be completed, but the CISO must review each system-level plan to ensure that dates entered are realistic and are consistent with the risk the weakness poses. The CISO should be prepared to slap the hands of any system owner who approves a milestone five years in the future.

These are the primary columns that need to be included in the risk remediation plan. Because of the usefulness of sorting each of these data fields, the use of a spreadsheet tool is ideal. A sample risk remediation plan is provided in Appendix Q.

Using the Plan

Like the security plan, the risk remediation plan is a living document. It needs to be used and updated to reflect the current status of the mitigation effort as it evolves. It should serve as the primary tool in the facilitation of correction of security weaknesses as well as for management oversight. The plan should also serve as a record of action taken. Once a weakness has been addressed and corrective action has been completed, the plan needs to be updated to record this activity and the action should be marked as completed. However, it should always remain a part of the plan and not be removed when completed. By keeping both open and closed issues in the plan this more effectively allows measurement of progress toward a goal. This is particularly true with significant vulnerabilities that require subdivision into multiple tasks and activities with varying kinds and degrees of resources involved. In this case the plan should show corrected and pending tasks together. Also, risks that management chooses to accept rather than correct should remain in the plan to allow the plan to function as a clearinghouse document for addressing all risks to the system. If it is demonstrated that the costs of mitigating a risk do not warrant correction, then the plan is the place to document this acceptance (as well as in other more formal documentation, such as the accreditation letter). This allows management to manage risks using a common plan.

In general, this discussion has concentrated on system-level remediation plans that are used to measure progress of corrective action for an individual system. These should not be confused with program-level remediation plans that document weaknesses and corrective actions applicable to the entire enterprise. However, when taken together, system-level plans of action and milestones also document the security of the entire enterprise. To do this, a tool for managing collected remediation plans is necessary so as to provide a means of performing trend analysis to identify common controls and other solutions that apply to multiple systems. When selecting tools to perform this function, do not forget to address access controls and auditing controls to ensure the integrity of the information. Only system owners or their designated ISSOs should have the capability of adding, updating, or inactivating remediation plan data for their own systems. To maintain a record of all actions related to an entry, entries for which corrective action is complete should never be deleted. Instead they should be deactivated, so that they are still available for historical purposes. Although the security manager should have access to this remediation plan data, it should be limited to view access only.

When to Create the Plan

Because it is so important to risk mitigation efforts, consideration should be given to creating a risk remediation plan whenever vulnerabilities are first identified, irrespective of the status of other certification and accreditation documentation. Naturally, the plan is prepared following a certification test after weaknesses have been verified. However, to support management needs for elevating the visibility of the mitigation effort, the plan can be prepared based on the results of a minimum security baseline assessment, a risk assessment, a vulnerability scan, development of a security plan, upon receipt of results of an audit or inspection, or following an incident where new weaknesses become known. In cases where a risk remediation plan already exists for the system, additional vulnerabilities identified on these occasions should be appended into the existing remediation plan to allow a central repository for corrective action information. This avoids the confusing problem of having multiple remediation plans pertaining to a single system. The sooner corrective action is initiated, the sooner the security of the system will begin to improve. Early development of the risk remediation plan supports this goal.

The plan is a highly valuable tool in mitigating weaknesses in a system's security controls. It should be the focal point of regular, periodic meetings in which progress toward correcting vulnerabilities is evaluated and measured. The plan should be in a continuous state of update, refinement, and completion. Feedback from those involved in executing the plan must be integrated into the plan in a controlled manner. A keeper of the plan should be appointed to be solely responsible for approving additions and updates, and for enforcement of version control (with an iron hand). The plan will not only change as tasks are completed, but also tasks will lead to identification of other tasks and subtasks that will need their own milestones, resources, and responsible points of contact. Additionally, it is doubtful that the system will remain static throughout the risk mitigation period, so the system owner will need to be prepared to update the plan to include addressing impacts stemming from changes to the system's environment, from security incidents, and from results from periodic vulnerability scans. Each of these will probably impact ongoing mitigation efforts and the plan must document these impacts in measurable tasks.

To be useful the plan must be logically organized, should resist excessive detail, and must provide the information necessary to track actions through to their completion. It should not be forgotten that the plan is a management document and its primary purpose is to track the status of corrective action. Anything falling short of this objective is inadequate and anything going beyond this goal is excessive and unnecessary. The plan should comprise high-level summary information that links to more specific data as necessary. It is possible for recommended corrective actions to be overly detailed and therefore too restrictive. The manager should be open to and should in fact seek solutions that best suit his or her system's environment rather than unthinkingly accepting courses of action recommended by outsiders. Continued reliance on solutions that have always been used and are thought to be time tested could result in unnecessary costs and time and might turn out to be overkill. The corrective action should be written to give the system owner and his or her staff some latitude in identifying novel solutions that fit a precise need.

In all likelihood the risk remediation plan will never be entirely completed. Because of ever-changing operating conditions, security needs are identified, changed, expanded, or eliminated in a continuing cycle. The system owner will find that he or she will probably never have sufficient resources to mitigate all the risks that are identified. The risks that remain after safeguards have been implemented may be too expensive to correct or corrective action may be impractical given the current status or nature of the system. Though they cannot be mitigated, they must still be addressed, and the risk remediation plan is the mechanism for doing this. The plan documents these residual risks for the approving authority's acceptance and approval.

The risk remediation plan should have a close relationship with the organization's capital planning process. The resources identified in the plan should be fully integrated into the planning, programming, and budgeting system. Entries in the organization's budget request that are based on the risk remediation plan are particularly well documented and have an increased chance of being supported. Labor hours projected in the plan can be consolidated and serve to scope projects for budgeting purposes.

The organization's audit function will without doubt be a key user of the risk remediation plan because it can play a role in assessing firsthand the status of corrective action. As an independent entity, an auditor can assess risk remediation plan activities to see that they are complete and effective, and to validate that due diligence has been performed.

The ISSO looks to risk remediation plan with the aim of improving system security. System owners use it to manage the correction of deficiencies so that their system is as secure as possible. Organization management relies on the plan to prove that they have exercised due diligence. The organization information technology security manager makes use of the plan as one of many to determine trends, to identify resource requirements, to consolidate mitigation efforts organizationwide, and to monitor the status of corrective action on a broad base to establish and manage compliance with security standards. The organization information technology staff relies on the remediation plan to integrate corrective actions into the strategic information technology plan. And the approving authority uses the plan to gain assurance that he or she is accepting no more risk than is absolutely necessary.

The costs identified in the plan only have to be detailed enough to allow planning for budgeting and resourcing requirements. Normally, measuring costs by rough order of magnitude (in tens of man-hours and in thousands of dollars) offers sufficient precision. Of course, as corrective actions are refined, costs can be more precisely defined as necessary. Consultants are often a good source for providing costing information because they have a good perspective on resource costs based on their experience in implementing corrective actions across many types of organizations.

Risk Mitigation Meetings

Periodic meetings where the risk remediation plan serves as the focal point need to be held frequently enough to maintain visibility of the mitigation effort. Systems with substantial weaknesses either in severity or number of corrective actions should meet perhaps weekly until the most significant weaknesses are mitigated fully or in part. Less significant systems or those with only minor issues to resolve need not meet as frequently or with decreasing frequency as progress is made. It is important, at least in the beginning, to go through each weakness and corrective action in the plan to ensure it is understood and to establish a baseline for follow-on activities. If the weakness is unclear, a call for additional information should be channeled to the appropriate source (for example, the certifying agent for weaknesses and the ISSO or system administrator for corrective actions). This exercise also builds a team mentality toward problem solving and provides a forum for further specific corrective actions necessary, as well as milestones, schedules, resources, and priorities. This meeting should be chaired by the system owner to give emphasis to its importance and should be attended by all those who have responsibility for the corrective actions being discussed. It is obvious that this should be distributed more broadly than the ISSO or else it would be a very small meeting.

Additionally, the CISO should conduct periodic meetings with elements of the organization to review progress in mitigating risks. This can be with individuals or groups of system owners according to mission needs, and risk remediation plans should be the focus of such meetings.

Summary

You've heard it said, "Don't fix what ain't broke." The goal of certification and accreditation is to identify what's "broke" and to ensure that corrective action to fix what is "broke" is applied where needed. The risk remediation plan identifies what is broken and, moreover, it provides a road map for correcting identified weaknesses in a logical and cost-effective way. The risk remediation plan along with the accreditation letter (with which it goes hand in hand) is one of the two most important documents generated by the certification and accreditation effort. Although the accreditation letter documents the approving authority's authorization for the system to process and his or her acceptance of residual risks, the risk remediation plan documents the plan for mitigating these risks to the minimum extent possible. Both of these documents must be totally synchronized.

Assessment of security controls is an important part of the certification and accreditation methodology, but assessment must be followed by remediation of any identified vulnerabilities. This ensures that system security is improved sufficiently to meet minimum standards applicable to the system. It provides a means of tracking the status of corrective action to ensure that these minimum standards are met and establishes a baseline from which to monitor the system to ensure minimum standards *continue* to be met. Without mitigation the organization is caught in an endless loop of assessing without ever getting around to solving security problems. Therefore, the entire certification and accreditation methodology must point toward the risk mitigation process with an aim toward improving security. The risk remediation plan is ideally suited to meet this need and is the capstone of the certification and accreditation methodology.

Chapter 15

Essential Certification and Accreditation Documentation

What sort of documentation should be included in the certification package? The answer is driven by the definition of what information is required by the approving authority to make an informed decision about the security of the system. The list of major documents required for inclusion in the certification package varies by methodology. As shown in Table 15.1, several formal certification and accreditation methodologies have lengthy lists that require a multitude of documentation to substantiate that security has been adequately implemented. The documentation required by these methodologies records the results of the certification process but also includes extensive evidence of implemented controls if not the actual controls themselves. The logical question that results is, What form of proof is necessary to substantiate to the approving authority that controls are adequate? And is an assessment report that documents and provides evidence of the existence of a control sufficient? For example, does the approving authority need to see the configuration management plan for the system as part of the certification and accreditation package to be convinced, or is it sufficient to have an independent certifier review the plan and attest that it exists and that it meets requirements? The answer lies in the definition of the purpose of certification. Certification is an assessment exercise and not a remediation exercise. Certification is

Table 15.1   DITSCAP and NIACAP Documentation

Example of DITSCAP Documentation	Example of NIACAP Documentation
■ Mission Need Statement ■ System Security Authorization Agreement (SSAA) ■ System Architecture Analysis ■ Software Design Analysis ■ Network Connection Rule Compliance Analysis ■ Integrity Analysis of Integrated Products ■ Life-Cycle Management Analysis ■ Vulnerability Assessment ■ Security Test and Evaluation ■ Penetration Test Results ■ TEMPEST and Red-Black Verification ■ COMSEC Compliance Validation ■ System Management Analysis ■ Site Accreditation Survey ■ Contingency Plan Evaluation ■ Risk-Based Management Review ■ Certification Authority's Recommendations ■ Accreditation Decision	■ System Security Authorization Agreement (SSAA) ■ Security Test and Evaluation (ST&E) ■ Penetration Testing Results ■ TEMPEST and Red-Black Verification ■ Communication Security (COMSEC) Compliance Validation ■ System Management Analysis ■ Site Evaluation ■ Contingency Plan Evaluation ■ Risk Management Review ■ System Certification Statement ■ Authorization to Operate

designed to assess whether the controls implemented to protect a given system meet a set of predefined requirements. Certification is not intended to assess and to remediate weaknesses found during the assessment. This is the reason that many certification programs fail; they lose sight of what they are intended to do.

So, getting back to the original question of what documentation needs to be included in the certification package, one must decide how much evidence the approving authority needs. NIST SP 800-37 has refined the contents of the certification to the system security plan, the risk assessment report, the security test and evaluation report, the plan of action and milestones, and the certification statement. By comparison, this was quite a departure from the list associated with most previous methodologies. But this revision refocused requirements for documentation to match the purpose of the effort — to assess controls. By reducing the amount of documentation to five primary documents, requirements increased for the system security plan and the certification test to be more descriptive and complete based on solid evidentiary and testing requirements for each control. To eliminate the need for inclusion of a technical architecture document, the security plan's system description and environment had to be more complete. To remove the disaster recovery plan from the package necessitated detailed findings in the certification test report and system security plan on the contents and effectiveness of various aspects addressed in the plan (i.e., identification of a recovery strategy, specification of an alternate processing site, documentation of critical resources required for recovery, etc.). And if actual procedures were not to be included as proof of their existence, then the certification test needed to specifically relate the extent to which procedures supporting each NIST SP 800-18 topic have been prepared, with any weaknesses being documented in the plan of action and milestones.

The approving authority is responsible for making the decision regarding the operation of the system. As such, he or she can require that any and all controls be fully implemented before processing is authorized. The approving authority can decide to accredit the system either based on direct observation and proof that required controls have been implemented (a time-consuming process) or based on an assessment that documents the status of controls. The decision on what belongs in the certification package should take into consideration the nature of the role of the approving authority. One should not expect the approving authority to be or to become a security expert as part of his or her accreditation responsibilities. Rather, the objective should be on the certifying agent to prepare and present reliable and objective evidence as to the existence of controls, with emphasis on the responsibility of the certifying agent, who is (or should be) an expert in information technology security and who holds a trusted position as an independent evaluator of the system.

Normally the approving authority is a member of the executive leadership of the organization and for him or her, time is a luxury. Because time is at such a premium, the certification should be complete but should also be summarized to facilitate ready understanding of security issues that affect the decision to accredit the system. For instance, the approving authority needs to be aware of the weaknesses in security controls for the system. However, this does not mean that the approving authority needs to be informed of each buffer overflow vulnerability detected. Instead, vulnerabilities should be summarized to the extent that the approving authority knows that technical vulnerabilities in database controls exist. Corrective actions proposed should also be presented in summarized fashion. On the other hand, the approving authority should be able to acknowledge specifically what residual risks he or she needs to accept to accredit the system.

The purpose of certification and accreditation documentation is to record the security of the information technology system and to present information to the approving authority to provide a basis to make an informed decision on the operation of the system. Further, it provides a historical record for auditing purposes and documents that management has exercised its due diligence responsibilities. The certification and accreditation package records what activities were performed in the process of certifying and accrediting the system, when they were performed, who performed them, the purpose for which they were performed, and the results of the certification and accreditation activities. The certification and accreditation documentation must record all findings, vulnerabilities, requirements, and recommendations relating to the security of the system that result from certification and accreditation activities.

Authority

Under the authority of senior leadership, the CISO, acting in his or her capacity as certification and accreditation program manager, should be the individual granted the authority to define minimum requirements for the contents of certification packages. This decision should not be left to approving authorities or business unit managers because of the potential for other officials to add requirements without understanding the need to keep the certification and accreditation process clean and simple. The CISO must be on guard for violations of this nature, knowing full well that the more things are added to the certification process the greater the likelihood that nothing will ever get certified. Therefore, the CISO should establish a process for spot-checking certification packages for compliance with program requirements. Certification package guidance should be available in the organization's policy library where it can be easily accessed by system owners initiating certification activities. This guidance may be posted on the organization's information technology security Web site and could include templates for all documents that have to be included in the package along with samples to assist in developing the documents. The most current template versions should be available to avoid the wrath of a system owner who has just completed his or her certification package using out-of-date templates.

Certification Package Contents

So, to be properly informed, the approving authority normally needs only documentation that describes the system and its environment, that identifies the controls that are required to protect the system, and that gives the status of those controls. The security plan provides that information.

Table 15.2   Certification Package Contents

- System Security Plan
- Risk Assessment (which includes a Minimum Security Baseline Assessment)
- Certification Test Plan and Results Report
- Remediation Plan
- Certification Statement

The approving authority must be made aware of the assets that need to be protected, the threats to those assets, the vulnerabilities in controls implemented to protect system resources, and necessary safeguards to reduce risks to the system and its operations. A risk assessment is designed to provide such information. The approving authority must have a record of the results of testing of security controls to ensure that they perform as required, all functions of the certification test, and an accompanying certification statement. Finally, the approving authority must also have information that describes what must be done to address weaknesses in security controls. This information requirement is satisfied by a remediation plan or plan of action and milestones. Table 15.2 depicts the essential documentation that should be included in the certification and accreditation package.

Excluded Documentation

Care must be taken to avoid making the certification and accreditation process a paperwork exercise. This can be avoided by carefully scrutinizing what should be excluded from the package. Normally, there is a wide variety of documentation that should be prepared for the development or operation of an information technology system. Although it may be tempting, it is neither practical nor necessary to include much of it in the certification package. A minimalist point of view should be taken when deciding what documentation should be included in the package. This perspective rules out a substantial amount of documentation that, although necessary and worthwhile for the operation of the system, is not required to provide assurance of the security of the system and does not belong in the certification package. Its inclusion can merely result in delays in submission of the package for the period that it takes to accumulate the superfluous information. This documentation can be omitted from the package because the documents that are included in the package should be written so as to clearly report on the security posture rather than to prove the security posture. Following this line of thinking, procedures, life-cycle methodologies, contingency plans, emergency plans, configuration management plans, service-level agreements, appointment orders, security clauses of governing contracts, audit reports, hardware/software documentation, templates and forms, maintenance records, access lists, notification lists, and interconnection agreements generally do not belong in the package. Exceptions should possibly be considered in the case of a system with a higher level of sensitivity or criticality, which is being certified at a higher level of scrutiny. But even in such cases as this, the inclusion of additional documentation in the certification package should be based on written guidance from the CISO, which specifies circumstances warranting these exceptions and which defines specifically what supplemental documentation is to be included.

The Certification Statement

The certification statement is prepared by the certifying agent to provide a summary document that assures the authorizing authority that the system has been properly certified. The statement summarizes activities involved in the certification process and documents at a high level findings, recommendations for remediation, and identification of residual risks. The essential elements of the certification statement should include the following:

- The identification of the system being certified
- The purpose of the certification and why it was performed
- The inclusive dates of certification testing
- The locations involved in testing
- Organizations involved in the certification (i.e., owning business units)
- The identity of the team conducting the certification and its authority for performing the certification
- The operating status of the system (in development, in operation)
- Reference to primary source documents by name and with date (i.e., security plan, risk assessment)
- The certification level at which the certification was performed
- A summary of weaknesses found in security controls
- A summary of recommendations for corrective actions
- Specific residual risks for which acceptance is recommended

Transmittal Letter

Once the package has been constructed, a concise memorandum should be prepared for transmittal of the package to the accrediting authority.

This document will in very brief terms describe why the package has been prepared, what it contains, and what is to be done with it. This document should state what action is to be taken, state who is responsible for taking the action, and give a deadline for taking action. This transmittal memo ties the certification together and establishes requirements for its handling. An example of a transmittal letter is presented in Table 15.3.

Administration

Although the original of the certification package is submitted to the accrediting authority for review and approval, a copy must be retained by the system owner. This copy should be held until the original has been approved and returned by the authorizing official. The package will be maintained until it is replaced by an updated package whenever an update is required (either periodically or after changes to the system). Normally, both hard-copy and electronic versions of the package need to be maintained to facilitate its update when required. Final versions of all files should be burned onto a CD and stored securely to ensure the unalterable copy is maintained. The package must be labeled according to the sensitivity of information it contains — usually quite sensitive because it describes in detail vulnerabilities in system controls. Hence, the documentation should be securely handled and stored to prevent unauthorized disclosure of any sensitive information it contains. The CISO should consider establishing a central repository for all certification and accreditation documentation. This will allow him or her to not only maintain a record copy for ease of access but also use the repository as a knowledge base for other system owners who may benefit from using approved documents as examples for developing documentation for their own systems.

Summary

The certification and accreditation package is designed to provide to the authorizing official necessary information to make an informed decision regarding the secure operation of the system. The purpose of the package is to inform, not to overwhelm. Therefore, it should contain only the documentation necessary to allow this senior management official to decide if the system should be allowed to operate or to continue to operate. If a package is properly prepared, it will contain the system security plan, risk assessment, certification test report, remediation plan, and certification statement.

Table 15.3 Example Transmittal Memo

Subject:	Security Certification and Accreditation of the Nutria System
From:	Chief Information Technology Security Officer
To:	Ron Noteworthy
	System Owner — Nutria System
	Finance and Accounting Office

Under my direction, a team of security analysts has completed a certification review of the Nutria System in accordance with Office of Management and Budget Circular A-130, Appendix III; *Security of Federal Automated Information Resources*; applicable National Institute for Standards and Technology (NIST) guidelines; and the XYZ Agency Certification and Accreditation Program.

The results of the security certification effort and supporting evidence for accrediting the system are provided in the attached Nutria System certification package. Please review the contents of this certification package, which includes a system security plan, minimum security baseline assessment, risk assessment report, security test and evaluation (ST&E) results report, plan of action and milestones, and certification statement. Comments and questions regarding these reports should be returned to Bill Inkwell, in the office of the Chief Information Security Officer. Please note that your review need only address findings and content of the deliverables. Completion of corrective actions stipulated in the certification package is not required at this time. However, monitoring of the status of necessary corrective actions will begin upon notification that the system has been authorized for operation. Please provide comments to the attached deliverables within five business days. If we do not receive comments by April 19, 2003, we will assume you concur and will generate a final certification package for the system.

Following review of the certification package, I request that you coordinate with the responsible authorizing official for approval and signature of the attached accreditation memo to accredit the system for continued operation. This authorization serves as the authorizing official's formal declaration regarding the level of implementation of security controls and the need for any additional controls to ensure that the system is adequately protected. Upon approval, a copy of the signed accreditation memo should be returned to Enterprise IT Security.

Attachment: Nutria System Certification Package

Chapter 16

Documenting the Accreditation Decision

The culminating event in the certification and accreditation process is accreditation, or the approval by a senior management official for the system to process. The act of signing an accreditation letter for the system is the physical substantiation of upper-level management involvement in assuring the security of the system. The accreditation letter fixes responsibility for the operation of the system. It is the end link in the chain of accountability.

By requiring a signature, management involvement at least to this extent must occur. Authorizing officials may be totally removed from the certification and accreditation process up to this time, but they are indispensable in this, the final step in the process. This is a function that authorizing officials should never delegate to someone else. With his or her signature, the approving authority indicates that he or she has considered the risks to operating the system and has decided to allow the system to begin processing or to continue processing. To ensure that the security of the system is given thoughtful consideration by the approving authority and to provide assurance that the approving authority is aware of risks to system processing, ample documentation in the form of the certification and accreditation package accompanies the accreditation letter. I suppose that there might be an approving authority out there somewhere that would sign an accreditation letter without having had the system first certified. However, this would not only be risky but also would not meet the requirements for exercising due care. From another angle, however, this is exactly what happens every day when systems go into production or continue to operate without a certification and accreditation process being implemented. In such cases responsibility for security is not fixed except at the highest level of the organization. Of course, we attempt to cushion the impact of not assigning security accountability with talk that "security is everyone's responsibility." However, such evasion does little to really improve security.

The Accrediting Authority

Accreditation establishes accountability for system operation and is a function of ownership of the system. The accrediting authority, while not being the actual, direct owner of the system, owns the business process that the system supports and owns the resources on which the system derives its sustenance. Being in the ownership chain while being removed from the day-to-day operations of the system puts the approving authority in a good position to oversee the security of the system from a higher perspective in the context of the broader mission of the organization. The approving authority should be able to see the "big picture." Because the approving authority controls the "purse strings" he or she holds a commanding position with respect to the manner in which risks will be mitigated or accepted.

Timing

Authorization to process should occur during the implementation phase of the system's life cycle. Any system currently in development should not be allowed to go into production until it has been accredited on the basis of certification of its security posture. For legacy systems the accreditation decision should be a priority with emphasis being given to the most critical systems first.

The Accreditation Letter

The accreditation letter must be clearly and carefully worded to reflect the desires of the approving authority with respect to security of the system. It should state the authority of the individual to accredit the system or should specify who appointed him or her to that position. It should provide a background of the certification and accreditation process on which the accreditation decision is being made (i.e., who performed it, over what period of time, the locations, for what purpose, using what methodology, and over what resources). The statement should declare its purpose — to document management's decision to permit the system to process in a stated security environment. It needs to specify the duration of the authorization — not normally more than three years. It is essential that the statement document the specific risks that are being accepted as part of the accreditation, either in the document itself or in an attached or associated document like a risk mediation plan. If the approving authority establishes conditions of authorization processing in light of residual risks, the accrediting statement is the place to document them. Often, the statement includes additional information such as approved mode of operation, identification of data types, sensitivity levels, criticality categorization, risk level, and certification level to classify the accreditation according to predetermined standards. An example of an accreditation letter is provided in Appendix S.

Approving authorities must understand that there may be both personal and operational consequences to their accreditation decision. Not only will accreditation affect the security of the system in an operational way, but it will also affect the responsibility, accountability, credibility, and reputation of the approving authority in a personal sense. However, system accreditation should be considered a normal management function, and there are no special rules for punishing malfeasance or negligence in this area any more so than in any other normal management function. However, the Computer Security Act of 1987 requires that systems processing federal data be authorized to process by a management official, and failure to do so constitutes a violation of a federal directive. Failure to do so demonstrated that management had not exercised due care in protecting the system if there was a security incident.

Suppose the approving authority does not wish to authorize processing. Perhaps the risks of continued operation are too great, or perhaps the system's design is inadequate and data will be compromised should the system be allowed to go into production. The approving authority can deny and perhaps should deny accreditation on any number of grounds: potential disclosure of customer data, lack of assurance of integrity of payment data; inability to meet customer uptime demands; potential loss of financial resources; potential impact on health, safety, and welfare; loss of credibility and embarrassment; or inability to establish trust with an interconnected system. The approving authority's denial of accreditation is just as important as an approved accreditation. It will certainly be treated more expeditiously and with more emphasis. The reason for the nonaccreditation decision should be clearly stated so that corrective action can be initiated. Of course, it is within the authority of the approving authority to say "forget the whole thing," or to cut losses and retire the system immediately or to stop development altogether. But that is an exception. However, the potential for this provides justification for applying the certification and accreditation methodology into the system's life cycle.

Conditional and Interim Accreditation

Because full accreditation is often impractical, conditional or interim accreditation may prove suitable. A conditional accreditation permits the system to operate under certain conditions for the full term of a normal accreditation. For instance, the system will be permitted to continue to process but only if compensatory controls are employed until necessary controls have been fully implemented. An interim accreditation on the other hand limits the length of time the system is permitted to operate in a degraded mode, usually a six-month period. If at the end of that six-month period prescribed corrective action has not been taken or completed, the accreditation expires and the system must cease processing. Interim accreditation must be used judiciously because there will be a great temptation to extend the temporary approval to process for another interim period ad infinitum. Interim accreditation may be appropriate for an operational system to allow it to continue to operate following a change to its processing environment or in response to a serious incident. Or an interim accreditation may be considered for a system in development that must meet a strict implementation date but that does not yet meet all conditions for full accreditation. Compensatory controls should be considered in addressing the most significant risks. They compensate for the lack of normal controls by providing equal or greater protection temporarily until the residual risk can be permanently mitigated. For example, the approving authority may require that audit trails be reviewed on a daily basis until background checks on all admin users can be completed. Similar to compensatory controls are operational restrictions, which temporarily limit actions that can be performed until residual risks can be mitigated. For example, if the trust level of a connected system cannot be fully established, sharing data with that system will be suspended. An example of an interim accreditation letter is provided in Appendix T.

Designation of Approving Authorities

Organizations must clearly define their policies regarding the role and responsibilities of individuals appointed as approving authorities. Such a policy should define the minimum level of authority of position that the approving authority must hold. The policy should require that each approving authority be a senior management official who has authority over and responsibility for the information technology system and the business process it supports and who manages the resources required to support both. In every case, the approving authority must be able to commit necessary resources for remedial action or correction of deficiencies (not necessarily all deficiencies but a clear majority of them). If total responsibility for all mitigation activities was a requirement, then the president or CEO would probably be required to serve as the approving authority in every case. It is sensible to set aside facility-related corrective actions as an example because this will in most cases fall outside most approving authorities' span of authority. The policy should also implement separation of duties by restricting system owners from being approving authorities for their own systems; by restricting COOs from being approving authorities for any system that does not directly support the CIO function; and restricting individuals in information technology from security positions.

Most organizations will find it necessary to appoint several individuals to serve as approving authorities, because they are normally organized according to distinct lines of business. It is important to assemble an approving authority matrix that indicates the approving authorities in association with the systems they are responsible for. A viable system inventory process (as shown in Table 16.1) will facilitate identification of individuals performing as approving authorities.

Table 16.1   Approving Authority Matrix

Approving Authority	Business Unit	System Name	Reaccreditation Due Date
John Hanson	Office of Administration	Zeus	July 15, 2007
		Prometheus	April 30, 2006
Catherine Bulloch	Office of the Chief Financial Officer	Apollo	August 2, 2006
		Mercury	January 31, 2007
		Bacchus	September 30, 2008
Vernon VanFleet	Research Department	Eros	February 10, 2006
Ray Horner	Office of Information Technology	Corporate LAN	November 12, 2005
		Corporate Intranet	June 30, 2007
		Corporate Internet	June 30, 2007

Approving Authority Qualifications

Not everyone is qualified to be an approving authority, just as not everyone is qualified to serve as a senior manager in an organization. The same qualities of integrity, competence, common sense, involvement, and initiative required to lead a major organizational element are the same qualities necessary to function effectively as an approving authority. According to federal certification and accreditation guidance found in NIST SP 800-37, the approving official must have budget authority over the system that is to be accredited as well as responsibility for the process supported by the system. The approving authority must also have solid knowledge of operations of his or her line of business and the broader organization as well and must also understand the necessity of implementing appropriate corrective actions. This means that the approving official must know security to some extent. Certainly, it does not need to be at the level of an experienced practitioner, but the approving authority must be familiar with the principles of risk management and certification testing. Development of a presentation specifically for those serving as approving authorities is time well spent by the CISO and can reap benefits when provided to newly appointed approving authorities and periodically thereafter.

The duties of the approving authority entrust the position with substantial authority, which must be judiciously exercised. An approving authority that chooses to flex his or her muscles by refusing to authorize processing cannot only be aggravating to the system owner but can also hamper future compliance. The authority to take a live system offline through deaccreditation should not be taken lightly and decisions of this nature should be taken only when there are no compensatory controls available or no ways that operations can be restricted to minimize risks temporarily. Of course, when a severe incident has occurred, temporary cessation of operations may be warranted until the extent of damage is known, but this should not immediately provoke deaccreditation.

For the accreditation process to be effective it must be tied to the budget process, and the approving authority more than anyone should understand the connection between these two processes. Funding for a new project should be made contingent upon certification and accreditation of the system. Likewise, continued funding for an operational system should also be associated with reaccreditation of the system.

Accreditation Decision Process

The process for documenting the accreditation decision begins with a completed, approved certification package for the system. As described in the previous chapter, the package includes only documentation germane to the certification effort. The package needs to be signed by the certifying agent and must be reviewed by the system owners and their staffs for completeness, accuracy, feasibility of recommendations, and applicability of findings. Once this has been done, and all comments and questions have been addressed to their satisfaction by the certifier, system owners will document their concurrence with the findings and recommendations of the certification. This concurrence should also address and open issues identified in the remediation plan. The system owner should update the risk mitigation plan and fine-tune tasks, responsibilities, and schedules for corrective action. System owners should signify their concurrence and the plan for corrective action in a written endorsement of the package for the approving authority. The owner should also prepare an accreditation letter for the approving authority's signature. The package should be routed through standard review channels to ensure that all affected parties have an opportunity to comment on the findings of the certification. This may include the general consul, CISO, CFO, and chief of staff. Because this approval process touches on individuals not previously involved in the certification and accreditation process, one must ensure that documentation is clearly written and easily understood and that terms used are well defined. In case the approving authority or other reviewers involved in the approval process wish to dig deeper into findings and recommendations, supporting documentation must be readily available. Screen shots made during the certification test; the risk ranking methodology; references to documentation reviewed during the certification process; and details of mitigation plans must be easily referenced during the review.

Time is always an issue with approval of certification and accreditation packages. This is because it is an important decision that plays a large role in expenditures of resources and has long-term implications for system security. Consequently, management normally involves a number of offices in the preliminary review, requiring them to make recommendations to the approving authority within their areas of responsibility. The need to minimize the number of preliminary approvers in the interest of timeliness must be balanced against the need to be thorough in protecting the interests of the approving authority.

With so many eyes potentially reviewing the package, there is a tendency for reviewers to pick it apart at many levels. Therefore, every mistake, typo, misstatement, incomplete statement, or error contributes to delays in final approval of the documents. Preparers must be very, very careful to spell names correctly and to designate organizational elements, position titles, name assignments, and system descriptions correctly. Although this seems comparatively trivial from a security point of view, such errors are easily spotted by staff members and provide them grounds for rejecting the certification and accreditation package. It is best to get it right the first time.

The system owner should offer to meet with the approving authority early on to explain the certification and accreditation package in the interest of speeding up the process. The hour it takes to explain the certification process, findings and recommendations, and residual risks can go a long way in ensuring the approving authority prioritizes his or her accreditation decision and speeds the approval process. Such a presentation should attempt to graphically portray data to ease understanding in the shortest amount of time. The presentation can benefit from providing the approving authority a comparison with like systems and organizations to help explain the consequences of approval or disapproval as does a description of system dependencies.

System owners should continually press for resolution. If the approving authority has the package, he or she should be prodded weekly until a decision is made; if the package is in the hands of reviewers, they should be encouraged to complete their reviews speedily because the security of the system is at stake; and, if the package has been returned for corrective action, then the system owner should facilitate resolution as rapidly as possible. Perhaps the biggest mistake the system owner can make is to assume that the package is progressing toward approval. It is far more realistic to assume that it has been delayed somewhere along the way, needing intervention to help get it back on track.

Actions Following Accreditation

Once the approving authority has approved the certification and accreditation package and has accredited the system, the system owner should safeguard the signature page with his or her life. It should be maintained on file in hard copy as part of the certification and accreditation package and it should be scanned into an electronic format as well. Also, the authorization of the system to operate should be registered in the system inventory system, and the master organization accreditation plan and schedule should be updated to show when the next periodic recertification and reaccreditation will be required based on this date. Although important, obtaining authorization to operate is clearly not the end of the process. The system owner still needs to track corrective actions to their conclusions, keeping the approving authority informed with periodic updates as directed. Or, when additional resources are required, the system owner should demand to brief the approving authority so that the approving authority can be apprised of resource issues. Completed corrective actions have to be documented and reported to the approving authority to provide assurance that residual risks have been addressed. This may be done as they are mitigated individually or after they have all been completed. Although accreditation is tied to a particular date based on conditions at a particular point in time, the security posture of the system must continue to be managed. Compliance reviews need to take place using frequent self-assessments, and automated tools need to detect vulnerabilities and malicious software. Incidents must be reported, investigated, tracked, and resolved to ensure security controls continue to function as designed and as implemented at the time of accreditation.

Changes in the environment must be monitored and assessed for their impact on security controls. Because of change, systems need to be evaluated to determine if reaccreditation needs to take place. As discussed in Chapter 3, the approving authority needs to be aware of the identification of new threats identified, evolving risks, changes in data sensitivity and criticality, and changes in the operating environment to make a conscious decision to require the system to be recertified irrespective of where the system is in the cycle for periodic recertification. Consolidation of systems may also require a reevaluation of system accreditation status, in that multiple accredited systems when combined may need to be reaccredited as a single, redesigned system.

Not only does the environment change but so do approving authorities. Reorganizations, reassignments, terminations, promotions, mergers, and acquisitions occur with great regularity and affect the identity of the responsible approving authority. There is normally no need to reaccredit a system based solely on a change in the responsible approving authority. However, that is a decision that the approving authority must make and should be considered and planned for by the CISO and system owners. The completeness, currency, and usability of the system certification and accreditation package will play a key role in the approving authority's decision on the need for reaccrediting the system, as will the security awareness of the individual newly assigned to that role. When the approving authority changes, the CISO and system owner should provide him or her with a briefing or at least a memo outlining the current accreditation with the objective of informing the approving authority of risks to the system, resource concerns, and the status of any ongoing corrective action.

Summary

The accreditation decision is an important one for at least two reasons: it demonstrates that due care has been exercised in the protection of the system, and it establishes accountability for the security of the system with a high-level official of the organization. Certification and accreditation is a highly effective approach to ensure that those in upper-level management are involved in the security of information technology resources, and it makes them directly accountable from a security perspective for the decision to allow a system to go into production or to continue to operate. Authorizing officials who understand the importance of the certification and accreditation process and the important role that they play in the process can also play a significant role in the implementation of the organization's overall information technology security program.

CERTIFICATION AND ACCREDITATION CASE STUDY

The purpose of this section is to provide an overview of how a major U.S. government department set about establishing and implementing an effective certification and accreditation program. This case study illustrates the certification and accreditation concepts and principles described in this book. Because I was contracted by the department to serve as its on-site certification and accreditation program manager and oversaw its Fiscal Year 2003 and 2004 certification and accreditation efforts as project manager, I have an ideal perspective from which to describe the events recorded in this case study. In that capacity I was in a position to assess the advantages and disadvantages of courses of action taken, the costs and benefits of approaches used, and lessons learned from this experience.

Situation

At the end of fiscal year 2002, the department had received a failing score in its level of compliance with FISMA standards. The FISMA scorecard indicated that the department's information technology security program had performed very poorly, particularly in the area of certification and accreditation. Although the department management had published certification and accreditation guidance and had documented a certification and accreditation policy, neither had been effectively enforced, and less than 10 percent of the department's mission critical systems and practically none of its noncritical systems were accredited. Up to that point, most of the department's certification and accreditation efforts had wisely been focused on life safety systems, which were being effectively managed; high standards for certification testing were being maintained; and effective tracking of risk mitigation was being accomplished.

Action Plan

The department CISO under the direction of the CIO was tasked with meeting the recently established FISMA guidance, which called for executive branch organizations to accredit all of their mission critical systems no later than October 1, 2003, and 90 percent of all department systems by July 1, 2004, to achieve an acceptable score. This meant that virtually all department general support systems and major applications would have to be certified and accredited, and this called for a concerted effort to meet this aggressive timetable. This newly assigned CISO constructed a strategy for meeting these milestones that included the following components:

- Update the department certification and accreditation process and establish a more responsive certification and accreditation oversight capability. This included a decision to implement NIST guidance related to certification and accreditation processes. Key objectives in the step were to achieve consistency in the development of certification and accreditation documentation and to develop a risk remediation process to document and correct weaknesses.
- Achieve certification and accreditation in two stages: first, concentrate efforts on mission critical general support systems and major applications, targeting them for completion in FY03; second, focus on non–mission critical systems with a goal of accrediting 100 percent of all systems by June 30, 2004. The decision to achieve the final goal in two years rather than one ensured that quality would not be sacrificed in the performance of project tasks.
- Provide system owners department-managed and department-funded certification and accreditation support on a nonreimbursable basis on request. The CIO would create a dedicated certification and accreditation capability at the department level to augment ongoing business unit–level efforts to speed up the work rate.

■ Build on current certification and accreditation efforts. This meant continued reliance on current efforts of major subordinate organizations relative to the most sensitive (high sensitivity) systems and on certification and accreditation work currently underway on other systems with the provision that their results would comply with the updated methodology as fully as possible.

■ Simultaneously develop and integrate the department's incident response, contingency planning, compliance management, and vulnerability scanning capabilities with the certification and accreditation program.

Lessons Learned

There were numerous significant lessons that were learned during the execution of the project, which are instructive in the implementation of certification and accreditation programs in general. These included:

■ *Data Collection*: The gathering of data necessary to complete certification and accreditation documentation became the biggest challenge to maintenance of the project schedule. Coordinating the availability of personnel to be interviewed by certification and accreditation team members and the slow pace of document collection often resulted in one- to three-week delays in established timetables. To counter this, analysts were required to communicate with system owners daily via phone, e-mail, or in person and to record these communications. They were instructed to escalate issues that could cause delays to the organization ISSO and to the project manager for assistance in resolving them. Finally, the project manager reported regularly to the CISO any scheduling difficulties, who would enlist the assistance of the responsible major subordinate element CIO.

■ *Project Schedule*: From start to finish, the project spanned a period of 13 months. Availability of personnel proved to be a major consideration in trying to stay on schedule, and progress was limited during the months of July, and most of November, December, and January by large numbers of personnel being away on vacation during the holidays and summer. The most productive months for accomplishing work proved to be February, March, April, May, August, and September. We found that there is little depth on government staffs and the schedule had to accommodate the availability of a single worker in many cases.

- *Methodology Development*: The effort expended to ensure that the certification and accreditation methodology was well thought out, was coordinated with subordinate organizations, and was compliant with NIST guidance was time well spent. The department developed documented certification and accreditation processes that were well integrated and permitted flexibility while ensuring consistency of format and methodology; these processes were simple to understand and to employ. Additionally, the CISO provided an overview presentation on the new methodology to the NIST staff to increase assurance that the methodology would be technically acceptable and would not be discredited at a later date.

- *System Inventory*: The project revealed significant flaws and inaccuracies in the system inventory. Systems on the list were found to be nearing retirement, in the early stages of development, not qualified to be a system, or previously certified within the scope of another system. Continual coordination and negotiation with ISSOs, system owners, and the CISO was necessary to justify and verify additions and deletions from the system inventory. Such coordination was required in cases where it appeared logical to combine the certifications of several systems into a single certification and accreditation package. This was continually sought as a means of achieving economies of scale. The general rule used in determining if such combining was warranted was to consider system ownership, system environment, and security environment. If all three of these tests could be satisfied and if a combining was considered cost-effective, then a single certification package would be prepared for multiple systems. A combined certification and accreditation package would seek to first describe the controls common to all the combined systems. However, care would be taken to also ensure that each system in the combined package was properly described and variances in controls would be fully addressed for each system specifically. This approach, though it caused deviations from the formatting in standard templates, proved to be well worth the trouble because it resulted in significant savings of time and effort required in the certification.

- *Level of Effort*: The project also proved the value in scaling the level of effort to the sensitivity of the system being certified. By focusing the project on systems that were less sensitive, the existing vigorous certification process that incorporated robust security testing and full documentation was maintained for the most sensitive systems, using contractors who were most familiar with these systems because they had been performing certifications of this nature on these specific systems for many years. Other low and moderate sensitivity systems could then be subjected to the new abbreviated certification treatment in either of two forms: SCL-1 for simple, low sensitivity systems, and SCL-2 for more sensitive systems categorized as having a moderate level of sensitivity. This permitted the effort to be scaled in terms of the level of detail required in each of the documents in the certification package.

■ *Use of Specialized Services*: As the project began, 42 systems were identified as having certification adherence activities initiated but had not as yet been completed. These systems required that only certification testing be performed and a remediation plan be prepared for each. This permitted the project manager to design an adjunct project for assignment to a specialized contractor who could select analysts skilled in this single discipline, to focus their efforts on a single aspect of the overall certification and accreditation methodology and to coordinate with a single organization within the department for its completion. This subproject allowed the department to certify these 42 systems in approximately six weeks.

■ *Expertise*: Contractors who were hired to perform certification and accreditation services were placed under the control of a senior subject matter expert who was responsible for selecting and training all team members and ensuring that each met established standards of quality. The team was tasked with providing dedicated certification and accreditation work and was not redirected to perform any other types of tasks for the duration of the project.

■ *Centralized Support*: The provision of centralized certification and accreditation services to subordinate organizations by the CIO proved to be an advantage in that the subordinate element did not have to concern itself with whether or not the services would meet department standards. This was implied. This permitted these organizations to shield themselves from the responsibility for compliance of work products delivered by the certification and accreditation team.

■ *Type Certification*: An additional way that was found to economize was to perform a type certification of enterprise architecture, budgeting, training, and travel software used throughout the department. Executive agents or these software products were named and were assigned responsibility as system owners. This eliminated the need for each user organization to certify their instance of the software individually.

■ *Travel Consolidation*: Savings in time and funds were realized by developing a consolidated plan for out-of-town travel and then closely monitoring adherence to it. This plan identified all potential travel requirements for multiple contractors and projected potential costs so as to identify situations in which travel could be combined to reduce costs. For instance, a team traveling to a destination for data collection would be assigned to conduct a certification test for another system while there to preclude another team having to travel there solely for that specific purpose. Possible alternatives to on-site data collection were identified to eliminate travel costs. If documentation could be obtained by mail, pouch, or transmission, and if interviews could be effectively conducted via conference call, then remote data collection would be strongly considered. However, this did not prove to be practical for complex systems with significant security issues and risks. Nor was this practice considered for certification test activities, which were required to be conducted on site in all cases.

■ *Cooperation*: The project manager was able to make use of the fact that requirements applicable to the program stemmed from sources that department managers readily recognized, increasing the credibility of program efforts. Because certification and accreditation compliance was established in federal law (FISMA) and compliance oversight was being driven by the Office of Management and Budget, and exercised by the Office of the Inspector General, the program was immediately recognized throughout the department as a substantial government initiative that could not be avoided.

■ *Training*: To ensure that program participants would be able to understand their roles and to equip them to further expedite implementation of the program, specialty training was provided to ISSOs, system development personnel, and designated approving authorities. Training ranged from as little as one hour for approving authorities to twelve hours for system developers. Additionally, information technology security personnel assigned to the dedicated certification and accreditation team were provided with 40 hours of hands-on training in the department's methodology during their first week of assignment.

■ *Deliverable Review*: Another schedule-related problem was the time required for deliverable review and final approval. Two weeks were planned for draft deliverable review and another two weeks for final accreditation. Approximately one-third of the systems failed to meet this schedule, however. Much effort had to be extended to follow up with organizations to determine the status of their review and approval efforts, requiring frequent requests for assistance to the CISO and CIO.

These were the most immediate lessons learned in execution of the project, but there were several others for which the significance developed less rapidly. These longer-term observations are described in the following paragraphs.

Tools

In the early stages of the project, tools were not considered for use. However, as the number of analysts declined over the term of the project, coupled with the sheer volume of collected data, the project team rapidly concluded that an automated tool could be useful in organizing data, ensuring consistency of results, and speeding the data collection and deliverable preparation process. A number of tools were considered, each having its own strengths and weaknesses. Because the department's selection of an automated tool turned on the availability of funding, the reduction of the budget for the project demonstrated that the most practical alternative would be the development of a homegrown software solution. Using a spreadsheet-based risk assessment tool that had been previously developed by a contractor for one of the department's major subordinate organizations, the project team began modifying and expanding this risk assessment tool to support data collection for all the major processes of the certification and accreditation methodology. The goal was to develop a single tool that would integrate the minimum security baseline assessment, the risk assessment, the certification test, the remediation plan, and the system security plan, as well as to be capable of generating charts and graphs to summarize findings for these deliverables and for a certification statement.

The tool was designed to map precisely to the department's certification and accreditation process. It included a NIST SP 800-26–based questionnaire, which could be extracted and sent to system owners for completion prior to data collection interviews, with the results being easily imported back into the tool. Analysts could also use the questionnaire to identify vulnerabilities in system controls during data collection interviews with systems personnel and during observations. The risk assessment methodology detailed in NIST SP 800-30 was also incorporated into the tool. From the NIST SP 800-26, minimum controls that were not implemented or that were only partially implemented populated the vulnerability list. From this list the analyst would select the most applicable threat for each vulnerability by using a pull-down menu. Should there be a need to pair the vulnerability with more than a single threat, the analyst could choose to select a threat group (i.e., human threats) or could duplicate the vulnerability as often as necessary to ensure that all reasonable threat/vulnerability pairs were identified. For instance, failure to have true floor-to-ceiling walls in the server room would be paired with the threat of unauthorized physical access as well as with the threat of fire and smoke.

Once threat/vulnerability pairs were identified, the tool permitted the analyst to select appropriate values for threat likelihood and impact according to each security concern (i.e., confidentiality, integrity, availability). The range of values was taken directly from NIST SP 800-30, and the software limited entry to exact values specified in drop-down menus. From these six variables the tool would then calculate the risk factor, which ranged from 3 to 300 points, and would translate the sum into a quantitative risk ranking. Scores from 3 to 100 ranked as low risk; moderate risk ranged from scores of 101 to 200; and scores greater than a score of 200 were ranked as high risk.

The analyst, based on his or her knowledge of the system and its environment, could then add additional threat/vulnerability pairs. This provided a mechanism for evaluating the adequacy of controls specified in the minimum security baseline and to document additional or alternative controls required to protect the system, as well as controls that were not applicable to the system, or for which risk should be accepted. The use of the tool deferred safeguard selection until after security testing had been performed and was integrated into the remediation plan development process.

The tool then allowed the analyst to generate certification test plan input specific to the system that showed controls reported to be implemented, not implemented, partially implemented, or for which risk had been accepted. The certification test plan also reflected the risk ranking for each applicable control not fully implemented. The certification test plan generated from the tool also included a procedure for testing each control and the expected results or minimum criteria for determining if a control had been fully implemented. The certification test plan incorporated a set of industry-standard best practice configurations for common technologies that the analyst could select from according to the system environment. Standards for Windows NT, Windows 2000, Solaris, Oracle, SQL Server, IIS, and Linux were documented in the tool. Other less frequently encountered platforms had to be manually added to the plan by the analyst based on leading practices identified by the project team.

Analysts used the tool-generated plan to perform the certification test and to record pass/fail findings to document whether or not controls requirements had been met. The certification test results report that documented certification test findings also included findings from the vulnerability scan conducted as part of the certification test. After reviewing these results of the scan for accuracy, they would be integrated into the tool by either mapping them to the most applicable minimum security baseline control or by appending them to the controls list with a new control number. Typically, scan findings ranked as high or moderate (or their equivalents) were entered as separate findings, while those ranked as low severity were grouped to keep the results report brief. However, scan results produced by vulnerability assessment tools utilized were included in full in an appendix to the certification test results report.

The tool then generated a plan of action and milestones that included a list of weaknesses from the certification test. For each of these weaknesses the analyst tailored certification test results to create specific corrective action deemed necessary to mitigate the weakness, along with projected resources associated with the recommended corrective action (man-hours and funding) and estimated milestone dates for each corrective action. The tool incorporated the OMB-specified POA&M format with one key exception: a column was added to show the risk assigned to each weakness resulting from the risk assessment process. This permitted the system owner to quickly see which weaknesses were judged to be the most severe. Recommendations in the remediation plan might also include acceptance of risk as an alternative to full implementation of a control when the analyst considered the return on investment to be too low.

The final functionality of the tool permitted the results of the certification test to be fed into the text-based system security plan. Once this merge function was performed, the analyst could tailor the certification test findings to describe the level of implementation of each security control according to NIST SP 800-18 format.

An additional advantage of using a tool such as this was that all deliverables were fully synchronized. As the certification test was conducted, the minimum security baseline assessment was automatically updated with the results. And because all data was housed in a common storehouse, all templates could be updated consistently and could all be dated the same to facilitate ease of use.

Document Templates

Once all data had been entered in the tool and after the analyst had completed all certification and accreditation processes, the draft deliverables for the system could be prepared using preestablished document templates. This set of Microsoft Word–based templates included the risk assessment, certification test plan and results report, and system security plan. The risk assessment template served as the starting point for describing the system, its environment, its assets, data sensitivity, general exposure levels, and certification levels. This same information was copied into the security plan template. The risk matrix section of the risk assessment was copied from the tool and pasted into the risk assessment template. The risk matrix listed each threat/vulnerability pair, threat likelihood and impact rankings for each of three security concerns, and the risk factor for each pair. This was the "meat" of the risk assessment. Graphics generated from the tool were also pasted into the template to show the relative number and percentages of high, moderate, and low risks relative to the system.

The certification test template was updated by the analyst to record certification test activities, dates, scope, and personnel involved as well as the certification test results appendix, which documented controls requirements, test procedures for each, expected results, the actual results, an indication if the certification test found the control to pass or fail, and reference to the evidence collected to substantiate each of the analyst's findings. Other appendices in the template included the platform-specific test procedures and results and vulnerability scanning results. The certification test template would be further updated with pie charts generated by the tool to graphically show the level of implementation of technical, operational, and management controls categories plus the overall control implementation status.

The tool generated an initial remediation plan that included all 280-some controls listed in the minimum security baseline, irrespective of whether the control had been implemented or not. The analyst would begin with this version to pare it down to only those controls listed as having failed the certification test, including those for which risk had been accepted. The remediation plan would then be updated to include resources required, corrective action, and milestone information input by the analyst. The remediation plan was maintained in the original spread-sheet format based on an OMB requirement that they be submitted in that format.

The system security plan template as described earlier was updated with information taken directly from the risk assessment and was further updated with controls status merged into the template from the certification test section of the tool. This information was then customized by the analyst to accurately describe in place or planned controls according to NIST SP 800-18.

Templates for the certification agent's statement and a recommended accreditation letter for the approving authority's use were then updated to reflect the details specific to the system being certified to include certification scope, dates, results, and recommendations. The certification statement template was also updated to include a bar chart produced by the tool to show the relative number of high, moderate, and low risks to the system.

The final template used was a standard transmittal memo used by the department information technology security manager to provide instructions to the system owner regarding required actions and deadlines for providing comments to the deliverables in the certification and accreditation package and for accrediting the system.

The draft version of the package was initially provided in hard copy with page updates being provided in response to comments made by the system owner and with the final version of all files provided electronically in Microsoft Word and Excel format on a CD. However, it proved to be more efficient to convert initial drafts into Adobe files with a "draft" overprint and with distribution being made electronically for system owner review. Then after all comments had been received and addressed, the final certification and accreditation package would be printed out and distributed in hard copy along with final versions of all files on CD. Because the package would contain vulnerability information, all files were page marked for sensitivity and were encrypted when transmitted outside the protected department network.

Coordination

For the project to be successful, the CISO had to emphasize the importance of gaining the full support and cooperation of its network of full-time information technology security managers or ISSOs. Each major subordinate organization in the department had the benefit of an assigned government employee dedicated to performing information technology security functions. Each of these individuals assisted in the project by identifying and categorizing systems to be certified and accredited by the centralized certification and accreditation team, gathering resources for in-house certification and accreditation efforts, facilitating the activities of the centralized certification and accreditation team through identification of systems owners, scheduling coordination interviews and data gathering, expediting the deliverable review process, assisting in problem resolution, and being the general "go to" person for all communications with systems owners and organization management. The cooperation of this trained staff contributed mightily to the eventual success of the project as much as any single factor.

Role of the Inspector General

The department inspector general staff was tasked with assuring compliance with FISMA requirements and would play a significant role in judging whether or not the department achieved its FISMA-mandated goals. It was clear that it would do little good to conduct certification activities based on inadequate guidance, which did not follow the prescribed standards or which were performed based on a systems list that was inaccurate or incomplete. Therefore, the inspector general was given full access to certification and accreditation guidance that had been developed to measure its compliance with FISMA requirements and NIST standards, and any issues for which there were questions a full explanation and justification were provided. The details of the project management plan were shared with the inspector general regularly to ensure that realistic milestones were set and to ensure that appropriate resources had been committed to the project; the inspector general reviewed the résumés and qualifications of contractor certification and accreditation analysts. The project management staff coordinated systems inventory with the inspector general to validate the number, categorization, sensitivity, and criticality of systems being certified and the prioritization of the work effort. Finally, individual deliverables were checked by the inspector general to verify coherence, consistency, completeness, and compliance with standards. Overall, time expended in support of inspector general review activities, although time-consuming, provided a high degree of assurance that the project was being performed according to high standards.

Compliance Monitoring

Once all systems had been certified, the CISO was successful in establishing a quarterly compliance review process to ensure that security documentation was being properly maintained in response to changes in the system but primarily to ensure that plans for implementing corrective actions were being exercised. Certification and accreditation team members were charged with performing these reviews and utilized a compliance checklist to measure the adequacy of security documentation. The review also included a technical vulnerability scan using automated software. Weaknesses identified during the review were added to the plan of action and milestones for the system and would also be subject to quarterly review.

Measuring Success

The CISO required the project manager to track the status of work performed at all times. Information was documented to allow the project manager to track the status of work by organization supported, by type of system being certified, by types of deliverables completed, and by dates of work to be performed and work accomplished. Metrics for the project included risks to project costs to ensure the project budget was adhered to, associated travel expenses, technical risks that were related to the use of the designed methodology, and performance risks relative to delivery of work products. The project manager also tracked totals of work performed (i.e., security plans, risk assessments, etc.) by system count and reviewed content of deliverables to ensure minimum requirements were adhered to. The measurements were included in weekly, monthly, and special purpose reports, which allowed the CISO and other managers to respond before they could risk compromise to the project. As certifications were completed the project management staff collected signed, hard-copy signature pages to be able to rapidly provide record documentation to substantiate proof of accreditation.

It was fortunate that all SCL-3 systems that required accreditation belonged to the same major subordinate organization. This eased accomplishment of coordination and oversight requirements. Additionally, this organization had a stable of qualified contractors who were familiar with certification and accreditation requirements, who had been previously cleared to work for the organization, and who had proved their trustworthiness to organization management.

Project Milestones

The establishment of extremely firm deadlines for completion of the project proved to be very important in completing the project on time. Strict OMB submission dates driven by FISMA allowed equally firm deadlines for project tasks and milestones to be established and enforced. Department management was committed to the position that failure was not an option and maintained that stance throughout the project.

Getting an early start allowed the department to design a project that could be implemented over a period of two fiscal years. This permitted the department to fine-tune its methodology during the first year and to benefit from application of economies of scale during the second year. It also avoided the temptation to seek shortcuts, which would have diminished the effectiveness of the certification and accreditation methodology and the quality of its results.

Interim Accreditation

Because of the aggressive nature of the schedule and because most of the systems requiring accreditation were already in operation, the CISO discouraged the practice of accrediting systems on an interim or temporary basis. FISMA guidelines stipulated that only fully accredited systems would be recognized for achieving certification and accreditation program milestones. This presented no real obstacle because most of the department's systems had never been previously certified. Accreditation letters for these systems were closely reviewed to ensure that systems being fully accredited did in fact meet the conditions for full accreditation.

Management Support and Focus

The most critical discriminator in determining the difference between project success and failure was the level of support provided from the highest levels of government. This support began with the department secretary establishing his intent to fully comply with Congress' mandate to certify and accredit all his systems; this support was amplified in the planning and pronouncements of the CIO and echoed by CIOs across the organization. This support was realized in provision of resources, continual monitoring of program status, and maintaining a high level of visibility for the effort. From the perspective of the project manager, there was never a question about the extremely high priority of the project, which facilitated the cooperation of managers across all lines of business deep into the organization. The success of the project demonstrated the effect of an organization to focus on a task and to carry it through to completion.

Results and Future Challenges

The department was able to achieve the goals that it established. All mission-critical systems were certified by the end of fiscal year 2003. And, by the end of fiscal year 2004, 96 percent of the department's IT systems had been certified and accredited. The inspector general had verified to the Office of Management and Budget that the department's inventory was correct, that the methodology met NIST standards, and that it was being implemented effectively with minor exceptions. These exceptions were the need for improving tracking of remedial actions and the need for adjustments in the formatting of security documentation (i.e., the wording of the accreditation letter and the inclusion of specific risks in the security plan). This allowed the department information technology security program to be removed from the list of material weaknesses.

To ensure that the certification and accreditation program remains effective, the department has integrated the topic into its annual information technology security training and awareness program, has fine-tuned its inventory process to solidify the ownership of information technology systems, and has consolidated its compliance review process with privacy, Section 508 accessibility, capital investment, and enterprise architecture oversight requirements. The program has moved into this new post-certification phase where the program manager now provides increased oversight of the security of systems in development, tracks changes to information systems and updates documentation, enhances the capabilities of existing automated tools and seeks software products to automate other project tasks, and schedules and manages recertification efforts.

Summary

This case study documents how one of the government's largest departments developed and implemented a plan to meet FISMA standards. Through its efforts the department experienced almost complete success, increasing its FISMA score by four letter grades. This case study shows what can be achieved when there is a combination of concentrated effort with a clearly defined goal, full support from management, application of workable methodology, and a committed project team.

THE FUTURE OF CERTIFICATION AND ACCREDITATION

With the passage of FISMA and other federal legislation that mandates implementation of security controls, compliance has become a primary business requirement for federal agencies and private companies that have contractual relationships with the federal government. With an increased emphasis on compliance, it appears that the future of certification and accreditation is secure. The body of guidance that has been developed by the National Institute of Standards and Technology and the promise of continued refinement of that guidance have provided a strong foundation for a practical and simplified approach to certification and accreditation that should to be able to withstand the test of time.

Though certification has for the most part been restricted to the public sector, there is anticipation of increased acceptance by the commercial sector over the next decade as compliance with federal laws such as HIPAA, Graham–Leach–Bliley, Clinger–Cohen, and Sarbanes–Oxley increasingly drive demand for security programs that can demonstrate that private firms are exercising due diligence in their operations. This should lead to steady integration of the NIST methodology and the one described in this book into usable approaches for private firms and organizations. This will undoubtedly lead to changes in terminology and fine-tuning of processes to more closely meet the needs of commercial organizations. Perhaps this will lead to even more streamlining and simplification of processes and greater flexibility in how certification and accreditation is applied.

As the guidance solidifies, we can expect to see more and better tools available to automate the various processes associated with certification and accreditation, and more successful integration of these processes with the use of expert systems. The day will soon come when a single automated tool will permit completion of self-assessment, development of the security plan, performance of the risk assessment, certification testing, creation of the remediation plan and generation of periodic FISMA reports into a single, integrated, automated process. The process where automation will reap the greatest reward is management of remedial actions. As more systems are brought into the scope of certification and accreditation programs, as security-related incidents continue to occur, and as external drivers increase business needs for security, more and more weaknesses in system security controls will be identified, and an effective means of managing this ever-increasing set of corrective actions will increase in importance.

I fully expect that certification and accreditation will solidify its position as the primary vehicle for managing risk in government organizations over the next five years and that expenditures for its implementation will grow in the near term but will then stabilize as the methodology matures and organizations become more adept in its maintenance. As expenditures level off, organizations will seek to become more efficient and cost-effective in the implementation and maintenance of their certification and accreditation programs. This should drive increased demand for the use of automation of the methodology, as well as formalized training in certification and accreditation processes and procedures.

As organizations become more familiar with certification and accreditation they will extend the reach of their programs to address smaller systems and systems in development more fully. The need for increased efficiency will change the focus of certification and accreditation from individual systems toward groups of systems, consolidation of systems, and concentration on certification of common controls that support multiple systems. Certification and accreditation will prove to be a generally accepted prerequisite for interconnection of systems because it provides a common standard for measuring the security posture of information systems.

There will be increased demand for individuals and organizations that can perform certification tasks effectively. Efforts to "certify the certifiers" should meet with increased acceptance as the demand for value will increase the demand for those who can meet commonly accepted standards of performance and will weed out less qualified performers, both individually and collectively. As we have seen in other industry certification efforts, commonly accepted standards of practice will be established for certification and accreditation, as will mechanisms for measuring the competence of individuals and companies seeking credentials. For certification, NIST will no doubt play a large part in establishing these minimum standards of practice, and industry recognized entities can be expected to develop certification and accreditation credentialing programs.

The broadening acceptance of certification and accreditation as the primary risk management approach for organizations can be expected to promote synergy with various other security processes such as security awareness and training, incident response, contingency planning, and facility security. In each of these related areas, immediate access to risk information (nature and location of vulnerabilities, potential impacts from interconnection of systems, and threat/vulnerability trends) will allow the development of more realistic awareness presentations and identification of more targeted training requirements. The certification and accreditation program will allow more effective implementation of security controls necessary to mitigate vulnerabilities that result from reported security incidents and events, and it will provide mechanisms for ensuring that corrective actions are thoroughly tracked. Certification and accreditation processes support organization contingency planning efforts and facility physical security enterprisewide through the application of oversight mechanisms offered by controls identification, risk determination, and controls implementation processes that the certification and accreditation methodology offers to those information technology security–related functional areas.

Certification and accreditation's place as a permanent information technology security methodology is assured because it provides an approach that satisfies organizational requirements for both regulatory compliance and for managing risk. The certification and accreditation methodology described in this volume represents a practical melding of both standards-based and risk-based approaches and is a proven management process for both public and private organizations that seek to ensure that practical, risk-based controls are identified, implemented, and continuously monitored.

APPENDICES V

Appendix A

Certification and Accreditation References

- Privacy Act of 1974 (Public Law 93-579), September 1975.
- Computer Security Act of 1987 (Public Law 100-235), January 1988.
- Paperwork Reduction Act of 1995 (Public Law 104-13), May 1995.
- Information Technology Management Reform Act of 1996 (Public Law 104-106), August 1996.
- Clinger–Cohen Act of 1996 (Public Law 104-208, which amended Public Law 104-106, the Information Technology Management Reform Act of 1996), 1996.
- Federal Information Security Management Act of 2002 (Public Law 107-347), December 2002.
- Office of Management and Budget, Circular A-130, Appendix III, Transmittal Memorandum #4, *Management of Federal Information Resources*, November 2000.
- Federal Information Processing Standard (FIPS) Publication 102, *Guideline for Computer Security Certification and Accreditation*, September 1983.
- FIPS Publication 199, *Standards for Security Categorization of Federal Information and Information Systems*, December 2003.
- FIPS Publication 200, *Security Controls for Federal Information Systems* (projected for publication December 2005).

- National Institute of Standards and Technology (NIST) Special Publication 800-12, *An Introduction to Computer Security: The NIST Handbook*, October 1995.
- NIST Special Publication 800-18, *Guide For Developing Security Plans for Information Technology Systems*, December 1998.
- NIST Special Publication 800-26, *Security Self-Assessment Guide for Information Technology Systems*, August 2001.
- NIST Special Publication 800-30, *Risk Management Guide for Information Technology Systems*, July 2002.
- NIST Special Publication 800-34, *Contingency Planning Guide for Information Technology Systems*, June 2002.
- NIST Special Publication 800-37, *Guide for the Security Certification and Accreditation of Federal Information Systems*, May 2004.
- NIST Special Publication 800-47, *Security Guide for Interconnecting Information Technology Systems*, August 2002.
- NIST Special Publication 800-53, *Recommended Security Controls for Federal Information Systems*, February 2005.
- NIST Special Publication 800-53A, *Techniques and Procedures for Verifying the Effectiveness of Security Controls in Federal Information Systems* (Draft).
- NIST Special Publication 800-60, *Guide for Mapping Types of Information and Information Systems to Security Categories*, June 2004.
- General Accounting Office GAO/AIMD-12.19.6, *Federal Information System Controls Audit Manual (FISCAM)*, January 1999.
- National Security Telecommunications and Information Systems Security Instruction (NSTISSI) No. 1000, *National Information Assurance Certification and Accreditation Process (NIACAP)*, April 2000.
- Department of Defense Instruction 5200.40, *Department of Defense Information Technology Security Certification and Accreditation Process (DITSCAP)*, December 1997.
- National Computer Security Center (NCSC) Technical Guideline NCSC-TG-029, *Introduction to Certification and Accreditation*, January 1994.
- International Organization for Standardization/International Electrotechnical Commission FDIS 17799, *Code of Practice for Information Security Management*, November 2004.

Appendix B

Glossary

Acceptable risk A concern that is acceptable to responsible management, due to the cost and magnitude of implementing countermeasures. [NIST SP 800-18]

Accountability The security goal that generates the requirement for actions of an entity to be traced uniquely to that entity. This supports nonrepudiation, deterrence, fault isolation, intrusion detection and prevention, and after-action recovery and legal action. [NIST SP 800-30]

Accreditation The official management decision given by a senior organization official to authorize operation of an information system and to explicitly accept the risk to organization operations (including mission, functions, image, or reputation), assets, or individuals, based on the implementation of an agreed-upon set of security controls. [NIST SP 800-37]

Accreditation boundary All components of an information system to be accredited by designated approving authority and excluding separately accredited systems, to which the information system is connected. [NIST SP 800-37]

Accreditation letter The accreditation letter documents the decision of the authorizing official and the rationale for the accreditation decision and is documented in the final accreditation package, which consists of the accreditation letter and supporting documentation. [NIST SP 800-37]

Accreditation package The evidence provided to the designated approving authority to be used in the security accreditation decision process. Evidence includes, but is not limited to (1) the system security plan;

(2) the assessment results from the security certification; and (3) the plan of action and milestones. [NIST SP 800-37]

Accrediting authority See *authorizing official.*

Application The use of information resources (information and information technology) to satisfy a specific set of user requirements. [OMB Circular A-130, Appendix III]

Assurance Grounds for confidence that the other four security goals (integrity, availability, confidentiality, and accountability) have been adequately met by a specific implementation. "Adequately met" includes (1) functionality that performs correctly, (2) sufficient protection against unintentional errors (by users or software), and (3) sufficient resistance to intentional penetration or bypass. [NIST SP 800-30]

Authorization See *accreditation.*

Authorize processing See *accreditation.*

Authorizing official Official with the authority to formally assume responsibility for operating an information system at an acceptable level of risk to agency operations (including mission, functions, image, or reputation), agency assets, or individuals. [NIST SP 800-37]

Availability The security goal that generates the requirement for protection against intentional or accidental attempts to perform unauthorized deletion of data, or otherwise deny service or data; and protection against unauthorized use of system resources. [NIST SP 800-30]

Awareness Awareness programs set the stage for training by changing organizational attitudes toward realization of the importance of security and the adverse consequences of its failure. [NIST SP 800-18]

Business impact analysis An analysis of an information technology (IT) system's requirements, processes, and interdependencies used to characterize system contingency requirements and priorities in the event of a significant disruption. [NIST SP 800-34]

Certification A comprehensive assessment of the management, operational, and technical security controls in an information system, made in support of security accreditation, to determine the extent to which the controls are implemented correctly, operating as intended, and producing the desired outcome with respect to meeting the security requirements for the system. [NIST SP 800-37]

Certification agent The individual, group, or organization responsible for conducting a system security certification. [NIST SP 800-37]

Certification level A combination of techniques and procedures used during a certification and accreditation process to verify the correctness and effectiveness of security controls in an information technology system. Security certification levels represent increasing levels of intensity and rigor in the verification process and include such techniques as reviewing and examining documentation; interviewing personnel;

conducting demonstrations and exercises; conducting functional, regression, and penetration testing; and analyzing system design documentation. [NIST SP 800-37]

Certification package Product of the certification effort documenting the detailed results of the certification activities. The certification package includes the security plan, developmental or operational certification test reports, risk assessment report, and certifier's statement. [NIST SP 800-37]

Certification statement The certifier's statement provides an overview of the security status of the system and brings together all of the information necessary for the DAA to make an informed, risk-based decision. The statement documents that the security controls are correctly implemented and effective in their application. The report also documents the security controls not implemented and provides corrective actions. [NIST SP 800-37]

Certifier See *certification agent.*

CEO Chief executive officer.

CFO Chief financial officer.

CIO Chief information officer.

CISM Certified information security manager.

CISO Chief information security officer.

CISSP Certified information systems security professional.

Clinger–Cohen Act of 1996 Also known as the Information Technology Management Reform Act. A statute that substantially revised the way that information technology resources are managed and procured, including a requirement that each agency design and implement a process for maximizing the value and assessing and managing the risks of information technology investments. [NIST SP 800-64]

Common security control A security control that can be applied to one or more organization information systems and has the following properties: (1) the development, implementation, and assessment of the control can be assigned to a responsible official or organizational element (other than the information system owner); and (2) the results from the assessment of the control can be used to support the security certification and accreditation processes of an organization information system where that control has been applied. [NIST SP 800-37]

Confidentiality The security goal that generates the requirement for protection from intentional or accidental attempts to perform unauthorized data reads. Confidentiality covers data in storage, during processing, and in transit. [NIST SP 800-30]

Contingency plan/planning Management policy and procedures designed to maintain or restore business operations, including computer operations, possibly at an alternate location, in the event of emergencies, system failures, or disaster. [NIST SP 800-34]

Countermeasure See *safeguard.*

Criticality See *mission criticality.*

Data owner See *information owner.*

Denial of service The prevention of authorized access to resources or the delaying of time-critical operations. [NIST SP 800-30]

Designated approving authority See *authorizing official.*

DITSCAP Department of Defense Information Technology Security Certification and Accreditation Process.

DOD Department of Defense.

Due care Managers and their organizations have a duty to provide for information security to ensure that the type of control, the cost of control, and the deployment of control are appropriate for the system being managed. [NIST SP 800-30]

FIPS Federal information processing standard.

FISMA Federal Information Security Management Act.

General support system An interconnected set of information resources under the same direct management control that shares common functionality. It normally includes hardware, software, information, data, applications, communications, and people. [OMB Circular A-130, Appendix III]

GLBA Gramm–Leach–Bliley Act.

HIPAA Health Insurance Portability and Accountability Act.

Information owner An official having statutory or operational authority for specified information and having responsibility for establishing controls for its generation, collection, processing, dissemination, and disposal. [CNSS Inst. 4009]

Information system A discrete set of information resources organized for the collection, processing, maintenance, use, sharing, dissemination, or disposition of information. [44 U.S.C., Sec. 3502; OMB Circular A-130, Appendix III]

Information system owner (or program manager) See *system owner.*

Information system security A system characteristic and a set of mechanisms that span the system both logically and physically. [NIST SP 800-30]

Information system security officer Individual responsible to the OA ISSO, designated approving authority, or information system owner for ensuring that the appropriate operational security posture is maintained for an information system or a closely related group of systems. [CNSS Inst. 4009, Adapted]

Integrity The security goal that generates the requirement for protection against either intentional or accidental attempts to violate data integrity (the property that data has when it has not been altered in an unauthorized manner) or system integrity (the quality that a system has when it performs its intended function in an unimpaired manner, free from unauthorized manipulation). [NIST SP 800-30]

Interconnection security agreement An agreement established between the organizations that own and operate connected information technology systems to document the technical requirements of the interconnection. The ISA also supports a memorandum of understanding or agreement (MOU/A) between the organizations. [NIST SP 800-47]

Interim accreditation Temporary authorization granted by a designated approving authority for an information technology system to process, store, and transmit information based on preliminary results of security certification of the system. [NIST SP 800-37]

ISACA Information Systems Audit and Control Association.

ISSO Information system security officer.

Major application An application that requires special attention to security due to the risk and magnitude of harm resulting from the loss, misuse, or unauthorized access to or modification of the information in the application. [OMB Circular A-130, Appendix III]

Management controls The security controls (i.e., safeguards or countermeasures) for an information system that focus on the management of risk and the management of information system security. [NIST SP 800-18]

Memorandum of understanding/agreement A document established between two or more parties to define their respective responsibilities in accomplishing a particular goal or mission. In this guide, an MOU/A defines the responsibilities of two or more organizations in establishing, operating, and securing a system interconnection. [NIST SP 800-47]

Minimum security baseline A set of minimum acceptable security controls, which are applicable to a range of information technology systems.

Minimum security baseline assessment An evaluation of controls protecting an information system against a set of minimum acceptable security requirements.

Minor application An application, other than a major application, that requires attention to security due to the risk and magnitude of harm resulting from the loss, misuse, or unauthorized access to or modification of the information in the application. Minor applications are typically included as part of a general support system. [NIST SP 800-37]

Mission criticality The property that data, resources, and processes may have, which denotes that the importance of that item to the accomplishment of the mission is sufficient to be considered an enabling/disabling factor. [NCSC-TG-029]

National security information Information that has been determined pursuant to Executive Order 12958 as amended by Executive Order 13292, or any predecessor order, or by the Atomic Energy Act of 1954, as amended, to require protection against unauthorized disclosure and is marked to indicate its classified status. [NIST SP 800-37]

National security system Any information system (including any tele-communications system) used or operated by an organization or by a contractor of the organization, or by other organization on behalf of the organization: (1) the function, operation, or use of which involves intelligence activities; involves cryptologic activities related to national security; involves command and control of military forces; involves equipment that is an integral part of a weapon or weapons system; or is critical to the direct fulfillment of military or intelligence missions (excluding a system that is to be used for routine administrative and business applications, for example, payroll, finance, logistics, and personnel management applications); or (2) is protected at all times by procedures established for information that have been specifically authorized under criteria established by an executive order or an Act of Congress to be kept classified in the interest of national defense or foreign policy. [44 U.S.C., Sec. 3542]

Networks Includes communication capability that allows one user or system to connect to another user or system and can be part of a system or a separate system. Examples of networks include local area network or wide area networks, including public networks such as the Internet. [NIST SP 800-18]

NIACAP National Information Assurance Certification and Accreditation Process.

NIST National Institute of Standards and Technology.

OMB Office of Management and Budget.

Operational controls The security controls (i.e., safeguards or countermeasures) for an information system that primarily are implemented and executed by people (as opposed to systems). [NIST SP 800-18]

Operational status For the purpose of identifying the operational status in the system security plan, the system is categorized as either (a) operational — system is currently in operation; (b) under development — system is currently under design, development, or implementation; or (c) undergoing a major modification — system is currently undergoing a major conversion or transition. [NIST SP 800-18]

Penetration testing Security testing in which the evaluators attempt to circumvent the security features of a system based on their understanding of the system design and implementation. The evaluators may be assumed to use all system design and implementation documentation, which may include listings of system source code, manuals, and circuit diagrams. The evaluators work under no constraints other than those applied to ordinary users or implementers of untrusted portions of the component. [NCSC-TG-029]

Plan of action and milestones A document that identifies tasks needing to be accomplished. It details resources required to accomplish the elements of the plan, any milestones in meeting the tasks, and scheduled completion dates for the milestones. [OMB Memorandum 02-01]

Policy See *security policy.*

Reaccreditation The official management decision to continue operating a previously accredited system. [NCSC-TG-029]

Recertification A reassessment of the technical and nontechnical security features and other safeguards of a system made in support of the reaccreditation process. [NCSC-TG-029]

Remediation plan See *plan of action and milestones.*

Residual risk Portion of risk remaining after security controls have been applied. [NIST SP 800-37]

Risk The net mission impact considering (1) the probability that a particular threat source will exercise (accidentally trigger or intentionally exploit) a particular information system vulnerability and (2) the resulting impact if this should occur. Information technology–related risks arise from legal liability or mission loss due to:

1. Unauthorized (malicious or accidental) disclosure, modification, or destruction of information
2. Unintentional errors and omissions
3. Information technology disruptions due to natural or man-made disasters
4. Failure to exercise due care and diligence in the implementation and operation of the information technology system [NIST SP 800-30]

Risk analysis See *risk assessment.*

Risk assessment The process of identifying the risks to system security and determining the probability of occurrence, the resulting impact, and additional safeguards that would mitigate this impact. This is part of risk management and synonymous with risk analysis. [NIST SP 800-30]

Risk management The total process of identifying, controlling, and mitigating information system–related risks. It includes risk assessment; cost-benefit analysis; and the selection, implementation, test, and security evaluation of safeguards. This overall system security review considers both effectiveness and efficiency, including impact on the mission and constraints due to policy, regulations, and laws. [NIST SP 800-30]

Risk mitigation See *risk management.*

Rules of behavior The rules that have been established and implemented concerning use of, security in, and acceptable level of risk for the system. Rules will clearly delineate responsibilities and expected behavior of all individuals with access to the system. Rules should cover such matters as working at home, dial-in access, connection to the Internet, use of copyrighted works, unofficial use of federal government equipment, the assignment and limitation of system privileges, and individual accountability. [NIST SP 800-18]

Safeguards Protective measures prescribed to meet the security requirements (i.e., confidentiality, integrity, and availability) specified for an information system. Safeguards may include security features, management constraints, personnel security, and security of physical structures, areas, and devices. Synonymous with security controls and countermeasures. [CNSS Inst. 4009, adapted]

SCL Security certification level (see *certification level*).

SDLC System development life cycle.

Security accreditation See *accreditation*.

Security authorization See *accreditation*.

Security category The characterization of information or an information system based on an assessment of the potential impact that a loss of confidentiality, integrity, or availability of such information or information system would have on organizational operations, organizational assets, or individuals. [FIPS 199]

Security controls See *safeguards*.

Security objective Confidentiality, integrity, or availability of information.

Security plan See *system security plan*.

Security policy The set of laws, rules, and practices that regulate how sensitive or critical information is managed, protected, and distributed. [NCSC-TG-029]

Security test and evaluation The techniques and procedures employed during a C&A process to verify the correctness and effectiveness of security controls in an information technology system. There are typically two types of certification test activities (i.e., developmental and operational certification test) that can be applied during the certification phase depending on where the system is in the system development life cycle. [NIST SP 800-37]

Sensitive information Information that requires protection due to the risk and magnitude of loss or harm that could result from inadvertent or deliberate disclosure, alteration, or destruction of the information. The term includes information whose improper use or disclosure could adversely affect the ability of an agency to accomplish its mission, proprietary information, records about individuals requiring protection under the Privacy Act, and information not releasable under the Freedom of Information Act. [NIST SP 800-18]

Sensitivity An information technology environment consists of the system, data, and applications, which must be examined individually and in total. All systems and applications require some level of protection for confidentiality, integrity, and availability. This level of protection is determined by an evaluation of the sensitivity and criticality of the information processed, the relationship of the system to the organization's mission, and the economic value of the system components. [NIST SP 800-18]

Site accreditation An accreditation where all systems at a location are grouped into a single management entity. A DAA may determine that a site accreditation approach is optimal given the number of information technology systems, major applications, networks, or unique operational characteristics. Site accreditation begins with all systems and their interoperability and major applications at the site being certified and accredited. The site is then accredited as a single entity, and an accreditation baseline is established. [NIST SP 800-37]

Subsystem A major subdivision or component of an information system consisting of information, information technology, and personnel that performs one or more specific functions. [NIST SP 800-53]

System See *information system.*

System development life cycle The scope of activities associated with a system, encompassing the system's initiation, development and acquisition, implementation, operation and maintenance, and, ultimately, its disposal, which instigates another system initiation. [NIST SP 800-34]

System interconnection The direct connection of two or more information technology systems for the purpose of sharing data and other information resources. [NIST SP 800-47]

System owner Official having responsibility for the overall procurement, development, integration, modification, or operation and maintenance of an information system. [CNSS Inst. 4009, adapted]

System security plan Formal document that provides an overview of the security requirements for the information system and describes the security controls in place or planned for meeting those requirements. [NIST SP 800-18]

System-specific security control A security control for an information system that has not been designated as a common security control. [NIST SP 800-37]

Technical controls The security controls (i.e., safeguards or countermeasures) for an information system that are primarily implemented and executed by the information system through mechanisms contained in the hardware, software, or firmware components of the system. [NIST SP 800-18, adapted]

Threat The potential for a threat source to exercise (accidentally trigger or intentionally exploit) a specific vulnerability. [NIST SP 800-30]

Threat agent See *threat source.*

Threat analysis The examination of threat sources against system vulnerabilities to determine the threats for a particular system in a particular operational environment. [NIST SP 800-30]

Threat source Either (1) intent and method targeted at the intentional exploitation of a vulnerability or (2) a situation and method that may accidentally trigger a vulnerability. [NIST SP 800-30]

Type accreditation In some situations, a major application or general support system is intended for installation at multiple locations. The application or system usually consists of a common set of hardware, software, and firmware. Type accreditations are a form of interim accreditation and are used to certify and accredit multiple instances of a major application or general support system for operation at approved locations with the same type of computing environment. [NIST SP 800-37]

User representative An individual that represents the operational interests of the user community and serves as the liaison for that community throughout the system development life cycle of the information system. [NIST SP 800-37]

VPN Virtual private network.

Vulnerability A flaw or weakness in system security procedures, design, implementation, or internal controls that could be exercised (accidentally triggered or intentionally exploited) and result in a security breach or a violation of the system's security policy. [NIST SP 800-30]

Vulnerability assessment Formal description and evaluation of the vulnerabilities in an information system. [NIST SP 800-37]

Appendix C

Sample Statement of Work

Technical Requirements Section

2.1 Task Description

Certification and accreditation services for the ABC System.

2.1.1 Scope of Work

The XYZ Company requires the performance of computer security services on a major application operating in a time-shared and networked environment. Federal laws, regulations, and corporate standards applicable to security analyses, security plans, testing, and the certification and accreditation process will be followed. The certification and accreditation effort will identify and evaluate ABC System hardware and software assets, organizational personnel structure, and continuity of operations, emergency action, business resumption, and disaster recovery plans and procedures currently in effect for the system. Using this information, a preliminary contingency plan will identify roles and responsibilities, critical files, backup procedures, restoration procedures, off-site storage locations, and a list of hardware and software needed to restore the system. The contractor will assist XYZ Company staff personnel in providing training to personnel and in testing and implementing developed contingency plans.

2.1.2 Statement of Work

The contractor will complete this effort for the XYZ Company in five milestones, resulting in specific deliverables as described in Section 2.2.

Milestone 1: Work Plan and Presentation

The contractor will conduct a review of the XYZ Company processing environment and the ABC System application environment to determine operational risks. Based on this review, the contractor will determine appropriate risk assessment, security planning, and certification testing approaches and methodologies to be used in completion of the task.

The contractor will prepare a project work plan and will present it to selected XYZ Company staff personnel.

Milestone 2: Risk Assessment

The contractor will conduct a formal risk assessment of the ABC System operating environment to identify potential undesirable or unauthorized events; to identify risks that could have a negative impact on the integrity, confidentiality, or availability of information processed or stored by ABC System; to identify potential controls to reduce or eliminate the impact of risk events; and to establish responsibilities and milestones for the implementation of mitigating controls. The approach selected by the contractor should permit expeditious completion and should result in qualitative measurement of risks.

The contractor will develop an ABC System risk assessment report to document the methodology, findings, and recommendations of this milestone.

Milestone 3: Security Plan Development

Should it be found that the security plan for ABC System is inadequate or nonexistent, the contractor shall update or develop an ABC System security plan in accordance with NIST Special Publication 800-18. Based on documentation obtained during Milestone 1, and upon risk assessment findings, the contractor will identify and request access to documentation related to ABC System. The contractor will interview cognizant XYZ Company personnel, physically inspect countermeasures protecting the system, and observe operations and demonstrations of security procedures. The contractor will compile necessary data to construct a system security plan for ABC System. Plan development will also include a preliminary estimation of the status of necessary safeguards (i.e., in place, not in place, planned, or not applicable). Concurrently, the contractor will prepare a plan for reviewing/testing the control measures protecting ABC System using the NIST Special Publication 800-37 certification methodology.

The contractor will first prepare and submit a draft system security plan/test plan for ABC System to the XYZ Company client representative for review. Based on this review, the contractor will produce the final ABC System security plan.

Milestone 4: System Certification

Upon approval of the ABC System security plan/test plan deliverable prepared in Milestone 3, the contractor will conduct system testing of safeguards for the ABC System. The contractor will make recommendations for improvements based on evaluation of the system test results and will incorporate recommendations into an action plan. Each safeguard shall be categorized as follows:

- *High Priority:* Corrective action should be taken prior to formal accreditation of the system
- *Moderate Priority:* Corrective action should be taken irrespective of formal system accreditation
- *Low Priority:* Corrective action should be taken as soon as it is practical and cost-effective

The contractor will prepare a certification report that will summarize the results of each step of this task. This report will be prepared for the XYZ Company management official responsible for accrediting ABC System. Preparation of certification statements and all worksheets and documentation required by FIPS Pub 102 will be submitted for the certification of the system. The deliverables for Milestone 4 will be a draft and final certification report for the ABC System that includes the security plan, system testing documentation, an action plan, and worksheets 1 through 6 from the DOC certification methodology.

Milestone 5: Exit Briefing

During this milestone, the contractor shall conduct an exit briefing, with no more than ten XYZ Company staff in attendance. The presentation shall include a brief summary of the work performed and documents prepared and will answer XYZ Company staff questions. The contractor will prepare a written agenda identifying the task, project, contractor, and document titles. The deliverable for this effort will be an exit briefing agenda and presentation.

2.2 Deliverables

Deliverables are due as specified in the contractor's accepted proposal.

Any product delivered under this task order shall meet the conditions specified in the warranty section of the basic contract.

All written deliverables shall be identified with its delivery date and an indication of whether it is draft or final. Draft copies, requiring review shall be marked "DRAFT" and submitted to the client representative for comment on the deliverable due date. The XYZ Company will have ten working days to complete the review of each deliverable and either accept the deliverable through oral notification or reject the deliverable in writing. Once the draft document is reviewed and commented on by the client representative, the contractor shall incorporate client comments and produce a final document within 15 working days (unless the first draft is accepted by the XYZ Company).

All deliverables shall become the property of the XYZ Company. All working papers shall be delivered to the XYZ Company at the exit briefing and shall also become company property.

Deliverable product acceptance forms shall be submitted concurrently to the client representative and the XYZ contracting officer in conjunction with the final deliverable.

Except where specified below, all deliverables shall conform to the following generic guidelines:

- When printed reports are required: The contractor shall provide two paper (hard copy) copies on 8-1/2" × 11" white, single-sided, GBC-bound bond paper.
- When electronic copies are required: The contractor shall provide one copy on disk of the product. This copy must be verified and asserted as being free of viruses.

To complete this task, the contractor must furnish the deliverables referenced in paragraph 2.1, as specified in the following list and sub-paragraphs to paragraph 2.2.

Deliverable Number	Milestone Number	Deliverable Description
1	1	Work plan
2	2	ABC System risk assessment report
3	3	ABC System security plan/test plan
4	4	ABC System certification report
5	5	Exit briefing

2.2.1 Work Plan (Deliverable 1)

Description

The contractor shall present a project work plan briefing to designated XYZ Company personnel detailing project schedules, deliverable schedules (that incorporate dates/milestone objectives), and a management plan. The briefing shall be no more than 60 minutes long with the exception of questions or issues that may be initiated by XYZ Company staff, as described in Milestone 1.

Criteria for Acceptance

The effort shall result in a project work plan and oral presentation that conform to the XYZ Company's stated intent for this project and that are acceptable to the XYZ Company.

Number of Copies

In addition to the two work plan copies (stated in the above chart), the contractor shall provide ten paper copies of GBC-bound presentation slides, as well as the foils (or software-based presentation).

2.2.2 ABC System Risk Assessment Report (Deliverable 2)

Description

The contractor shall prepare a draft and final risk assessment report for ABC System, as described in Section 2.1 above. The documents will include formal accreditation recommendations.

Criteria for Acceptance

The effort shall result in a risk assessment report that is acceptable to the XYZ Company.

Number of Copies

The contractor shall submit an original and one copy of the draft and of the final report. A disk copy of the final report will also be provided.

2.2.3 ABC System Security Plan/Test Plan (Deliverable 3)

Description

The contractor shall prepare an ABC System security plan/test plan, as described in Section 2.1 above. The plan shall follow the format of NIST SP 800-18, which shall be used as a foundation for the analysis and presentation of essential security plan information. Plan development shall also include a preliminary estimation of the status of necessary safeguards (i.e., in place, partially in place, not in place, planned, or not applicable). The deliverable shall include plans for testing the adequacy of system security controls in accordance with applicable XYZ Company standards and NIST guidance.

Criteria for Acceptance

The effort shall result in an ABC System security plan/test plan that is acceptable to the XYZ Company.

Number of Copies

The contractor shall submit an original and one copy of the deliverable. A disk copy is not required.

2.2.4 ABC System Certification Report (Deliverable 4)

Description

The contractor will document system testing results based on the approved system review/test plan prepared for the ABC System. The contractor will prepare a certification report containing recommendations, test results, an action plan, and recommendations to the accrediting official. The certification report will be prepared in accordance with the Computer Security Act of 1987, federal statutes and regulations, and XYZ Company directives. Government comments to the draft deliverable will be reviewed and discussed with the XYZ Company client representative as necessary, and will be incorporated into the final deliverable.

Criteria for Acceptance

The effort will result in an ABC System certification report that is acceptable to the XYZ Company.

Number of Copies

The contractor shall provide one typewritten original and one copy of the ABC System certification report deliverable to the XYZ Company. In addition, one electronic copy will be provided.

2.2.5 Exit Briefing Agenda and Presentation (Deliverable 5)

Description

The contractor shall conduct an exit briefing to include a presentation of work performed and deliverables prepared during the task. The agenda will be prepared according to Milestone 5.

Criteria for Acceptance

The effort will result in an exit briefing agenda and presentation that are acceptable to the XYZ Company.

Number of Copies

The contractor will provide an original and ten copies of the exit briefing agenda to the XYZ Company at the time of presentation of the exit briefing.

Appendix D

Sample Project Work Plan

Task	Duration	Start Date	End Date
Certify ABC System	52 days	10-Nov-03	9-Jan-04
Project Preparation	2 days	10-Nov-03	11-Nov-03
Coordinate project with system owner	1 day	10-Nov-03	10-Nov-03
Obtain system inventory information	2 days	10-Nov-03	11-Nov-03
Set up project directory	1 day	10-Nov-03	10-Nov-03
Develop project plan	0 days	11-Nov-03	11-Nov-03
Project Kickoff	5 days	11-Nov-03	17-Nov-03
Schedule kickoff briefing	2 days	11-Nov-03	12-Nov-03
Prepare kickoff briefing	1 day	12-Nov-03	12-Nov-03
Present kickoff briefing	1 day	17-Nov-03	17-Nov-03
Update project plan	0 days	17-Nov-03	17-Nov-03
Data Collection	9 days	18-Nov-03	28-Nov-03
Collect documentation	4 days	18-Nov-03	21-Nov-03
Schedule interviews	4 days	18-Nov-03	21-Nov-03
Review documentation	1 day	24-Nov-03	24-Nov-03
Conduct interviews	5 days	24-Nov-03	28-Nov-03
Coordinate and perform vulnerability scan	5 days	24-Nov-03	28-Nov-03
Data Analysis/Deliverable Preparation	12 days	1-Dec-03	16-Dec-03
Review and analyze collected data	1 day	1-Dec-03	1-Dec-03

Prepare draft risk assessment	2 days	2-Dec-03	3-Dec-03
Prepare draft ST&E plan	1 day	4-Dec-03	4-Dec-03
Submit draft risk assessment and ST&E plan	0 days	4-Dec-03	4-Dec-03
Obtain and address comments to drafts	5 days	10-Dec-03	16-Dec-03
Security Test and Evaluation	6 days	5-Dec-03	12-Dec-03
Coordinate ST&E requirements	1 day	5-Dec-03	5-Dec-03
Conduct ST&E	2 days	11-Dec-03	12-Dec-03
C&A Package Preparation	20 days	15-Dec-03	9-Jan-04
Prepare draft ST&E results report	2 days	15-Dec-03	16-Dec-03
Prepare draft POA&M	1 day	17-Dec-03	17-Dec-03
Develop system security plan	3 days	18-Dec-03	22-Dec-03
Compile C&A package	2 days	23-Dec-03	24-Dec-03
Submit C&A package	0 days	24-Dec-03	24-Dec-03
Obtain and address comments	10 days	25-Dec-03	7-Jan-04
Update and submit changes to C&A package	2 days	8-Jan-04	9-Jan-04
Project Closeout			
Coordinate and present wrap-up briefing	3 days	12-Jan-04	14-Jan-04
Finalize project plan	1 day	15-Jan-04	15-Jan-04
Archive files	1 day	16-Jan-04	16-Jan-04

Appendix E

Sample Project Kickoff Presentation Outline

Title Slide

- Certification and Accreditation for the ABC System
- Kickoff Briefing
- December 15, 2004
- John Doe, Project Manager

Briefing Agenda

- XYZ Company C&A program overview
- ABC System C&A project overview
- Data collection tasks
- Questions

XYZ Company C&A Program Overview

- CISO-initiated C&A effort
- Permit lines of business to concentrate resources on remediation activities

- Scope: Certify and accredit 50 XYZ Company systems in FY05
- C&A work to be performed according to OMB A-130 and NIST publications
- Focus on assessment and identification of weaknesses in security controls

ABC System C&A Project Objectives

- Prepare certification package for the system that includes:
  - Risk assessment
  - Security testing and evaluation (ST&E) results
  - Plan of action and milestones
  - System security plan
  - Certification and accreditation statement
- Identify necessary security improvements
- Permit accreditation of the system by March 30th

Deliverable Standards

- Risk assessment: NIST SP 800-30
- Security testing and evaluation (ST&E): NIST SP 800-26 and 800-53
- System security plan: NIST SP 800-18
- Certification statement: NIST SP 800-37
- Plan of action and milestones: NIST SP 800-37

ABC System C&A Project Plan

- Conduct data collection to define the system and establish the certification boundary
- Review system security requirements and system documentation
- Develop draft risk assessment — submit to system owner for review
- Draft ST&E plan and procedures — submit to system owner for review
- Conduct testing of system security controls
- Prepare and submit draft certification package that includes the risk assessment, ST&E results, security plan, plan of action and milestones (POA&M), certification statement, and accreditation statement

Project Organization

- Acme Consulting has organized a team of five security professionals for this effort:
  - Project management — John Doe
  - Data collection tasks — Hank Johnson
  - Other project tasks — Bill Black
- All personnel have appropriate personnel security screening/clearance

Immediate Objective

- Data collection to permit development of ABC System –
  - Risk assessment
  - Security test and evaluation plan
  - Obtain data through –
    - Interviews
    - Observation
    - Documentation review
    - Vulnerability scanning

Documentation Review

Collect and review the following types of information concerning the system:

- Completed NIST SP 800-26 self-assessment
- System inventory submission
- Governing external regulations
- Mission statement
- Operating procedures
- Previous security analyses/audits and incident reports
- System application architecture/design or flowcharts
- User manuals
- Memoranda of understanding
- Vendor contracts/service-level agreements
- Configuration management plan
- Disaster recovery/contingency plan

Interviews

Interview personnel who have knowledge of system name security controls/operations (each interview should take 60–90 minutes):

- System management
- System security
- System administration
- Database administration
- Applications programming
- Systems programming
- Facility management
- Personnel

Vulnerability Scanning

- Nonintrusive
- SAN Top 100 vulnerabilities
- Use of various public domain tools
- Full advance coordination

Other Data Collection Goals

- Limit interference with daily operations
- Objectively review system security controls
- Provide on-the-spot suggestions on best practice improvements
- Identify points of contact for follow-up questions/information

Project Schedule

- Data collection: January 10–14
- Follow-up data collection: January 20–21
- Submit draft risk assessment: January 28
- Submit ST&E plan: February 4
- Conduct ST&E: February 14–18
- Submit C&A package: March 4

Administrative Requirements

- Facility/office access — normal duty hours only
- Space requirements
- Work area
- Meeting room
- Interview area
- Phone/fax access
- Reproduction support

Next Steps

- Identify system points of contact
- Arrange data collection interviews
- Obtain written documentation
- Confirm date for ST&E

Other Comments

- Scope does not include development of contingency plan, configuration management plan, or detailed procedures
- Anticipate need to expedite review of deliverables and approval of C&A package
- User-level access to the system will not be required

Team Contact Information

- John Doe
- Office phone: (123) 245-7890
- E-mail: john.doe@xyz.com
- Team will operate out of Room 13B, XYZ Corporate Headquarters Building

Questions

Appendix F

Sample Project Wrap-Up Presentation Outline

Title Slide

Briefing Agenda

- Project objective
- Tasks and deliverables
- Findings
- Recommendations
- Next steps
- Questions

ABC System C&A Objective

- Prepare certification package for the system that prospectively includes:
    - Risk assessment
    - Security testing and evaluation (ST&E) results
    - Plan of action and milestones

- System security plan
- Certification and accreditation statement
- Identify security improvements necessary
- Permit accreditation of the system by March 30th

ABC System C&A Project Tasks and Deliverables

- Conducted data collection between January 10–14 to define the system and establish the certification boundary
- Reviewed system security requirements and system documentation
- Developed draft risk assessment and submitted it on January 28
- Conducted testing of system security controls between February 14–18
- Prepared and submitted a draft certification package on March 4 that included the risk assessment, ST&E report, security plan, plan of action and milestones (POA&M), certification statement, and accreditation statement
- Addressed XYZ Company comments and submitted the final certification package on March 8

Project Findings

- The security plan documents the sensitivity of the system as moderate
- The risk assessment verified the validity of the minimum security baseline selected for the system (ISO 17799) and identified 26 weaknesses in applicable controls (3 high, 11 moderate, and 12 low)
- Certification testing verified the adequacy of technical and procedural controls currently implemented on ABC System servers
- The POA&M records corrective actions, resource requirements, responsibilities, and milestones for each of the 26 identified weaknesses in system controls

Recommendations

- Mitigate high-severity vulnerabilities over next 30 days
- Mitigate moderate-severity risks over next 60 days
- Mitigate low-severity risks when resources are available
- Accept the risks specified in the certification report

Next Steps

- Complete plan of action and milestones
- Monitor corrective action
- Obtain approval of accrediting official

Questions

Appendix G

Sample System Inventory Policy

Statement of Policy

Subject:	System Inventory Policy	File code:	Q14-05-008
Function:	Information Services	Release date:	5/24/06
Issued by:	Chief Information Officer	Supersedes:	N/A
Approved by:	Chief Executive Officer	Reference:	N/A
Applicability:	Worldwide	Total pages:	2

Purpose

This document establishes system inventory policy for the XYZ Company, including all of its affiliates and subsidiaries. This policy governs the inventory of information systems in use throughout the company to ensure they are protected according to their sensitivity, criticality, and risk level.

Definition

System: A discrete set of information resources organized for the collection, processing, maintenance, use, sharing, dissemination, or disposition of information.

Policy

The XYZ Company will implement and maintain a process for identifying and classifying information systems according to the sensitivity of the information that they process, transmit, or store, and according to the criticality of the system to the corporation as a whole. The system inventory process will be designed to support the corporation certification and accreditation process through the identification of all general support systems and major applications that require accreditation by a senior management official. The system inventory process will be automated as fully as possible and the ability to add, modify, and delete inventory information will be strictly limited to those demonstrating a need to know.

The chief information security officer will develop inventory process requirements, ensure they are implemented within the process, and manage the inventory system. The system inventory will be verified quarterly or no less than annually in accordance with guidelines published by the office of the chief information security officer.

Applicability

This policy applies to all XYZ Company information systems in use at all corporate locations (corporate, group, local) worldwide.

Authority and Responsibility

This policy is issued by authority of the chief information security officer. It is the responsibility of general management at each level within the organization (corporate, group, local) to ensure compliance with this policy.

Document History

Q14-05-008   Released
01   5/24/06
02   6/16/06

Appendix H

Sample Business Impact Assessment

XYZ Corporate Intranet Business Impact Analysis

Organization	IT Operations				
Date BIA Completed	September 1, 2005				
BIA POC	Bill Black				
	Confidentiality	Integrity	Availability	System Criticality	
	Moderate	Moderate	Moderate	Mission Critical	

System Description

The XYZ Corporate Intranet is a collection of predefined HTML templates into which information stored in a relational database is contextually extracted based on how the visitor navigates through the site. The site is publicly available to everyone within the XYZ Company intranet domain.

The XYZ Corporate Intranet Web site system (http:// XYZnet.com) is located in Room 1005 of the corporate headquarters building. The system consists of two servers: INTRANET1.XYZ.COM — Production server and INTRANET2.XYZ.COM — Hot standby and testing server.

All servers run MS Windows NT 4.0 Service Pack 6a and Security Rollup Package. Servers also run Internet Information Server (IIS) 4.0 with the IIS lockdown tool and the latest patches and hotfixes. Microsoft SQL 7.0 Server is used as the database engine for the system. The SQL servers have SP-3 installed along with the appropriate hotfixes. The system consists of two Compaq Proliant ML370 servers with 4x700MHz P-III processors and 1024MB RAM with approximately 96GB of disk space in a RAID5 configuration.

Recovery Priority	Critical Resource/ Function	Critical Role	Department	Maximum Allowable Outage	Business Impact	
					Impact	Comments
1	Servers (Primary and Secondary) Hardware Operating system	System administrator	IT operations	72 hours	High	The consequences of loss of system resource or to data or information in the system are only marginally acceptable.

	Resource				Impact
	Servers (Primary and Secondary) Hardware Operating system Security Data archive				Impact to resource would adversely affect the XYZ corporate mission.
2	Web Application – HTML Code	Web programming team	IT operations	72 hours	High	Impact to resource would adversely affect XYZ corporate mission.
3	Database Software – SQL	System administrator/ Web programming team	IT operations	72 hours	High	Impact to resource would adversely affect XYZ corporate mission.
4	Web Services Software – IIS	Web programming team	IT operations	72 hours	High	Impact to resource would adversely affect XYZ corporate mission.
5	Content Management System	Web programming team	IT operations	1 week	Low	Impact to resource would affect upload to primary (production) Web server.

Appendix I

Sample Rules of Behavior (General Support System)

XYZ Company Local Area Network (LAN) Rules of Behavior

- I will comply with XYZ Company policies, regulations, and guidelines regarding the protection, handling, printing, duplication, processing, transmission, distribution, and destruction of sensitive information designated "restricted."
- I will not knowingly introduce any malicious code into the XYZ Company LAN and I will not attempt to bypass or circumvent network security features or mechanisms.
- I will protect all passwords issued to me and will not disclose them to anyone. I understand that password sharing or the use of another user's ID and password is prohibited. I will change my password when I suspect that it may have been compromised.
- I will protect sensitive information from unauthorized access, disclosure, modification, misuse, copying, damage, destruction, or theft.
- I will immediately notify the system security officer when I no longer require access to the XYZ Company LAN because of transfer, completion of project, retirement, or termination of employment.
- I will not copy or remove copies of software licensed to the XYZ Company without proper authorization and I will not import or

use unauthorized software, firmware, or hardware in the work environment.

- I will only access XYZ Company LAN resources for which I am authorized.
- I will not embed passwords in log-on scripts.
- I will report all security incidents, including password compromises, violations of software licensing agreements, and computer viruses, to the system security officer and my supervisor.
- I will use the XYZ Company LAN for processing, transmission, and storage of official Company-related or authorized work only.
- I will not relocate XYZ Company LAN equipment or software without proper authorization.
- Upon final checkout or departure from the company, I will not have in my possession or in my home any sensitive information in any form or any government-owned equipment, software, storage media (e.g., diskettes), user manuals, or system documentation.

I understand that failure to comply with any or all of the above security requirements could result in the loss of my system privileges, other administrative sanctions, and civil or criminal penalties.

I acknowledge receipt of, understand my responsibilities, and will comply with the rules of behavior for the XYZ Company LAN.

Name	Signature	Date

Annual Update:

	Signature	Date

Annual Update:

	Signature	Date

Annual Update:

	Signature	Date

Appendix J

Sample Rules of Behavior (Major Application)

ABC System Rules of Behavior

- I will comply with XYZ Company policies, regulations, and guidelines regarding the protection, handling, processing, transmission, distribution, and destruction of sensitive unclassified information designated "restricted."
- I will not knowingly introduce any malicious code and I will not attempt to bypass or circumvent security features or mechanisms.
- I will protect all passwords issued to me and will not disclose them to anyone. I understand that password sharing or the use of another user's ID and password is prohibited. I will change my password when I suspect that it may have been compromised.
- I will protect sensitive information from unauthorized access, disclosure, modification, misuse, damage, or theft.
- I will immediately notify the security officer for my area when I no longer require access to the ABC System because of transfer, completion of project, retirement, or termination of employment.
- I will only access ABC System resources for which I am authorized.
- I will report all security incidents, including password compromises, anomalous system behavior, and illegal activity to the security officer and my supervisor.

■ Upon final checkout or departure from the XYZ Company, I will not have in my possession or in my home any sensitive ABC System information in any form.

I understand that failure to comply with any or all of the above security requirements could result in the loss of my system privileges, other administrative sanctions, and civil or criminal penalties.

I acknowledge receipt of, understand my responsibilities, and will comply with the rules of behavior for the ABC System.

_____	_____	_____
Name	Signature	Date
Annual Update:	_____	_____
	Signature	Date
Annual Update:	_____	_____
	Signature	Date
Annual Update:	_____	_____
	Signature	Date

Appendix K

Sample System Security Plan Outline

The following sample system security plan outline is based on guidance contained in NIST SP 800-18.

Security Plan Outline

System Identification
    System name
    Responsible organization
    Information contact(s)
    Assignment of security
    Operational status
    General description/purpose
    System environment
        Technical description
        Principal system components
        Security software
    System interconnection/information sharing
    Applicable laws or regulations affecting the system
    General description of information sensitivity
        Confidentiality
        Integrity

Availability
System risks (summarized from risk assessment)
System Controls
Management controls
Risk assessment
Planning
Systems and services acquisition
Certification, accreditation, and security assessments
Operational controls
Personnel security
Physical and environmental protection
Contingency planning
Configuration management
Maintenance
System and information integrity
Media protection
Incident response
Awareness and training
Technical controls
Identification and authentication
Access controls
Audit and accountability
System and communications protection

Appendix L

Sample Memorandum of Understanding

The following sample memorandum of understanding is based on guidance contained in NIST SP 800-47.

Memorandum of Understanding

Introduction

This memorandum will record the formal agreement between the Acme Corporation and the Ajax Company with regard to interconnection between the Zeus System, operated by the Acme Corporation, and the Athena System, owned by the Ajax Company, to include the development, management, operation, and security of the connection. This agreement is designed to govern the relationship between these two named entities and their personnel in the absence of common management authority.

Background

It is the intent of the agreeing parties to interconnect the two named information systems to permit the exchange of training-related data. The Acme Corporation requires access to the Ajax Company's Athena System to permit the update of personnel training records, and the Ajax Company

271

requires access to the Acme Corporation's Zeus System for the purpose of accessing training reports. The expected benefit of the interconnection is to expedite the processing of training information within prescribed timelines. Each information technology system is described as follows:

Zeus System

- Function: Training management system
- Location: Acme Corporation Headquarters, Anywhere, New Jersey
- Description of Data: Moderately sensitive data consisting of personnel training data, which includes training attended, dates of training, and completion status by employee name. Personal Social Security numbers are not used or stored by the system.

Athena System

- Function: Employee training repository
- Location: Ajax Company Headquarters, Smallplace, Pennsylvania
- Description of Data: Moderately sensitive data that consists of employee training information, which includes training attended, dates of training, and completion status by employee name. Personal Social Security numbers are not used or stored by the system.

Communications

To ensure the successful management and operation of the interconnection, frequent communications are essential. The parties agree to maintain open lines of communication between personnel at both the managerial and technical levels. All communications described in this agreement will be documented in writing unless otherwise noted.

To support the management and operation of the interconnection the owners of the Zeus System and the Athena System agree to designate points of contact for their respective system. To safeguard the confidentiality, integrity, and availability of the connected systems and the data they store, process, and transmit, the parties agree to provide notice of the following events within the time frames indicated:

- *Security Incidents*: Points of contact will immediately notify their designated counterparts by telephone or e-mail when a security incident is detected, so that the receiving party may take action to determine if its system has been compromised and to permit taking appropriate security precautions. The system owner will receive formal notification in writing within three business days after detection of the incident.

- *Disasters and Other Contingencies*: Points of contact will immediately notify their designated counterparts by telephone or e-mail in the event of a disaster or other contingency that disrupts the normal operation of one or both of the connected systems.
- *Material Changes to System Configuration*: Planned technical changes to the system architecture will be reported to the point of contact prior to their implementation. The initiating party agrees to conduct a risk assessment based on the new system architecture and to modify and re-sign the ISA within one month of implementation.
- *Additional Interconnections*: The initiating party will notify the other party at least one month before it connects its information technology system with any other information technology system, including systems that are owned and operated by third parties.
- *Personnel Changes*: The parties agree to provide notification of the separation or long-term absence of their respective system owners or technical leads. In addition, both parties will provide notification of any changes in point-of-contact information. Both parties also will provide notification of changes to user profiles, including users who resign or change job responsibilities.

Interconnection Security Agreement

The technical details of the interconnection will be documented in an interconnection security agreement (ISA). The parties agree to work together to develop the ISA, which must be signed by both parties before the interconnection is activated. Proposed changes to either system or the interconnecting medium will be reviewed and evaluated to determine the potential impact on the interconnection. The ISA will be renegotiated before changes are implemented. Signatories to the ISA shall be authorizing officials for each system.

Security

Both parties agree to work together to ensure the joint security of the connected systems and the data they store, process, and transmit, as specified in the ISA. Each party certifies that its respective system is designed, managed, and operated in compliance with all relevant federal laws, regulations, and policies.

Cost Considerations

Both parties agree to equally share the costs of the interconnecting mechanism and media, but no such expenditures or financial commitments shall be made without the written concurrence of both parties. Modifications to either system that are necessary to support the interconnection are the responsibility of the respective system owners' organizations.

Timeline

This agreement will remain in effect for one year after the last date on either signature in the signature block below. After one year, this agreement will expire without further action. If the parties wish to extend this agreement, they may do so by reviewing, updating, and reauthorizing this agreement. The newly signed agreement should explicitly supersede this agreement, which should be referenced by title and date. If one or both of the parties wish to terminate this agreement prematurely, they may do so upon 30 days' advanced notice or in the event of a security incident that necessitates an immediate response.

Signatory Authority

I agree to the terms of this memorandum of understanding.

(Organization A Official)   (Organization B Official)

_____   _____

(Signature Date)   (Signature Date)
Acme Corporation   Ajax Company

Appendix M

Sample Interconnection Security Agreement

The following sample interconnection security agreement is based on guidance contained in NIST SP 800-47.

Section 1: Statement of Requirements

The requirements for interconnection between the Acme Corporation and the Ajax Company are for the express purpose of exchanging data between the Zeus System, owned by the Acme Corporation, and the Athena System, owned by the Ajax Company. The Ajax Company requires the use of the Acme Corporation's personnel training database and the Acme Corporation requires the use of the Ajax Company's training data repository. The expected benefit is to expedite the processing of employee training data within prescribed timelines.

Section 2: System Security Considerations

General Information/Data Description

The interconnection between the Zeus System and the Athena System is a two-way path. The purpose of the interconnection is to deliver personnel data to the Acme Company's training management branch and to deliver training information to the Acme Corporation's personnel office.

Services Offered

No user services are offered. This connection only exchanges data between the Zeus System and the Athena System via a dedicated connection.

Data Sensitivity

The sensitivity of data exchanged between the Zeus System and the Athena System is considered high on the basis of its need for protection against disclosure.

User Community

All Acme Corporation users with access to the data received from the Ajax Company are U.S. citizens with a valid and current Acme Corporation background investigation. All Ajax Company users with access to the data received from the Acme Corporation are U.S. citizens with a valid and current Ajax Company background investigation.

Information Exchange Security

The security of the information being passed on this two-way connection is protected through the use of encryption mechanisms that meet federal requirements. The connections at each end are located within controlled access facilities, guarded 24 hours a day. Individual users will not have access to the data except through their systems security software inherent to the operating system. All access is controlled by authentication methods to validate the approved users.

Trusted Behavior Expectations

The Acme Corporation's system and users are expected to protect the Ajax Company's data, and the Ajax Company's system and users are expected to protect the Acme Corporation's data, in accordance with all applicable federal laws.

Formal Security Policy

Policy documents that govern the protection of the data are the Acme Corporation's computer security policy and the Ajax Company's information technology security policy and standards.

Incident Reporting

The organization discovering a security incident will report it in accordance with its incident reporting procedures. In the case of the Ajax Company, any security incident will be reported to the network operations center located in the company data center.

Audit Trail Responsibilities

Both parties are responsible for auditing application processes and user activities involving the interconnection. Activities that will be recorded include event type, date and time of event, user identification, workstation identification, success or failure of access attempts, and security actions taken by system administrators or security officers. Audit logs will be retained for one (1) year.

Section 3: Connectivity Drawing

Section 4: Approval

Signatory Authority

This ISA is valid for one (1) year after the last date on either signature below. At that time it will be updated, reviewed, and reauthorized. Either party may terminate this agreement upon 30 days' advanced notice in writing or in the event of a security incident that necessitates an immediate response.

Acme Corporation   Ajax Company

_____   _____   _____   _____
Signature   Date   Signature   Date

Appendix N

Sample Risk Assessment Outline

The following risk assessment outline is based on guidance contained in NIST SP 800-30.

Executive Summary

I. Introduction

- Purpose
- Scope
- System description

Describe the system components, elements, users, field-site locations (if any), and any other details about the system to be considered in the assessment.

II. Risk Assessment Approach

Briefly describe the approach used to conduct the risk assessment to include:

- Project participants
- The process used for information gathering (i.e., interviews, automated tools, questionnaires, etc.)

■ The methodology for identifying, evaluating, and pairing threats and vulnerabilities; for ranking risks; and for specifying risk mitigating controls

III. System Characterization

Characterize the system, including hardware (server, router, switch), software (e.g., application, operating system, protocol), system interfaces (e.g., communication link), data, and users. Also include a connectivity diagram or system input and output flowchart to show the scope of the risk assessment.

IV. Threat Statement

Compile and list the potential threats and associated threat actions applicable to the assessed system.

V. Risk Assessment Results

List the findings (threat/vulnerability pairs), which include:

■ Finding cross-reference number with a brief description of observation
■ A discussion of the threat/vulnerability pair
■ Specification of likelihood of occurrence and evaluation (e.g., high, medium, or low likelihood)
■ Impact identification and evaluation (e.g., high, medium, or low impact)
■ Risk rating based on the risk-level matrix (e.g., high, medium, or low risk level)
■ Recommended controls or alternative options for reducing the risk

VI. Summary

Provide a report of the findings, and summarize them, the associated risk levels, the recommendations, and any comments necessary to facilitate understanding.

Appendix O

Sample Security Procedure

Procedure 3-7: Incident Response
Satisfies Security Requirements (NIST SP 800-53): Controls IR-1 to IR-7

Responsibility for Implementation and Enforcement

- Group name: IT Operations
- Person's name: Joe Doaks
- Title: ABC System Information System Security Officer
- Phone: (123) 456-7890
- E-mail: joe.doaks@xyz.com

References

XYZ Company Policy 37, Computer Incident Reporting

Applicability

A security incident occurs whenever XYZ Company information is compromised, when there is a risk of compromise of such information, when recurring or successful attempts to obtain unauthorized access to the ABC System is detected, or where misuse of the system is suspected.

Reporting Process

The ISSO manages a reporting process as part of the security incident reporting procedure for ABC System users to keep them informed of security-relevant activity that they may observe on the ABC System. This reporting process shall not use the ABC System itself to report security-relevant activity about the system.

The reporting process includes:

- Description of the incident
- Identification of the individual reporting the security incident
- Identification of the loss, potential loss, access attempt, or misuse
- Identification of the perpetrator (if possible)
- Notification of appropriate security and management personnel, and support to civilian authorities, when required
- Reestablishment of protective controls, if required
- Restart of operations if the system had been shut down to facilitate investigation

Tasks

The ISSO will perform the following tasks in the implementation of this procedure:

- Monitor and react to system security warning messages and reports
- Immediately report security incidents through the appropriate security and management channels
- Submit an analysis of the security incident to the appropriate XYZ Corporate Incident Response Team for corrective and disciplinary actions
- Perform an initial evaluation of security problems, and, if necessary, temporarily deny access to affected systems
- Ensure that the system administrator evaluates, reports, and documents ABC System security problems and vulnerabilities
- Partially or completely suspend operations if any incident is detected that affects security of operations
- Ensure that all cases of actual or suspected compromise of passwords are investigated

- Ensure that occurrences within the ABC System that may affect the integrity and security of the data being processed are investigated
- Assist the investigating officials in analyzing actual or suspected compromises of information, if applicable

Appendix P

Sample Certification Test Results Matrix

Question	Vulnerability	ST&E Actions	Expected Results	Pass/ Fail	Actual Results Summary	Document Reference
9	1.2.1 Are final risk determinations and related management approvals documented and maintained on file? (FISCAM SP-1)	Review current risk assessment report.	Program officials understand the risk to their system and determined it to be acceptable.	P	Final risk determinations and related management approvals are documented and maintained on file.	ABC System risk assessment, dated Aug. 6, 2003
10	1.2.2 Has a mission/business impact analysis been conducted? (NIST SP 800-30)	Review current mission/business impact analysis.	A mission/business impact analysis has been conducted on the system by the system owners and presented to management.	F	A mission/business impact analysis has not been conducted.	Interview with program manager, Feb. 1, 2005
11	1.2.3 Have additional controls been identified to sufficiently mitigate identified risks? (NIST SP 800-30)	Review current risk assessment to determine whether additional controls have been identified to sufficiently mitigate identified risks.	Program officials have ensured that additional safeguards are identified and implemented.	P	Additional controls have been identified to sufficiently mitigate identified risks.	ABC System risk assessment, dated Aug. 6, 2003

13	2.1.1 Have the system and all network boundaries been subjected to periodic reviews? (FISCAM SP-5.1)	Review written procedures for conducting reviews and documentation showing evidence that periodic reviews have been conducted.	An independent security review has been performed once annually.	P	The system and all network boundaries are subjected to annual periodic reviews.	ABC Information System security plan, dated Jan. 11, 2005
14	2.1.2 Has an independent review been performed when a significant change occurred? (OMB Circular A-130, III FISCAM SP-5.1; NIST SP 800-18)	Review written procedures for conducting independent reviews and documentation showing that reviews have been conducted.	System security controls have been reviewed following major configuration changes.	P	An independent review was in July 2003. The review that led to the development of this report was performed in February 2005. There were no significant changes in the ABC processing environment between those dates.	ABC Information System security plan, dated Jan. 11, 2005

Appendix Q

Sample Risk Remediation Plan

Quarter 2
FY 2005

System Name	System Criticality	Confidentiality	Availability	Integrity	If no weakness, provide a reason
ABC System	Non-mission critical	Moderate	Low	High	N/A

ID	Weakness	POC	Resources Required	Scheduled Completion Date	Milestones with Completion Dates	Actual Completion Date	Status/ Comments	Risk Level
1	1.2.2 A mission/business impact analysis has not been conducted.	System owner	16 man-hours	9/30/2005	Prepare a business impact analysis in accordance with NIST SP 800-34.			Low
2	4.1.7 The vulnerability scan performed on the Unix server detected one medium risk (Telnet daemon is running) and one low risk vulnerability (XDMCP service detected).	System owner	8 man-hours	6/30/2005	Address the identified medium risk and low risk vulnerabilities by reviewing the necessity for using Telnet and XDMCP services, and remove them if possible.			Moderate

| 3 | 6.1.4 Critical system support functions are divided between the system administrator, application programmer, and DBA. However, the application programmer is granted permission to perform system modifications, testing, and production system updates. | System owner | 8 man-hours | 4/30/2005 | Establish procedures and implement mechanisms that require the functions of system modification, testing, and update of the production system to be performed by a minimum of two personnel. | High |

Appendix R

Sample Certification Statement

ABC System Certification Statement

Background

Between April 18–22, 2005, a security test and evaluation (ST&E) was conducted on the ABC System operated by the XYZ Company, located in Dusty Junction, Arizona. The ST&E was performed by an independent assessment team under the direction of the undersigned certifying agent at the direction of the chief information security officer, XYZ Company, and was conducted in accordance with Office of Management and Budget Circular A-130, Appendix III, *Security of Federal Automated Information Resources*, and XYZ Company policy on accreditation. The purpose of the ST&E was to demonstrate, through selected verification techniques and verification procedures documented in the ABC System ST&E plan (dated April 1, 2005) and ST&E report (dated May 1, 2005), that necessary security controls that are identified in the ABC System security plan (dated November 11, 2004) are implemented correctly, meet minimum security requirements, are effective in their applications, and that the controls adequately mitigate risks described in the ABC System risk assessment report (dated November 21, 2004). The certification effort provides the designated approving authority (DAA) with important information necessary to make an informed, risk-based decision regarding the operation of ABC System.

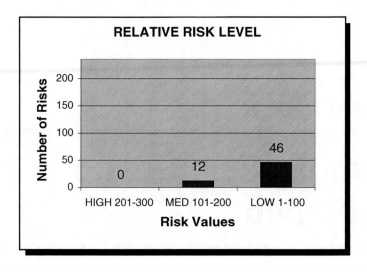

Figure R.1   Relative risk level.

Summary of Findings

The results of the certification effort are summarized in Figures R.1 and R.2.

There were 58 vulnerabilities found in ABC System controls. These were ranked according to risk as shown in Figure R.1. Based on these findings, the ABC System is categorized as having a moderate level of risk. This corresponds to the moderate security category identified in FIPS 199.

The results of the risk assessment of ABC System indicated that the primary risks to system resources related to unauthorized acts committed by authorized system users, and system intrusion, fraud, and spoofing.

Figure R.2   Total system controls.

Unintentional user errors and omissions were also found to be significant risks to system data and operations.

ABC System management has fully implemented 45 of 80 of the required information technology security controls (55 percent). Another two (2) controls (3 percent) have been partially implemented or are in the process of being implemented. Twenty-four (24) controls (30 percent) are not applicable to the system. Residual risk is being accepted for two (2) of the controls (3 percent). Seven controls (9 percent) have not been implemented at this time.

Statement of Compliance

Based on the state of security controls tested and evaluated during the ST&E, it is the judgment of the certifying agent that, with the exception of corrective actions specified in the attached plan of action and milestones, the ABC System complies with the general requirements of OMB Circular A-130, Appendix III, and with minimum security requirements defined by the XYZ Company in accordance with National Institute of Standards and Technology (NIST) guidance. The most significant areas of noncompliance identified are:

- Failure to review security controls on a quarterly basis
- Failure to update the risk assessment following significant changes to the system
- Failure to properly dispose of magnetic and optical media
- Failure to record successful user log-ons
- Failure to implement auditing

Recommendations

The security controls listed in the ABC System security plan have been tested and evaluated by an independent certification team using the verification techniques and the procedures described in the attached ST&E results report to determine if those controls meet minimum security requirements and are effective in their applications. Testing has reasonably demonstrated that the ABC System provides necessary assurance for secure processing. Based on the results of ST&E activities, the undersigned certifying agent recommends that the system owner take action to correct identified vulnerabilities according to the schedule documented in the plan of action and milestones (POA&M), which describes the necessary corrective measures to reduce or eliminate the stated vulnerabilities in system controls. I further recommend that the system be authorized for operation by the DAA and that identified residual risks be accepted.

_____   _____
Joe Doaks   Date
Certifying Agent
Acme Consulting, Inc.

Certification Statement

Based on my review of documentation contained in the accompanying certification package, I concur with the findings and recommendations of the certifying agent. I certify that ABC System security controls have been tested at the appropriate certification level and as of this date the ABC System meets applicable federal security requirements as it operates in its current environment with the exception of vulnerabilities identified in the attached POA&M. I recommend that the DAA accept identified residual risk and authorize ABC System processing in its current operational environment by accrediting the system under the provision that all risks be mitigated in accordance with the ABC System POA&M. A review of security controls protecting the system will be conducted upon any major changes to the current operating environment.

_____   _____
Jane Doe, CISO   Date
Certifying Official
XYZ Company

Appendix S

Sample Accreditation Letter

In accordance with the provisions of the Acme Corporation Certification and Accreditation Program, after reviewing the security controls that have been implemented and planned and weighing the remaining residual risks against operational requirements, I authorize continued operation of the Apollo System under the provision that necessary corrective action is taken to address the following weaknesses:

- Lack of a documented agreement regarding the interconnection with the Ajax System
- Failure to conduct contingency plan testing
- Lack of separation of duties between those administering the system and personnel charged with managing security controls
- Failure to identify a backup storage site that is more than ten miles from the primary processing location

This authorization is my formal declaration that security controls for the Apollo System have generally been implemented and are functioning correctly; however, additional security controls are needed to ensure that a heightened level of security has been achieved. The Apollo System may be operated in a restricted mode until all high and medium risks identified in the plan of action and milestones (POA&M) for the system can be implemented. This authorization is for the existing operating environment of the Apollo System, is contingent on continued operation and maintenance of the security controls in place, and is valid for a period of three (3) years from the date of this statement unless a significant change to the information technology system requires earlier reaccreditation. I authorize the Apollo System to operate with residual risks related to the following NIST SP 800-26 requirements:

- Lack of separation of duties between those administering the system and personnel charged with managing security controls
- Failure to identify a backup storage site that is more than ten miles from the primary processing location

I will ensure that the owner of the Apollo System analyzes any significant change in the system's configuration (i.e., hardware, software, and firmware) or in the system's operating environment to determine its impact on system security, and that the system owner takes appropriate action to maintain a level of security consistent with the requirements for this action.

The Acme Corporation information system security officer (ISSO) will retain a copy of this accreditation letter with all supporting documentation as a permanent record.

_____   _____

Theodore Postlewaithe   Date
Approving Authority
Office of the Chief Financial Officer

cc: Helen Bridgewater, Chief Information Officer

Attachments:

1. System security plan
2. Risk assessment
3. Security test and evaluation plan and results
4. Plan of action and milestones
5. Minimum security baseline assessment

Appendix T

Sample Interim Accreditation Letter

From: Accrediting Official
To: System Owner
Subject: Interim Authority to Operate for the ABC System

I have reviewed the results of the security certification of the ABC System and all supporting documentation provided in the ABC System accreditation package. Based on this review I have determined that the risk resulting from the operation of the system to XYZ Company operations, assets, and personnel is not presently acceptable. However, I recognize that there is a continuing need to allow the system to continue its operation due to existing business needs. Therefore, this interim authorization to operate the ABC System in its existing operating environment is being granted. This interim authorization constitutes a limited authorization to operate the system under specific conditions and acknowledges increased risk to company operations for a specified period of time until specified operating conditions are met. The terms and conditions of this interim authority to operate are described in the enclosure.

This interim authorization is valid for 90 days. During this period the system owner will submit weekly security status reports for the system. The system owner will take action to reduce or eliminate vulnerabilities in ABC System controls identified in the plan of action and milestones.

The system owner will immediately establish a process to monitor the effectiveness of the security controls in the information system during this period of limited authorization. Specific areas of concern identified during the security certification will be given priority for monitoring. The system owner will immediately report any significant changes in the security posture of the ABC System during the period of limited authorization. I will monitor the plan of action and milestones submitted with the accreditation package during the period of limited authorization.

At the end of the period of limited authorization, I will again review the risks to the ABC System and will either authorize it to operate or deny continued operation. I will not grant further renewals or extensions to this interim authorization to operate. The system owner will retain a copy of this authorization with all supporting security certification and accreditation documentation in accordance with the company's record retention schedule.

John Doe, Vice President for Operations
Enclosure

Index VI

Index